ARTIFICIAL INTELLIGENCE AND MACHINE LEARNING

Unleashing Intelligence

Kruger Brentt
Publishers

ARTIFICIAL INTELLIGENCE AND MACHINE LEARNING

Unleashing Intelligence

Helena Mentis
Nanette Simenas

Kruger Brentt

Publishers

2025

Kruger Brentt Publishers UK. LTD.
Company Number 9728962

Regd. Office: 68 St Margarets Road, Edgware, Middlesex HA8 9UU

© 2025 AUTHORS

ISBN: 978-1-78715-306-6

For information on all our publications visit our website at http://krugerbrentt.com/

PREFACE

"Artificial Intelligence and Machine Learning: Unleashing Intelligence" represents a holistic exploration into the transformative power of artificial intelligence (AI) and machine learning (ML), offering insights into their principles, applications, and implications for society. This book serves as an indispensable resource for students, professionals, and enthusiasts seeking to understand the foundational concepts, cutting-edge developments, and ethical considerations surrounding AI and ML.

Artificial intelligence and machine learning have emerged as central pillars of the digital age, revolutionizing industries, economies, and everyday life. From personalized recommendations and autonomous vehicles to medical diagnosis and predictive analytics, AI and ML technologies are reshaping the way we live, work, and interact with the world.

As editors of this volume, we have endeavored to compile a diverse array of perspectives, methodologies, and case studies from leading experts and practitioners in the fields of AI and ML. Through a blend of theoretical insights, practical examples, and real-world applications, this book covers a wide range of topics, including neural networks, deep learning, natural language processing, computer vision, reinforcement learning, and ethical AI.

Our overarching goal in presenting this book is to demystify AI and ML, making these complex technologies accessible and understandable to a broad audience. By providing clear explanations, illustrative examples, and thought-provoking discussions, we aim to empower readers to explore the possibilities of AI and ML, engage critically with their societal impacts, and contribute to the responsible development and deployment of intelligent systems.

We extend our sincere gratitude to all the contributors who have generously shared their expertise, experiences, and insights in the field of artificial intelligence and machine learning. It is our hope that this book will serve as a valuable resource and inspiration for students, professionals, policy makers, and enthusiasts as they embark on their journey to unleash the potential of intelligence in the digital age.

Helena Mentis
Nanette Simenas

CONTENTS

CHAPTER- 1
INTRODUCTION TO AL AND ML

DEFINING ARTIFICIAL INTELLIGENCE

"Artificial intelligence is that activity devoted to making machines intelligent, and intelligence is that quality that enables an entity to function appropriately and with foresight in its environment." - Nils J. Nilsson

Artificial intelligence, or AI, is technology that enables computers and machines to simulate human intelligence and problem-solving capabilities.

Artificial intelligence (AI) refers to computer systems capable of performing complex tasks that historically only a human could do, such as reasoning, making decisions, or solving problems.

Today, the term "AI" describes a wide range of technologies that power many of the services and goods we use every day – from apps that recommend tv shows to chatbots that provide customer support in real time. But do all of these really constitute artificial intelligence as most of us envision it? And if not, then why do we use the term so often?

Artificial intelligence (AI) is the theory and development of computer systems capable of performing tasks that historically required human intelligence, such as recognizing speech, making decisions, and identifying patterns. AI is an umbrella term that encompasses a wide variety of technologies, including machine learning, deep learning, and natural language processing (NLP).

Although the term is commonly used to describe a range of different technologies in use today, many disagree on whether these actually constitute artificial intelligence. Instead, some argue that much of the technology used in the real world today actually constitutes highly advanced machine learning that is simply a first step towards true artificial intelligence, or "general artificial intelligence" (GAI).

Yet, despite the many philosophical disagreements over whether "true" intelligent machines actually exist, when most people use the term AI today, they're referring to a suite of machine learning-powered technologies, such as Chat GPT or computer vision, that enable machines to perform tasks that previously only humans can do like generating written content, steering a car, or analyzing data.

Artificial intelligence examples

Though the humanoid robots often associated with AI (think *Star Trek: The Next Generation's* Data or *Terminator's* T-800) don't exist yet, you've likely interacted with machine learning-powered services or devices many times before.

At the simplest level, machine learning uses algorithms trained on data sets to create machine learning models that allow computer systems to perform tasks like making song recommendations, identifying the fastest way to travel to a destination, or translating text from one language to another. Some of the most common examples of AI in use today include:

- ◉ **ChatGPT:** Uses large language models (LLMs) to generate text in response to questions or comments posed to it.

- ◉ **Google Translate:** Uses deep learning algorithms to translate text from one language to another.

- ◉ **Netflix:** Uses machine learning algorithms to create personalized recommendation engines for users based on their previous viewing history.

- ◉ **Tesla:** Uses computer vision to power self-driving features on their cars.

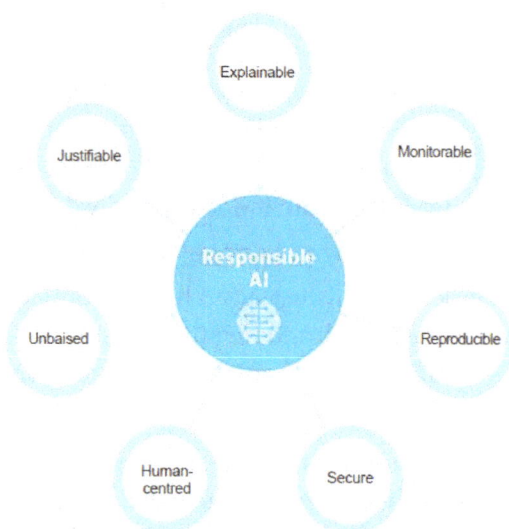

Fig. 1.1 Responsible AI

AI programming focuses on cognitive skills that include the following:

- ◉ **Learning.** This aspect of AI programming focuses on acquiring data and creating rules for how to turn it into actionable information. The rules, which are called *algorithms*, provide computing devices with step-by-step instructions for how to complete a specific task.

- ⦿ **Reasoning.** This aspect of AI programming focuses on choosing the right algorithm to reach a desired outcome.

- ⦿ **Self-correction.** This aspect of AI programming is designed to continually fine-tune algorithms and ensure they provide the most accurate results possible.

- ⦿ **Creativity.** This aspect of AI uses neural networks, rules-based systems, statistical methods and other AI techniques to generate new images, new text, new music and new ideas.

THE EVOLUTION OF MACHINE LEARNING

Machine Learning is the branch of computer science that deals with the development of computer programs that teach and grow themselves. According to Arthur Samuel, an American pioneer in computer gaming, Machine Learning is the subfield of computer science that "gives the computer the ability to learn without being explicitly programmed." Machine Learning allows developers to build algorithms that automatically improve themselves by finding patterns in the existing data without explicit instructions from a human or developer.

The Machine Learning development approach includes learning from data inputs and evaluating and optimizing the model results. Machine Learning is widely used in data analytics as a method to develop algorithms for making predictions on data. Machine Learning is related to probability, statistics, and linear algebra.

Machine learning can be broadly defined as computational methods using experience to improve performance or to make accurate predictions. Here, experience refers to the past information available to the learner, which typically takes the form of electronic data collected and made available for analysis. This data could be in the form of digitized human-labeled training sets, or other types of information obtained via interaction with the environment. In all cases, its quality and size are crucial to the success of the predictions made by the learner.

Machine learning consists of designing efficient and accurate prediction algorithms. As in other areas of computer science, some critical measures of the quality of these algorithms are their time and space complexity. But, in machine learning, we will need additionally a notion of sample complexity to evaluate the sample size required for the algorithm to learn a family of concepts. More generally, theoretical learning guarantees for an algorithm depend on the complexity of the concept classes considered and the size of the training sample.

Since the success of a learning algorithm depends on the data used, machine learning is inherently related to data analysis and statistics. More generally, learning techniques are data-driven methods combining fundamental concepts in computer science with ideas from statistics, probability and optimization.

Machine Learning is broadly classified into three categories depending on the nature of the learning 'signal' or 'feedback' available to a learning system.

- **Supervised learning:** Computer is presented with inputs and their desired outputs. The goal is to learn a general rule to map inputs to the output.

- **Unsupervised learning:** Computer is presented with inputs without desired outputs, the goal is to find structure in inputs.

- **Reinforcement learning:** Computer program interacts with a dynamic environment, and it must perform a certain goal without a guide or teacher.

Machine Learning takes advantage of the ability of computer systems to learn from correlations hidden in the data; this ability can be further utilized by programming or developing intelligent and efficient Machine Learning algorithms.

While Machine Learning may seem new, it has been around long before people observed it as popular technology. It has evolved to solve real problems of human life and automate the processes used in various industries such as banking, healthcare, telecom, retail, and so on. The software or application or solution developed using Machine Learning can learn from its dynamic environment and adapt to changing requirements.

In contrast to traditional software implementation, the lessons learned from Machine Learning algorithms can be scaled and transferred across multiple applications. Machine Learning naturally considers a large number of variables that influence the results or observations, which can be used in both science and business.

Because of all these features and advantages, today's software is developed for automated decision making and more innovative solutions, which makes an investment in Machine Learning a natural evolution of technology.

Evolution over the years

Machine Learning technology has been in existence since 1952. It has evolved drastically over the last decade and saw several transition periods in the mid-90s. The data-driven approach to Machine Learning came into existence during the 1990s. From 1995-2005, there was a lot of focus on natural language, search, and information retrieval. In those days, Machine Learning tools were more straightforward than the tools being used currently. Neural networks, which were popular in the 80s, are a subset of Machine Learning that are computer systems modeled on the human brain and nervous system. Neural networks started making a comeback around 2005.

It has become one of the trending technologies of the current decade. According to Gartner's 2016 Hype Cycle for Emerging Technologies, Machine Learning is among the technologies at the peak of inflated expectations and is expected to reach the mainstream adoption in the next 2–5 years. Technological capabilities such as infrastructure and technical skills also must advance to keep up with the growth of Machine Learning.

Machine Learning has been one of the most active and rewarding areas of research due to its widespread use in many areas. It has brought a monumental shift in technology and its applications.

Natural Language Processing

Natural language processing (NLP) defines the way or method of connecting computer systems with natural languages such as English. NLP helps computer systems perform the tasks and automate manual processes based on human input, which may be either spoken or written text. For example, shopping by user audio analysis (through speakers like Amazon's Alexa) and automating user preference list in a web page based on user interests.

NLP is applied widely to characterize, interpret, or understand the information content of the free-form text or unstructured data. It is estimated that 80% of the world's data is unstructured. Hence to handle and get valuable insights from unstructured data, NLP is essential. It allows computer systems to learn and draw insights from data such as email, social media response, audio, and videos, which helps computer systems understand human interaction, human response, and other associated events or activities related to an environment.

Unlike the older NLP algorithm generation, which involved manual categorization of text, the modern NLP algorithms are mainly based on statistical Machine Learning. Machine Learning algorithms are used to automatically learn the rules of categorizing the text through the analysis of a corpus (a set of text documents). Many different classes of Machine Learning algorithms such as Decision tree, Support vector machine, Naïve Bayes, and so on have been applied to NLP tasks. The process of NLP is explained in the following steps:

- **Lexical analysis:** This step deals with identifying and analyzing the structure of words. After this step, the whole chunk of raw text is divided into paragraphs, sentences, and words.

- **Syntactical analysis (parsing):** Analyzing the words in a sentence for grammar and arranging the words in a way that shows the relationship among them. The sentence such as "The school goes to the boy" is rejected by an English syntactic analyzer.

- **Semantic analysis:** Focuses on drawing dictionary meaning from the text. This step is to disregard the sentences, that are not meaningful such as "hot ice cream."

- **Discourse integration:** The meaning of any word or sentence is analyzed through the associated prefixes to words or sentences. The situations such as "looking for a great product" and "not looking like a great product" are analyzed and categorized as different (as positive and negative feedbacks) to draw meaning out of text data.

⊙ **Pragmatic analysis:** In this phase, the interpretation of results from the semantic analysis are performed concerning a context or environment. For example, the sentences such as "The large cat chased the rat." and "The large cat is Felix" derived from the semantic analysis are further interpreted to identify the large cat as Felix.

Deep Learning

Deep Learning is part of a broader family of Machine Learning methods, which is also called deep structured learning, hierarchical learning, or Deep Machine Learning. Deep Learning is a rebranding of a Machine Learning algorithm called an artificial neural network.

Artificial neural networks are a class of computing systems. They are inspired and derived by analyzing the structure and function of the brain. They are created from very simple processing nodes formed into a network. They are fundamentally patterned recognition systems and tend to be more useful for tasks which can be described regarding pattern recognition. They are 'trained' by feeding them with datasets of known outputs.

Deep learning is an extension of neural networks that have existed since the 1960s. According to Jeff Dean, an American computer scientist who is involved with the Google Brain Project and development of large-scale deep learning software Disbelief and Tenser flow, Deep Learning is as large as deep neural networks. He mentions that the scalability of neural networks gets better with more data and larger models that in turn require more computation power to train models (Machine Learning models) illustrates working of Deep Learning or deep neural network for solving a pattern recognition problem.

Cognitive Computing

Many enterprises are evolving and incorporating new technologies to keep pace with modern business. There are many technologies which are limited to research; narrow industry niches are now being considered for mainstream adoption. One such technology, which is gaining popularity is cognitive computing (or cognitive intelligence).

Cognitive computing is a simulation of human thought processes in the computerized model. Cognitive computing develops self-learning systems that use data mining and Machine Learning-related techniques such as pattern recognition and Natural Language Processing to mimic the way the human brain works. The goal of cognitive computing is to create automated IT systems that can solve problems without requiring human assistance or guidance.

Cognitive computing is a new kind of computing aimed at very complex problems. It can develop meaningful conclusions from diverse resources. IBM began a research project called Watson with the intent to successfully build a system which can learn, think, and understand like a human. It was specifically developed to answer questions on the quiz show called "Jeopardy" in 2011. Watson is developed by combining NLP, Machine Learning, and knowledge representation. Watson was given questions, searched its repository for information, developed and analyzed hypotheses, and produced answers that were also in natural language form.

IMPORTANCE AND APPLICATIONS OF AL AND ML

In simplest terms, AI is computer software that mimics the ways that humans think in order to perform complex tasks, such as analyzing, reasoning, and learning. Machine learning, meanwhile, is a subset of AI that uses algorithms trained on data to produce models that can perform such complex tasks.

Most AI is performed using machine learning, so the two terms are often used synonymously, but AI actually refers to the general concept of creating human-like cognition using computer software, while ML is only one method of doing so.

Artificial Intelligence (AI) and Machine Learning (ML) have revolutionized the way modern businesses operate, making them more efficient, effective, and profitable. In this article, we explore the significance of these transformative technologies and their impact on the business landscape.

- **Automation and Efficiency:** Organizations can start by identifying the tasks that are repetitive, time-consuming, and can be automated. Once identified, organizations can use tools such as robotic process automation (RPA) and ML algorithms to automate these tasks. Organizations can also create a roadmap for automation that prioritizes tasks based on their impact on efficiency and productivity.

- **Predictive Analytics and Personalization:** Collecting and organizing data is critical here. Once the data is collected, organizations can use ML algorithms to analyze the data and identify patterns and trends. This analysis can be used to make predictions about behavior and preferences if the data analyzed is about customers, enabling organizations to personalize their offerings. Organizations can then use this data to optimize their marketing strategies and improve customer retention.

- **Improved Customer Experience:** Organizations can start by identifying the touchpoints where customers interact with the business. These touchpoints can include websites, mobile apps, and customer service channels. Once identified, organizations can use AI-powered chatbots and virtual assistants to provide round-the-clock support and faster response times. Organizations can also use customer data to personalize the customer experience and provide relevant recommendations.

- ◉ **Fraud Detection and Cybersecurity:** AI and ML play a vital role here. Organizations can start by identifying the potential areas of vulnerability in their systems or business process. Once identified, organizations can use AI and ML algorithms to monitor these areas in real-time and detect potential threats. This monitoring can be used to flag suspicious behavior and prevent fraud before it occurs. Organizations can also use ML algorithms to analyze patterns in user behavior and detect anomalies that may indicate a security breach.

- ◉ **Competitive Advantage:** Organizations should focus on identifying impactful use cases where AI and ML can provide the most significant impact. This can be done by conducting a cost-benefit analysis and assessing the potential ROI of implementing AI and ML. Organizations can also invest in building a strong data infrastructure that can support AI and ML, such as data lakes and data warehouses.

When we talk about AI & ML, we often get lost on what tool sets to look at. There are many tools available that customers can consider when embarking on their journey towards AI and Machine Learning implementation. Some popular tools that can help organizations implement AI and ML are:

TensorFlow, an open-source platform developed by Google, Amazon SageMaker, a cloud-based platform, Microsoft Azure ML, a cloud-based platform, IBM Watson Studio, PyTorch, an open-source platform developed by Facebook, Google Cloud ML Engine, H2O.ai, an open-source platform, and many more.

There are many such tools available that can help organizations implement AI and Machine Learning. These tools can provide a range of functionality, from data preparation and feature engineering to model development and deployment. Organizations should consider their specific needs and use cases when choosing a tool and ensure that the tool is compatible with their existing infrastructure and workflows.

Implementing AI and Machine Learning requires a combination of strategy, technology, and people. Organizations that want to implement these technologies successfully should start by identifying the most impactful use cases and developing a roadmap for implementation. They should also invest in building a strong data infrastructure and developing the skills and expertise required to work with AI and ML technologies. By doing so, organizations can gain a competitive advantage and unlock new opportunities for growth and innovation.

Some of the common use-cases across industries that can be explored include:

- ◉ **Healthcare:** AI and ML can be leveraged to improve medical diagnosis, drug discovery, and personalized treatment plans. For instance, ML algorithms can analyze patient data to identify patterns and predict disease progression, while natural language processing (NLP) can be used to analyze medical records and identify potential treatment options.

- **Retail:** AI and ML can be utilized to enhance customer experience, increase sales, and optimize inventory management. For example, ML algorithms can analyze customer data to provide personalized recommendations and promotions, while computer vision can be used to monitor store traffic and optimize store layouts.

- **Finance:** AI and ML can be applied to improve fraud detection, risk management, and investment strategies. For instance, ML algorithms can analyze financial transactions to detect potential fraud, while predictive analytics can be used to forecast market trends and optimize investment portfolios. The Global AI in Banking Market Will Grow to $64.03 Billion by 2030, at a CAGR of 32.6% During 2021-2030 - Research And Markets.com

- **Manufacturing:** AI and ML can be employed to improve supply chain management, reduce downtime, and optimize production processes. For example, computer vision can be used to monitor production lines and identify potential issues, while ML algorithms can analyze data from IoT sensors to identify patterns and optimize processes.

- **Markets and Markets projects** that the global AI in manufacturing market will grow from $1.1 billion in 2020 to $16.7 billion by 2026, at a CAGR of 57.2%.

- **Transportation**: AI and ML can be utilized to improve logistics, reduce fuel consumption, and enhance safety. For instance, ML algorithms can analyze data from GPS trackers to optimize route planning and reduce delivery times, while computer vision can be used to monitor driver behavior and improve safety.

- According to a report by Grand View Research, the global AI in transportation market size was valued at USD 1.21 billion in 2020 and is expected to grow at a CAGR of 18.2% from 2021 to 2028. By 2028, the market size is projected to reach USD 10.3 billion

- **Marketing:** AI and ML can be used to improve customer targeting, campaign optimization, and lead generation. For example, ML algorithms can analyze customer data to identify potential high-value leads, while NLP can be used to analyze social media sentiment and optimize social media campaigns.

- **Scalability:** Cloud computing provides the necessary infrastructure to scale up or down the computing resources needed for AI and ML workloads. This allows businesses to easily expand or contract their AI and ML capabilities to meet changing demands.

- **Cost-effectiveness:** Cloud computing eliminates the need for businesses to invest in expensive hardware and infrastructure to run AI and ML workloads. Instead, businesses can leverage cloud services to pay only for the computing resources they use, which can result in significant cost savings.

- **Access to AI and ML tools:** Cloud providers like Amazon Web Services, Microsoft Azure, and Google Cloud Platform offer a wide range of AI and ML tools and services, such as machine learning algorithms, natural language processing, and computer vision. These tools are accessible to businesses of all sizes and can be integrated into existing workflows.

- **Flexibility:** Cloud computing provides businesses with the flexibility to choose the level of AI and ML capabilities they need. They can start with basic tools and gradually scale up as they become more comfortable with the technology.

- **Data Management:** Cloud computing also provides an effective way to manage large amounts of data that are required for AI and ML workloads. It allows businesses to store, process, and analyze large datasets from various sources in a secure and efficient manner.

- To ensure the success of any AI or ML project, it's crucial to understand the critical components and architecture that determine its outcome. By following the steps outlined below, organizations can ensure that they select the right data, algorithm, and architecture to solve the problem and achieve their desired outcome:

- **Define the Problem and Objective:** The first step in deciding the architecture for AI and ML is to define the problem and objective that needs to be solved. This includes identifying the data sources, types of data, and the desired outcome.

- **Select the Right Data:** Once you have defined the problem and objective, the next step is to select the right data for the project. This includes identifying the sources of data, cleaning and preprocessing the data, and selecting the features that are most relevant to the problem.

- **Choose the Right Algorithm:** The next step is to choose the right algorithm that is best suited to solve the problem. This involves understanding the strengths and weaknesses of different algorithms and selecting the one that is most appropriate for the task at hand.

- **Determine the Architecture:** The architecture for AI and ML involves determining the structure and organization of the system that will be used to train and deploy the algorithm. This includes selecting the hardware, software, and networking components that will be used to implement the system or look at the cloud options that we discussed.

- **Train and Test the Model:** This involves using the selected data and algorithm to train the model and then testing the model to ensure that it is accurate and reliable.

- **Deploy the Model:** Finally, the model can be deployed once it has been tested and validated. This involves integrating the model into the system architecture and making it available to end-users.

Applications of Artificial Intelligence and Machine Learning

So, here are some applications of artificial intelligence

- **Speech recognition:** AI algorithms are used in many speech recognition devices like Alexa to understand human language, convert them into commands, do the research and give appropriate results.

- **Navigation:** AI algorithms are used in navigation applications like Google maps. They (AI algorithms) are used to reach a destination in minimum time, look at real-time traffic data, and more.

- **Chatbots:** Nowadays, companies use chatbots as a lead generation tool. The idea of a chatbot is to respond to user queries with minimal human intervention. It helps improve the user experience by providing visitors guidance and support needed to navigate a website. With new techniques like Natural Language Processing (NLP) and AI, machines can also react to advanced queries, which involves looking at a user's history and profile before attending the query.

- **Autonomous cars:** Autonomous cars are the future. These automated cars use AI and ML algorithms to sense the environment and operate without human drivers.

Meanwhile, here's the application of artificial intelligence across different lines of business.

- AI in e-commerce can provide a personalised shopping experience, assistance, and fraud prevention.

- AI in education can help automate administrative tasks, digitise content like video lectures, conferences, and textbooks, and provide personalised learning.

- AI in human resources helps scan the job profile and resumes of candidates.

- AI in healthcare can help build modern and sophisticated machines to detect diseases. It can also be used to maintain the medical data of patients.

Moving on, here are the applications of machine learning

- **Image recognition:** Image recognition is the most common application of machine learning. Henceforth, ML algorithms are used to read and understand images and identify objects, persons, places, and digital images. However, the most popular use of image recognition is the automatic friend tagging suggestion on social media.

- **Automatic language translation:** Most people would have used automatic language translating apps to convert texts into their known language. Therefore, this process is called automatic translation, which is possible due to machine learning systems like Neural Machine Learning, which translates texts into known languages.

- ◉ **Product recommendation:** Machine learning is widely used across e-commerce companies to provide useful product recommendations.

- ◉ **Email spam and malware filtering:** Machine learning helps in automatically filtering emails into different folders like significant, usual or spam.

CHAPTER-2
FOUNDATIONS OF MACHINE LEARNING

Machine learning can be broadly defined as computational methods using experience to improve performance or to make accurate predictions. Here, experience refers to the past information available to the learner, which typically takes the form of electronic data collected and made available for analysis. This data could be in the form of digitized human-labeled training sets, or other types of information obtained via interaction with the environment. In all cases, its quality and size are crucial to the success of the predictions made by the learner.

Machine learning consists of designing efficient and accurate prediction algorithms. As in other areas of computer science, some critical measures of the quality of these algorithms are their time and space complexity. But, in machine learning, we will need additionally a notion of sample complexity to evaluate the sample size required for the algorithm to learn a family of concepts. More generally, theoretical learning guarantees for an algorithm depend on the complexity of the concept classes considered and the size of the training sample.

Since the success of a learning algorithm depends on the data used, machine learning is inherently related to data analysis and statistics. More generally, learning techniques are data-driven methods combining fundamental concepts in computer science with ideas from statistics, probability and optimization.

Learning scenarios

- **Supervised learning**: The learner receives a set of labeled examples as training data and makes predictions for all unseen points. This is the most common scenario associated with classification, regression, and ranking problems. The spam detection problem discussed in the previous section is an instance of supervised learning.

- **Unsupervised learning**: The learner exclusively receives unlabeled training data, and makes predictions for all unseen points. Since in general no labeled example is available in that setting, it can be difficult to quantitatively evaluate the performance of a learner. Clustering and dimensionality reduction are example of unsupervised learning problems.

- **Semi-supervised learning**: The learner receives a training sample consisting of both labeled and unlabeled data, and makes predictions for all unseen points. Semisupervised learning is common in settings where unlabeled data is easily accessible but labels are expensive to obtain. Various types of problems arising in applications, including classification, regression, or ranking tasks, can be framed as instances of semi-supervised learning. The hope is that the distribution of unlabeled data accessible to the learner can help him achieve a better performance than in the supervised setting. The analysis of the conditions under which this can indeed be realized is the topic of much modern theoretical and applied machine learning research.

- **Transductive inference**: As in the semi-supervised scenario, the learner receives a labeled training sample along with a set of unlabeled test points. However, the objective of transductive inference is to predict labels only for these particular test points. Transductive inference appears to be an easier task and matches the scenario encountered in a variety of modern applications. However, as in the semi-supervised setting, the assumptions under which a better performance can b

- **On-line learning**: In contrast with the previous scenarios, the online scenario involves multiple rounds and training and testing phases are intermixed. At each round, the learner receives an unlabeled training point, makes a prediction, receives the true label, and incurs a loss. The objective in the on-line setting is to minimize the cumulative loss over all rounds. Unlike the previous settings just discussed, no distributional assumption is made in on-line learning. In fact, instances and their labels may be chosen adversarially within this scenario.

- **Reinforcement learning**: The training and testing phases are also intermixed in reinforcement learning. To collect information, the learner actively interacts with the environment and in some cases affects the environment, and receives an immediate reward for each action. The object of the learner is to maximize his reward over a course of actions and iterations with the environment. However, no long-term reward feedback is provided by the environment, and the learner is faced with the exploration versus exploitation dilemma, since he must choose between exploring unknown actions to gain more information versus exploiting the information already collected.

- **Active learning**: The learner adaptively or interactively collects training examples, typically by querying an oracle to request labels for new points. The goal in active learning is to achieve a performance comparable to the standard supervised learning scenario, but with fewer labeled examples. Active learning is often used in applications where labels are expensive to obtain, for example computational biology applications.

In practice, many other intermediate and somewhat more complex learning scenarios may be encountered.

UNDERSTANDING BASIC CONCEPTS

Machine Learning is continuously growing in the IT world and gaining strength in different business sectors. Although Machine Learning is in the developing phase, it is popular among all technologies. It is a field of study that makes computers capable of automatically learning and improving from experience. Hence, Machine Learning focuses on the strength of computer programs with the help of collecting data from various observations. In this article, "Concepts in Machine Learning", we will discuss a few basic concepts used in Machine Learning such as what is Machine Learning, technologies and algorithms used in Machine Learning, Applications and example of Machine Learning, and much more. So, let's start with a quick introduction to machine learning.

Machine Learning is defined as a technology that is used to train machines to perform various actions such as predictions, recommendations, estimations, etc., based on historical data or past experience.

Machine Learning enables computers to behave like human beings by training them with the help of past experience and predicted data.

There are three key aspects of Machine Learning, which are as follows:

◉ **Task**: A task is defined as the main problem in which we are interested. This task/problem can be related to the predictions and recommendations and estimations, etc.

◉ **Experience**: It is defined as learning from historical or past data and used to estimate and resolve future tasks.

◉ **Performance**: It is defined as the capacity of any machine to resolve any machine learning task or problem and provide the best outcome for the same. However, performance is dependent on the type of machine learning problems.

Applications of Machine Learning

Machine Learning is widely being used in approximately every sector, including healthcare, marketing, finance, infrastructure, automation, etc. There are some important real-world examples of machine learning, which are as follows:

Healthcare and Medical Diagnosis

Machine Learning is used in healthcare industries that help in generating neural networks. These self-learning neural networks help specialists for providing quality treatment by analyzing external data on a patient's condition, X-rays, CT scans, various tests, and screenings. Other than treatment, machine learning is also helpful for cases like automatic billing, clinical decision supports, and development of clinical care guidelines, etc.

Marketing

Machine learning helps marketers to create various hypotheses, testing, evaluation, and analyze datasets. It helps us to quickly make predictions based on the concept of big data. It is also helpful for stock marketing as most of the trading is done through bots and based on calculations from machine learning algorithms. Various Deep Learning Neural network helps to build trading models such as Convolutional Neural Network, Recurrent Neural Network, Long-short term memory, etc.

Self-driving cars

This is one of the most exciting applications of machine learning in today's world. It plays a vital role in developing self-driving cars. Various automobile companies like Tesla, Tata, etc., are continuously working for the development of self-driving cars. It also becomes possible by the machine learning method (supervised learning), in which a machine is trained to detect people and objects while driving.

Speech Recognition

Speech Recognition is one of the most popular applications of machine learning. Nowadays, almost every mobile application comes with a voice search facility. This "Search By Voice" facility is also a part of speech recognition. In this method, voice instructions are converted into text, which is known as Speech to text" or "Computer speech recognition.

Google assistant, SIRI, Alexa, Cortana, etc., are some famous applications of speech recognition.

Traffic Prediction

Machine Learning also helps us to find the shortest route to reach our destination by using Google Maps. It also helps us in predicting traffic conditions, whether it is cleared or congested, through the real-time location of the Google Maps app and sensor.

Image Recognition

Image recognition is also an important application of machine learning for identifying objects, persons, places, etc. Face detection and auto friend tagging suggestion is the most famous application of image recognition used by Facebook,

Instagram, etc. Whenever we upload photos with our Facebook friends, it automatically suggests their names through image recognition technology.

Product Recommendations

Machine Learning is widely used in business industries for the marketing of various products. Almost all big and small companies like Amazon, Alibaba, Walmart, Netflix, etc., are using machine learning techniques for products recommendation to their users. Whenever we search for any products on their websites, we automatically get started with lots of advertisements for similar products. This is also possible by Machine Learning algorithms that learn users' interests and, based on past data, suggest products to the user.

Automatic Translation

Automatic language translation is also one of the most significant applications of machine learning that is based on sequence algorithms by translating text of one language into other desirable languages. Google GNMT (Google Neural Machine Translation) provides this feature, which is Neural Machine Learning. Further, you can also translate the selected text on images as well as complete documents through Google Lens.

Virtual Assistant

A virtual personal assistant is also one of the most popular applications of machine learning. First, it records out voice and sends to cloud-based server then decode it with the help of machine learning algorithms. All big companies like Amazon, Google, etc., are using these features for playing music, calling someone, opening an app and searching data on the internet, etc.

Email Spam and Malware Filtering

Machine Learning also helps us to filter various Emails received on our mailbox according to their category, such as important, normal, and spam. It is possible by ML algorithms such as Multi-Layer Perceptron, Decision tree, and Naïve Bayes classifier.

Commonly used Machine Learning Algorithms

Here is a list of a few commonly used Machine Learning Algorithms as follows:

Linear Regression

Linear Regression is one of the simplest and popular machine learning algorithms recommended by a data scientist. It is used for predictive analysis by making predictions for real variables such as experience, salary, cost, etc.

It is a statistical approach that represents the linear relationship between two or more variables, either dependent or independent, hence called Linear Regression. It shows the value of the dependent variable changes with respect to the independent variable, and the slope of this graph (Fig. 2.1) is called as Line of Regression.

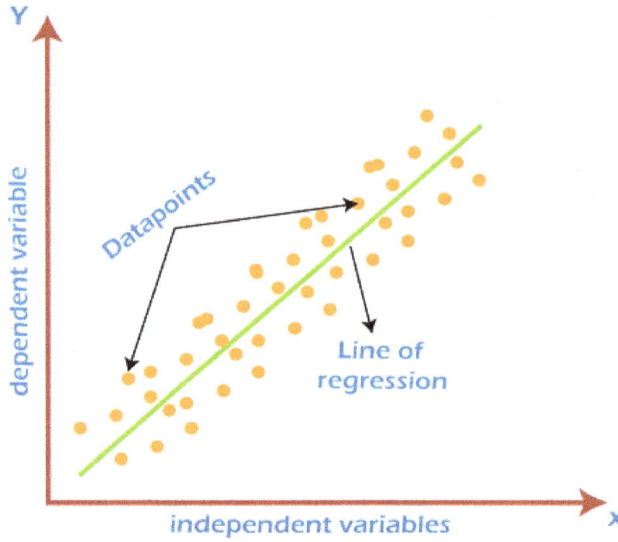

Fig. 2.1 Linear Regression

Linear Regression can be expressed mathematically as follows:

$y = a_0 + a_1x + e$

Y= Dependent Variable

X= Independent Variable

a_0 = intercept of the line (Gives an additional degree of freedom)

a_1 = Linear regression coefficient (scale factor to each input value).

e = random error

The values for x and y variables are training datasets for Linear Regression model representation.

Types of Linear Regression:

⦿ Simple Linear Regression

⦿ Multiple Linear Regression

Applications of Linear Regression

Linear Regression is helpful for evaluating the business trends and forecasts such as prediction of salary of a person based on their experience, prediction of crop production based on the amount of rainfall, etc.

Logistic Regression

Logistic Regression is a subset of the Supervised learning technique. It helps us to predict the output of categorical dependent variables using a given set of independent variables. However, it can be Binary (0 or 1) as well as Boolean (true/false), but instead of giving an exact value, it gives a probabilistic value between 0 or 1. It is much similar to Linear Regression, depending on its use in the machine learning model. As Linear regression is used for solving regression problems, similarly, Logistic regression is helpful for solving classification problems.

Logistic Regression can be expressed as an 'S-shaped curve called sigmoid functions. It predicts two maximum values (0 or 1).

Mathematically, we can express Logistic regression as follows:

Types of Logistic Regression:

⊙ Binomial

⊙ Multinomial

⊙ Ordinal

K Nearest Neighbour (KNN)

It is also one of the simplest machine learning algorithms that come under supervised learning techniques. It is helpful for solving regression as well as classification problems. It assumes the similarity between the new data and available data and puts the new data into the category that is most similar to the available categories. It is also known as Lazy Learner Algorithms because it does not learn from the training set immediately; instead, it stores the dataset, and at the time of classification, it performs an action on the dataset. Let's suppose we have a few sets of images of cats and dogs and want to identify whether a new image is of a cat or dog. Then KNN algorithm (Fig. 2.2) is the best way to identify the cat from available data sets because it works on similarity measures. Hence, the KNN model will compare the new image with available images and put the output in the cat's category.

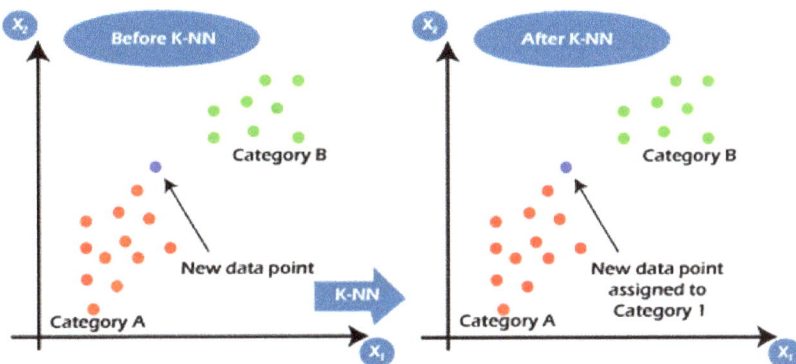

Fig. 2.2 KNN algorithm

Let's understand the KNN algorithm with the below screenshot, where we have to assign a new data point based on the similarity with available data points.

Applications of KNN algorithm in Machine Learning

Including Machine Learning, KNN algorithms are used in so many fields as follows:

- ◉ Healthcare and Medical diagnosis
- ◉ Credit score checking
- ◉ Text Editing
- ◉ Hotel Booking
- ◉ Gaming
- ◉ Natural Language Processing, etc.

K-Means Clustering

K-Means Clustering is a subset of unsupervised learning techniques. It helps us to solve clustering problems by means of grouping the unlabeled datasets into different clusters. Here K defines the number of pre-defined clusters that need to be created in the process, as if K=2, there will be two clusters, and for K=3, there will be three clusters, and so on.

Decision Tree

Decision Tree is also another type of Machine Learning technique that comes under Supervised Learning. Similar to KNN, the decision tree also helps us to solve classification as well as regression problems, but it is mostly preferred to solve classification problems. The name decision tree is because it consists of a tree-structured classifier in which attributes are represented by internal nodes, decision rules are represented by branches, and the outcome of the model is represented by each leaf of a tree. The tree starts from the decision node, also known as the root node, and ends with the leaf node (Fig. 2.3).

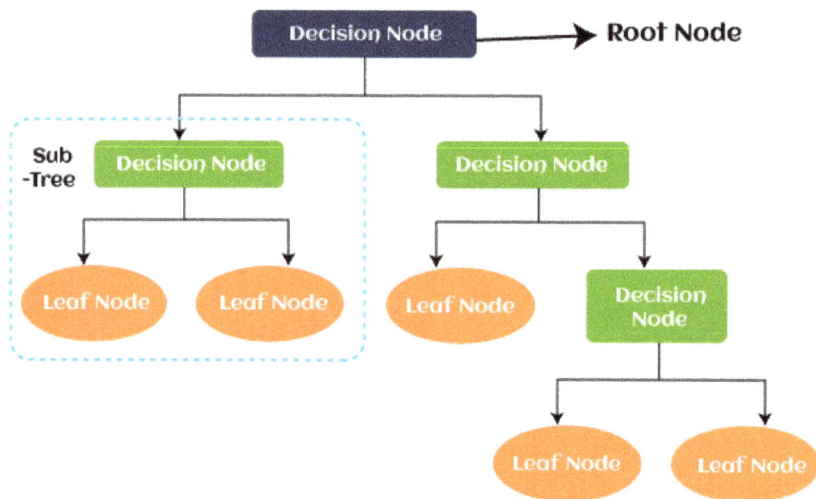

Fig. 2.3 A Decision Node Tree

Decision nodes help us to make any decision, whereas leaves are used to determine the output of those decisions.

A Decision Tree is a graphical representation for getting all the possible outcomes to a problem or decision depending on certain given conditions.

Random Forest

Random Forest is also one of the most preferred machine learning algorithms that come under the Supervised Learning technique. Similar to KNN and Decision Tree, It also allows us to solve classification as well as regression problems, but it is preferred whenever we have a requirement to solve a complex problem and to improve the performance of the model.

A random forest algorithm is based on the concept of ensemble learning, which is a process of combining multiple classifiers.

Random forest classifier is made from a combination of a number of decision trees as well as various subsets of the given dataset. This combination takes input as an average prediction from all trees and improves the accuracy of the model. The greater number of trees in the forest leads to higher accuracy and prevents the problem of overfitting. Further, It also takes less training time as compared to other algorithms.

Support Vector Machines (SVM)

It is also one of the most popular machine learning algorithms that come as a subset of the Supervised Learning technique in machine learning. The goal of the support vector machine algorithm is to create the best line or decision boundary that can segregate n-dimensional space into classes so that we can easily put the new data point in the correct category in the future. This best decision boundary is called a hyperplane. It is also used to solve classification as well as regression problems. It is used for Face detection, image classification, text categorization, etc.

Naïve Bayes

The naïve Bayes algorithm is one of the simplest and most effective machine learning algorithms that come under the supervised learning technique. It is based on the concept of the Bayes Theorem, used to solve classification-related problems. It helps to build fast machine learning models that can make quick predictions with greater accuracy and performance. It is mostly preferred for text classification having high-dimensional training datasets.

It is used as a probabilistic classifier which means it predicts on the basis of the probability of an object. Spam filtration, Sentimental analysis, and classifying articles are some important applications of the Naïve Bayes algorithm.

It is also based on the concept of Bayes Theorem, which is also known as Bayes' Rule or Bayes' law. Mathematically, Bayes Theorem can be expressed as follows:

Where,

- $P(A)$ is Prior Probability
- $P(B)$ is Marginal Probability
- $P(A|B)$ is Posterior probability
- $P(B|A)$ is Likelihood probability

Difference between Machine Learning and Artificial Intelligence

- Artificial intelligence is a technology using which we can create intelligent systems that can simulate human intelligence, whereas Machine learning is a subfield of artificial intelligence, which enables machines to learn from past data or experiences.

- Artificial Intelligence is a technology used to create an intelligent system that enables a machine to simulate human behavior. Whereas, Machine Learning is a branch of AI which helps a machine to learn from experience without being explicitly programmed.

- AI helps to make humans like intelligent computer systems to solve complex problems. Whereas, ML is used to gain accurate predictions from past data or experience.

- AI can be divided into Weak AI, General AI, and Strong AI. Whereas, IML can be divided into Supervised learning, Unsupervised learning, and Reinforcement learning.

- Each AI agent includes learning, reasoning, and self-correction. Each ML model includes learning and self-correction when introduced with new data.

- AI deals with Structured, semi-structured, and unstructured data. ML deals with Structured and semi-structured data.

- **Applications of AI:** Siri, customer support using catboats, Expert System, Online game playing, an intelligent humanoid robot, etc.

- **Applications of ML:** Online recommender system, Google search algorithms, Facebook auto friend tagging suggestions, etc.

TYPES OF MACHINE LEARNING: SUPERVISED, UNSUPERVISED, AND REINFORCEMENT LEARNING

Supervised learning

Supervised learning is a type of machine learning algorithm that learns from labeled data. Labeled data is data that has been tagged with a correct answer or classification.

Supervised learning, as the name indicates, has the presence of a supervisor as a teacher. Supervised learning is when we teach or train the machine using data that is well-labelled. Which means some data is already tagged with the correct answer. After that, the machine is provided with a new set of examples(data) so that the supervised learning algorithm analyses the training data(set of training examples) and produces a correct outcome from labelled data.

For example, a labelled dataset of images of Elephant, Camel and Cow would have each image tagged with either "Elephant", "Camel"or "Cow." (Fig. 2.4)

Key Points:

- ◉ Supervised learning involves training a machine from labeled data.

- ◉ Labeled data consists of examples with the correct answer or classification.

- ◉ The machine learns the relationship between inputs (fruit images) and outputs (fruit labels).

- ◉ The trained machine can then make predictions on new, unlabeled data.

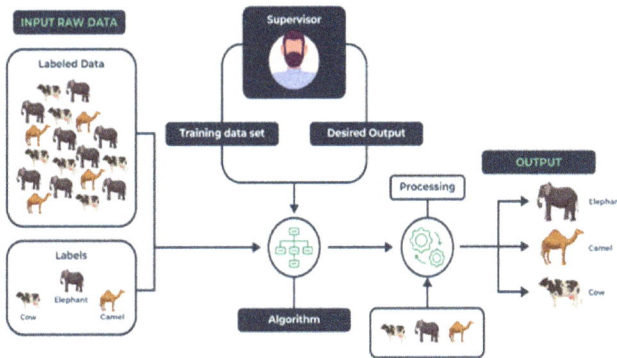

Fig. 2.4 Supervised learning

Example:

Let's say you have a fruit basket that you want to identify. The machine would first analyze the image to extract features such as its shape, color, and texture. Then, it would compare these features to the features of the fruits it has already learned about. If the new image's features are most similar to those of an apple, the machine would predict that the fruit is an apple.

For instance, suppose you are given a basket filled with different kinds of fruits. Now the first step is to train the machine with all the different fruits one by one like this:

- ◉ If the shape of the object is rounded and has a depression at the top, is red in color, then it will be labeled as –**Apple**.

- ◉ If the shape of the object is a long curving cylinder having Green-Yellow color, then it will be labeled as –**Banana**.

Now suppose after training the data, you have given a new separate fruit, say Banana from the basket, and asked to identify it.

Since the machine has already learned the things from previous data and this time has to use it wisely. It will first classify the fruit with its shape and color and would confirm the fruit name as BANANA and put it in the Banana category. Thus the machine learns the things from training data(basket containing fruits) and then applies the knowledge to test data(new fruit).

Types of Supervised Learning

Supervised learning is classified into two categories of algorithms:

⦿ **Regression**: A regression problem is when the output variable is a real value, such as "dollars" or "weight".

⦿ **Classification**: A classification problem is when the output variable is a category, such as "Red" or "blue" , "disease" or "no disease".

Supervised learning deals with or learns with "labeled" data. This implies that some data is already tagged with the correct answer.

Regression

Regression is a type of supervised learning that is used to predict continuous values, such as house prices, stock prices, or customer churn. Regression algorithms learn a function that maps from the input features to the output value.

Some common regression algorithms include:

⦿ Linear Regression

⦿ Polynomial Regression

⦿ Support Vector Machine Regression

⦿ Decision Tree Regression

⦿ Random Forest Regression

Classification

Classification is a type of supervised learning that is used to predict categorical values, such as whether a customer will churn or not, whether an email is spam or not, or whether a medical image shows a tumor or not. Classification algorithms learn a function that maps from the input features to a probability distribution over the output classes.

Some common classification algorithms include:

⦿ Logistic Regression

⦿ Support Vector Machines

⦿ Decision Trees

⦿ Random Forests

- Naive Baye

Evaluating Supervised Learning Models

Evaluating supervised learning models is an important step in ensuring that the model is accurate and generalizable. There are a number of different metrics that can be used to evaluate supervised learning models, but some of the most common ones include:

For Regression

- **Mean Squared Error (MSE):** MSE measures the average squared difference between the predicted values and the actual values. Lower MSE values indicate better model performance.

- **Root Mean Squared Error (RMSE):** RMSE is the square root of MSE, representing the standard deviation of the prediction errors. Similar to MSE, lower RMSE values indicate better model performance.

- **Mean Absolute Error (MAE):** MAE measures the average absolute difference between the predicted values and the actual values. It is less sensitive to outliers compared to MSE or RMSE.

- **R-squared (Coefficient of Determination):** R-squared measures the proportion of the variance in the target variable that is explained by the model. Higher R-squared values indicate better model fit.

For Classification

- **Accuracy:** Accuracy is the percentage of predictions that the model makes correctly. It is calculated by dividing the number of correct predictions by the total number of predictions.

- **Precision:** Precision is the percentage of positive predictions that the model makes that are actually correct. It is calculated by dividing the number of true positives by the total number of positive predictions.

- **Recall:** Recall is the percentage of all positive examples that the model correctly identifies. It is calculated by dividing the number of true positives by the total number of positive examples.

- **F1 score:** The F1 score is a weighted average of precision and recall. It is calculated by taking the harmonic mean of precision and recall.

- **Confusion matrix:** A confusion matrix is a table that shows the number of predictions for each class, along with the actual class labels. It can be used to visualize the performance of the model and identify areas where the model is struggling.

Applications of Supervised learning

Supervised learning can be used to solve a wide variety of problems, including:

- ◉ **Spam filtering:** Supervised learning algorithms can be trained to identify and classify spam emails based on their content, helping users avoid unwanted messages.

- ◉ **Image classification:** Supervised learning can automatically classify images into different categories, such as animals, objects, or scenes, facilitating tasks like image search, content moderation, and image-based product recommendations.

- ◉ **Medical diagnosis:** Supervised learning can assist in medical diagnosis by analyzing patient data, such as medical images, test results, and patient history, to identify patterns that suggest specific diseases or conditions.

- ◉ **Fraud detection:** Supervised learning models can analyze financial transactions and identify patterns that indicate fraudulent activity, helping financial institutions prevent fraud and protect their customers.

- ◉ **Natural language processing (NLP):** Supervised learning plays a crucial role in NLP tasks, including sentiment analysis, machine translation, and text summarization, enabling machines to understand and process human language effectively.

Advantages of Supervised learning

- ◉ Supervised learning allows collecting data and produces data output from previous experiences.

- ◉ Helps to optimize performance criteria with the help of experience.

- ◉ Supervised machine learning helps to solve various types of real-world computation problems.

- ◉ It performs classification and regression tasks.

- ◉ It allows estimating or mapping the result to a new sample.

- ◉ We have complete control over choosing the number of classes we want in the training data.

Disadvantages of Supervised learning

- ◉ Classifying big data can be challenging.

- ◉ Training for supervised learning needs a lot of computation time. So, it requires a lot of time.

- ◉ Supervised learning cannot handle all complex tasks in Machine Learning.

- ◉ Computation time is vast for supervised learning.

- ◉ It requires a labelled data set.

- ◉ It requires a training process.

Unsupervised learning

Unsupervised learning is a type of machine learning that learns from unlabeled data. This means that the data does not have any pre-existing labels or categories. The goal of unsupervised learning is to discover patterns and relationships in the data without any explicit guidance.

Unsupervised learning is the training of a machine using information that is neither classified nor labeled and allowing the algorithm to act on that information without guidance. Here the task of the machine is to group unsorted information according to similarities, patterns, and differences without any prior training of data.

Unlike supervised learning, no teacher is provided that means no training will be given to the machine. Therefore the machine is restricted to find the hidden structure in unlabeled data by itself.

You can use unsupervised learning to examine the animal data that has been gathered and distinguish between several groups according to the traits and actions of the animals. These groupings might correspond to various animal species, providing you to categorize the creatures without depending on labels that already exist (Fig. 2.5).

Key Points

- Unsupervised learning allows the model to discover patterns and relationships in unlabeled data.

- Clustering algorithms group similar data points together based on their inherent characteristics.

- Feature extraction captures essential information from the data, enabling the model to make meaningful distinctions.

- Label association assigns categories to the clusters based on the extracted patterns and characteristics.

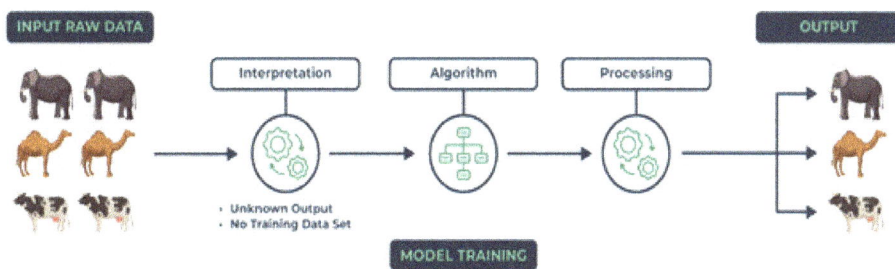

Fig. 2.5 Unsupervised learning

Example

Imagine you have a machine learning model trained on a large dataset of unlabeled images, containing both dogs and cats. The model has never seen an image of a dog or cat before, and it has no pre-existing labels or categories for these animals. Your task is to use unsupervised learning to identify the dogs and cats in a new, unseen image.

For instance, suppose it is given an image having both dogs and cats which it has never seen.

Thus the machine has no idea about the features of dogs and cats so we can't categorize it as 'dogs and cats '. But it can categorize them according to their similarities, patterns, and differences, i.e., we can easily categorize the above picture into two parts. The first may contain all pics having **dogs** in them and the second part may contain all pics having **cats** in them. Here you didn't learn anything before, which means no training data or examples.

It allows the model to work on its own to discover patterns and information that was previously undetected. It mainly deals with unlabelled data.

Types of Unsupervised Learning

Unsupervised learning is classified into two categories of algorithms:

- **Clustering**: A clustering problem is where you want to discover the inherent groupings in the data, such as grouping customers by purchasing behavior.
- **Association**: An association rule learning problem is where you want to discover rules that describe large portions of your data, such as people that buy X also tend to buy Y.

Clustering

Clustering is a type of unsupervised learning that is used to group similar data points together. Clustering algorithms work by iteratively moving data points closer to their cluster centers and further away from data points in other clusters.

- Exclusive (partitioning)
- Agglomerative
- Overlapping
- Probabilistic

Clustering Types

- Hierarchical clustering
- K-means clustering
- Principal Component Analysis
- Singular Value Decomposition
- Independent Component Analysis
- Gaussian Mixture Models (GMMs)
- Density-Based Spatial Clustering of Applications with Noise (DBSCAN)

Association rule learning

Association rule learning is a type of unsupervised learning that is used to identify patterns in a data. Association rule learning algorithms work by finding relationships between different items in a dataset.

Some common association rule learning algorithms include:

◉ Apriori Algorithm

◉ Eclat Algorithm

◉ FP-Growth Algorithm

Evaluating Non-Supervised Learning Models

Evaluating non-supervised learning models is an important step in ensuring that the model is effective and useful. However, it can be more challenging than evaluating supervised learning models, as there is no ground truth data to compare the model's predictions to.

There are a number of different metrics that can be used to evaluate non-supervised learning models, but some of the most common ones include:

◉ **Silhouette score:** The silhouette score measures how well each data point is clustered with its own cluster members and separated from other clusters. It ranges from -1 to 1, with higher scores indicating better clustering.

◉ **Calinski-Harabasz score:** The Calinski-Harabasz score measures the ratio between the variance between clusters and the variance within clusters. It ranges from 0 to infinity, with higher scores indicating better clustering.

◉ **Adjusted Rand index:** The adjusted Rand index measures the similarity between two clusterings. It ranges from -1 to 1, with higher scores indicating more similar clusterings.

◉ **Davies-Bouldin index:** The Davies-Bouldin index measures the average similarity between clusters. It ranges from 0 to infinity, with lower scores indicating better clustering.

◉ **F1 score:** The F1 score is a weighted average of precision and recall, which are two metrics that are commonly used in supervised learning to evaluate classification models. However, the F1 score can also be used to evaluate non-supervised learning models, such as clustering models.

Application of Unsupervised learning

Non-supervised learning can be used to solve a wide variety of problems, including:

◉ **Anomaly detection:** Unsupervised learning can identify unusual patterns or deviations from normal behavior in data, enabling the detection of fraud, intrusion, or system failures.

◉ **Scientific discovery:** Unsupervised learning can uncover hidden relationships and patterns in scientific data, leading to new hypotheses and insights in various scientific fields.

◉ **Recommendation systems:** Unsupervised learning can identify patterns and similarities in user behavior and preferences to recommend products, movies, or music that align with their interests.

◉ **Customer segmentation:** Unsupervised learning can identify groups of customers with similar characteristics, allowing businesses to target marketing campaigns and improve customer service more effectively.

◉ **Image analysis:** Unsupervised learning can group images based on their content, facilitating tasks such as image classification, object detection, and image retrieval.

Advantages of Unsupervised learning

◉ It does not require training data to be labeled.

◉ Dimensionality reduction can be easily accomplished using unsupervised learning.

◉ Capable of finding previously unknown patterns in data.

◉ Unsupervised learning can help you gain insights from unlabeled data that you might not have been able to get otherwise.

◉ Unsupervised learning is good at finding patterns and relationships in data without being told what to look for. This can help you learn new things about your data.

Disadvantages of Unsupervised learning

◉ Difficult to measure accuracy or effectiveness due to lack of predefined answers during training.

◉ The results often have lesser accuracy.

◉ The user needs to spend time interpreting and label the classes which follow that classification.

◉ Unsupervised learning can be sensitive to data quality, including missing values, outliers, and noisy data.

◉ Without labeled data, it can be difficult to evaluate the performance of unsupervised learning models, making it challenging to assess their effectiveness.

Reinforcement learning

Reinforcement learning is an area of Machine Learning. It is about taking suitable action to maximize reward in a particular situation. It is employed by various software and machines to find the best possible behavior or path it should take in a specific situation. Reinforcement learning differs from supervised learning in a way that in supervised learning the training data has the answer key with it so the model is trained with the correct answer itself whereas in reinforcement learning, there is no answer but the reinforcement agent decides what to do to perform the given task. In the absence of a training dataset, it is bound to learn from its experience.

Reinforcement Learning (RL) is the science of decision making. It is about learning the optimal behavior in an environment to obtain maximum reward. In RL, the data is accumulated from machine learning systems that use a trial-and-error method. Data is not part of the input that we would find in supervised or unsupervised machine learning.

Reinforcement learning uses algorithms that learn from outcomes and decide which action to take next. After each action, the algorithm receives feedback that helps it determine whether the choice it made was correct, neutral or incorrect. It is a good technique to use for automated systems that have to make a lot of small decisions without human guidance.

Reinforcement learning is an autonomous, self-teaching system that essentially learns by trial and error. It performs actions with the aim of maximizing rewards, or in other words, it is learning by doing in order to achieve the best outcomes.

Example

The problem is as follows: We have an agent and a reward, with many hurdles in between. The agent is supposed to find the best possible path to reach the reward. The following problem explains the problem more easily (Fig. 2.6).

Figure 2.6 below shows the robot, diamond, and fire. The goal of the robot is to get the reward that is the diamond and avoid the hurdles that are fired. The robot learns by trying all the possible paths and then choosing the path which gives him the reward with the least hurdles. Each right step will give the robot a reward and each wrong step will subtract the reward of the robot. The total reward will be calculated when it reaches the final reward that is the diamond.

Main points in Reinforcement learning

- ◉ **Input:** The input should be an initial state from which the model will start
- ◉ **Output:** There are many possible outputs as there are a variety of solutions to a particular problem
- ◉ **Training:** The training is based upon the input, The model will return a state and the user will decide to reward or punish the model based on its output.
- ◉ The model keeps continues to learn.
- ◉ The best solution is decided based on the maximum reward.

Fig. 2.6 Reinforcement Learning

FEATURE ENGINEERING AND DATA PREPROCESSING

Feature engineering is the pre-processing step of machine learning, which is used to transform raw data into features that can be used for creating a predictive model using Machine learning or statistical Modelling. Feature engineering in machine learning aims to improve the performance of models (Fig. 2.7).

Fig. 2.7 Feature Engineering and Data Preprocessing

What is a feature?

Generally, all machine learning algorithms take input data to generate the output. The input data remains in a tabular form consisting of rows (instances or observations) and columns (variable or attributes), and these attributes are often known as features. For example, an image is an instance in computer vision, but a line in the image could be the feature. Similarly, in NLP, a document can be an observation, and the word count could be the feature. So, we can say a feature is an attribute that impacts a problem or is useful for the problem.

Feature Engineering

Feature engineering is the pre-processing step of machine learning, which extracts features from raw data. It helps to represent an underlying problem to predictive models in a better way, which as a result, improve the accuracy of the model for unseen data. The predictive model contains predictor variables and an outcome variable, and while the feature engineering process selects the most useful predictor variables for the model (Fig. 2.8).

Since 2016, automated feature engineering is also used in different machine learning software that helps in automatically extracting features from raw data. Feature engineering in ML contains mainly four processes: Feature Creation, Transformations, Feature Extraction, and Feature Selection.

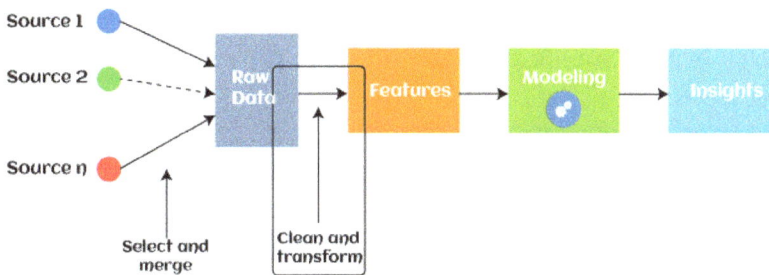

Fig. 2.8 Feature engineering

These processes are described as below:

- ◉ **Feature Creation**: Feature creation is finding the most useful variables to be used in a predictive model. The process is subjective, and it requires human creativity and intervention. The new features are created by mixing existing features using addition, subtraction, and ration, and these new features have great flexibility.

- ◉ **Transformations**: The transformation step of feature engineering involves adjusting the predictor variable to improve the accuracy and performance of the model. For example, it ensures that the model is flexible to take input of the variety of data; it ensures that all the variables are on the same scale, making the model easier to understand. It improves the model's accuracy and ensures that all the features are within the acceptable range to avoid any computational error.

- ◉ **Feature Extraction**: Feature extraction is an automated feature engineering process that generates new variables by extracting them from the raw data. The main aim of this step is to reduce the volume of data so that it can be easily used and managed for data modelling. Feature extraction methods include cluster analysis, text analytics, edge detection algorithms, and principal components analysis (PCA).

⦿ **Feature Selection:** While developing the machine learning model, only a few variables in the dataset are useful for building the model, and the rest features are either redundant or irrelevant. If we input the dataset with all these redundant and irrelevant features, it may negatively impact and reduce the overall performance and accuracy of the model. Hence it is very important to identify and select the most appropriate features from the data and remove the irrelevant or less important features, which is done with the help of feature selection in machine learning. "Feature selection is a way of selecting the subset of the most relevant features from the original features set by removing the redundant, irrelevant, or noisy features."

Below are some benefits of using feature selection in machine learning:

⦿ It helps in avoiding the curse of dimensionality.

⦿ It helps in the simplification of the model so that the researchers can easily interpret it.

⦿ It reduces the training time.

⦿ It reduces overfitting hence enhancing the generalization.

Need for Feature Engineering in Machine Learning

In machine learning, the performance of the model depends on data pre-processing and data handling. But if we create a model without pre-processing or data handling, then it may not give good accuracy. Whereas, if we apply feature engineering on the same model, then the accuracy of the model is enhanced. Hence, feature engineering in machine learning improves the model's performance. Below are some points that explain the need for feature engineering:

⦿ **Better features mean flexibility.** In machine learning, we always try to choose the optimal model to get good results. However, sometimes after choosing the wrong model, still, we can get better predictions, and this is because of better features. The flexibility in features will enable you to select the less complex models. Because less complex models are faster to run, easier to understand and maintain, which is always desirable.

⦿ **Better features mean simpler models.** If we input the well-engineered features to our model, then even after selecting the wrong parameters (Not much optimal), we can have good outcomes. After feature engineering, it is not necessary to do hard for picking the right model with the most optimized parameters. If we have good features, we can better represent the complete data and use it to best characterize the given problem.

⦿ **Better features mean better results.** As already discussed, in machine learning, as data we will provide will get the same output. So, to obtain better results, we must need to use better features.

Steps in Feature Engineering

The steps of feature engineering may vary as per different data scientists and ML engineers. However, there are some common steps that are involved in most machine learning algorithms, and these steps are as follows:

- ◉ **Data Preparation:** The first step is data preparation. In this step, raw data acquired from different resources are prepared to make it in a suitable format so that it can be used in the ML model. The data preparation may contain cleaning of data, delivery, data augmentation, fusion, ingestion, or loading.

- ◉ **Exploratory Analysis:** Exploratory analysis or Exploratory data analysis (EDA) is an important step of features engineering, which is mainly used by data scientists. This step involves analysis, investing data set, and summarization of the main characteristics of data. Different data visualization techniques are used to better understand the manipulation of data sources, to find the most appropriate statistical technique for data analysis, and to select the best features for the data.

- ◉ **Benchmark**: Benchmarking is a process of setting a standard baseline for accuracy to compare all the variables from this baseline. The benchmarking process is used to improve the predictability of the model and reduce the error rate.

Feature Engineering Techniques

Some of the popular feature engineering techniques include:

Imputation

Feature engineering deals with inappropriate data, missing values, human interruption, general errors, insufficient data sources, etc. Missing values within the dataset highly affect the performance of the algorithm, and to deal with them "Imputation" technique is used. Imputation is responsible for handling irregularities within the dataset.

For example, removing the missing values from the complete row or complete column by a huge percentage of missing values. But at the same time, to maintain the data size, it is required to impute the missing data, which can be done as:

- ◉ For numerical data imputation, a default value can be imputed in a column, and missing values can be filled with means or medians of the columns.

- ◉ For categorical data imputation, missing values can be interchanged with the maximum occurred value in a column.

Handling Outliers

Outliers are the deviated values or data points that are observed too away from other data points in such a way that they badly affect the performance of the model. Outliers can be handled with this feature engineering technique. This technique first identifies the outliers and then remove them out.

Standard deviation can be used to identify the outliers. For example, each value within a space has a definite to an average distance, but if a value is greater distant than a certain value, it can be considered as an outlier. **Z-score** can also be used to detect outliers.

Log transform

Logarithm transformation or log transform is one of the commonly used mathematical techniques in machine learning. Log transform helps in handling the skewed data, and it makes the distribution more approximate to normal after transformation. It also reduces the effects of outliers on the data, as because of the normalization of magnitude differences, a model becomes much robust.

Binning

In machine learning, overfitting is one of the main issues that degrade the performance of the model and which occurs due to a greater number of parameters and noisy data. However, one of the popular techniques of feature engineering, "binning", can be used to normalize the noisy data. This process involves segmenting different features into bins.

CHAPTER-3
ALGORITHMS AND MODELS

AI search and optimization algorithms are fundamental tools in artificial intelligence for solving complex problems efficiently. These algorithms are designed to navigate through large search spaces to find optimal solutions or make informed decisions. They range from uninformed search methods like depth-first search and breadth-first search to informed techniques such as A* search and genetic algorithms. Additionally, optimization algorithms like gradient descent and genetic programming help refine solutions to achieve desired outcomes. These algorithms play a crucial role in problem-solving, decision-making, and optimization tasks across various domains.

LINEAR REGRESSION AND LOGISTIC REGRESSION

Linear Regression is a machine learning algorithm based on supervised regression algorithm. Regression models a target prediction value based on independent variables. It is mostly used for finding out the relationship between variables and forecasting. Different regression models differ based on – the kind of relationship between the dependent and independent variables, they are considering and the number of independent variables being used. Logistic regression is basically a supervised classification algorithm. In a classification problem, the target variable(or output), y, can take only discrete values for a given set of features(or inputs), X.

Sl. No.	Linear Regression	Logistic Regression
1.	Linear Regression is a supevised regresion model	Logistic Regression is a supervised classification model
2.	Equation of linear regression: $y = a0 + a1x1 + a2x2 + \ldots + aixi$ Here, y = response variable xi = ith predictor variable ai = average effect on y as xi increases by 1	Equation of logistic regressiony $(x) = e(a0 + a1x1 + a2x2 + \ldots + aixi) / (1 + e(a0 + a1x1 + a2x2 + \ldots + aixi))$ Here, y = response variable xi = ith predictor variable ai = average effect on y as xi increases by 1
3.	In Linear Regression, we predict the value by an integer number.	In Logistic Regression, we predict the by 1 or 0.

Sl. No.	Linear Regression	Logistic Regression
4.	Here no activation function is used.	Here activation function is used to convert a linear regression equation to the logistic regression equation
5.	Here no threshold value is needed.	Here a threshold value is added.
6.	Here we calculate Root Mean Square Error(RMSE) to predict the next weight value.	Here we use precision to predict the next weight value.
7.	Here dependent variable should be numeric and the response variable is continuous to value.	Here the dependent variable consists of only two categories. Logistic regression estimates the odds outcome of the dependent variable given a set of quantitative or categorical independent variables.
8.	It is based on the least square estimation.	It is based on maximum likelihood estimation.
9.	Here when we plot the training datasets, a straight line can be drawn that touches maximum plots.	Any change in the coefficient leads to a change in both the direction and the steepness of the logistic function. It means positive slopes result in an S-shaped curve and negative slopes result in a Z-shaped curve.
10.	Linear regression is used to estimate the dependent variable in case of a change in independent variables. For example, predict the price of houses.	Whereas logistic regression is used to calculate the probability of an event. For example, classify if tissue is benign or malignant.
11.	Linear regression assumes the normal or gaussian distribution of the dependent distribution of the dependent variable.	Logistic regression assumes the binomial variable.
12.	Application of linear regression: Financial risk management Business insights Market analysis	Applications of logistic regression: Medicine Credit Scoring Hotel Booking Gaming Text editing

Linear Regression

⦿ Linear Regression is one of the most simple Machine learning algorithm that comes under Supervised Learning technique and used for solving regression problems.

⦿ It is used for predicting the continuous dependent variable with the help of independent variables.

⦿ The goal of the Linear regression is to find the best fit line that can accurately predict the output for the continuous dependent variable.

- If single independent variable is used for prediction then it is called Simple Linear Regression and if there are more than two independent variables then such regression is called as Multiple Linear Regression.

- By finding the best fit line, algorithm establish the relationship between dependent variable and independent variable. And the relationship should be of linear nature.

- The output for Linear regression should only be the continuous values such as price, age, salary, etc. The relationship between the dependent variable and independent variable can be shown in Fig. 3.1:

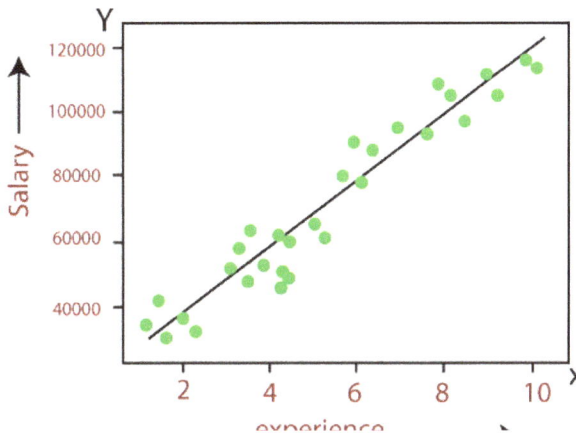

Fig. 3.1

In Fig. 3.1 the dependent variable is on Y-axis (salary) and independent variable is on x-axis(experience). The regression line can be written as:

$$y = a_0 + a_1 x + e$$

Where, a_0 and a_1 are the coefficients and e is the error term.

Logistic Regression

- Logistic regression is one of the most popular Machine learning algorithm that comes under Supervised Learning techniques.

- It can be used for Classification as well as for Regression problems, but mainly used for Classification problems.

- Logistic regression is used to predict the categorical dependent variable with the help of independent variables.

- The output of Logistic Regression problem can be only between the 0 and 1.

- Logistic regression can be used where the probabilities between two classes is required. Such as whether it will rain today or not, either 0 or 1, true or false etc.

- Logistic regression is based on the concept of Maximum Likelihood estimation. According to this estimation, the observed data should be most probable.

◉ In logistic regression, we pass the weighted sum of inputs through an activation function that can map values in between 0 and 1. Such activation function is known as sigmoid function and the curve obtained is called as sigmoid curve or S-curve. Consider Fig. 3.2:

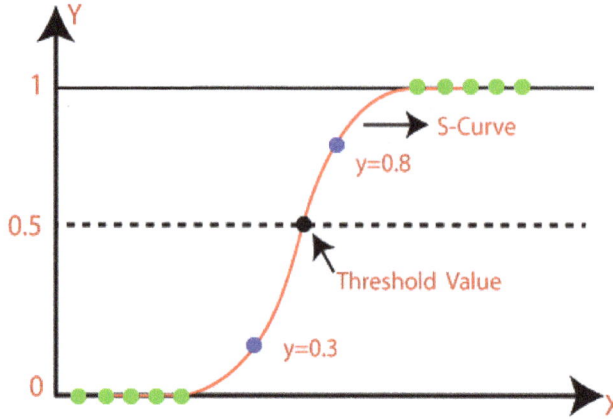

Fig. 3.2 Sigmoid curve or S-curve

◉ The equation for logistic regression is:

$$\log\left[\frac{y}{1-y}\right] = b_0 + b_1x_1 + b_2x_2 + b_3x_3 + \cdots + b_nx_n$$

Difference between Linear Regression and Logistic Regression:

Linear Regression	Logistic Regression
Linear regression is used to predict the continuous dependent variable using a given set of independent variables.	Logistic Regression is used to predict the categorical dependent variable using a given set of independent variables.
Linear Regression is used for solving Regression problem.	Logistic regression is used for solving Classification problems.
In Linear regression, we predict the value of continuous variables.	In logistic Regression, we predict the values of categorical variables.
In linear regression, we find the best fit line, by which we can easily predict the output.	In Logistic Regression, we find the S-curve by which we can classify the samples.
Least square estimation method is used for estimation of accuracy.	Maximum likelihood estimation method is used for estimation of accuracy.
The output for Linear Regression must be a continuous value, such as price, age, etc.	The output of Logistic Regression must be a Categorical value such as 0 or 1, Yes or No, etc.

Linear Regression	Logistic Regression
In Linear regression, it is required that relationship between dependent variable and independent variable must be linear.	In Logistic regression, it is not required to have the linear relationship between the dependent and independent variable.
In linear regression, there may be collinearity between the independent variables.	In logistic regression, there should not be collinearity between the independent variable.

DECISION TREES AND RANDOM FORESTS

- Decision Tree is a Supervised learning technique that can be used for both classification and Regression problems, but mostly it is preferred for solving Classification problems. It is a tree-structured classifier, where internal nodes represent the features of a dataset, branches represent the decision rules and each leaf node represents the outcome.

- In a Decision tree, there are two nodes, which are the Decision Node and Leaf Node. Decision nodes are used to make any decision and have multiple branches, whereas Leaf nodes are the output of those decisions and do not contain any further branches.

- The decisions or the test are performed on the basis of features of the given dataset.

- It is a graphical representation for getting all the possible solutions to a problem/decision based on given conditions.

- It is called a decision tree because, similar to a tree, it starts with the root node, which expands on further branches and constructs a tree-like structure.

- In order to build a tree, we use the CART algorithm, which stands for Classification and Regression Tree algorithm.

- A decision tree simply asks a question, and based on the answer (Yes/No), it further split the tree into subtrees.

Using of Decision Trees

There are various algorithms in Machine learning, so choosing the best algorithm for the given dataset and problem is the main point to remember while creating a machine learning model. Below are the two reasons for using the Decision tree:

- Decision Trees usually mimic human thinking ability while making a decision, so it is easy to understand.

- The logic behind the decision tree can be easily understood because it shows a tree-like structure.

Working of Decision Tree Algorithm

In a decision tree, for predicting the class of the given dataset, the algorithm starts from the root node of the tree. This algorithm compares the values of root attribute with the record (real dataset) attribute and, based on the comparison, follows the branch and jumps to the next node.

For the next node, the algorithm again compares the attribute value with the other sub-nodes and move further. It continues the process until it reaches the leaf node of the tree. The complete process can be better understood using the below algorithm:

- ⊙ **Step-1:** Begin the tree with the root node, says S, which contains the complete dataset.

- ⊙ **Step-2:** Find the best attribute in the dataset using **Attribute Selection Measure (ASM).**

- ⊙ **Step-3:** Divide the S into subsets that contains possible values for the best attributes.

- ⊙ **Step-4:** Generate the decision tree node, which contains the best attribute.

- ⊙ **Step-5:** Recursively make new decision trees using the subsets of the dataset created in step -3. Continue this process until a stage is reached where you cannot further classify the nodes and called the final node as a leaf node.

Example: Suppose there is a candidate who has a job offer and wants to decide whether he should accept the offer or Not. So, to solve this problem, the decision tree starts with the root node (Salary attribute by ASM). The root node splits further into the next decision node (distance from the office) and one leaf node based on the corresponding labels. The next decision node further gets split into one decision node (Cab facility) and one leaf node. Finally, the decision node splits into two leaf nodes (Accepted offers and Declined offer). Consider Fig. 3.3 below:

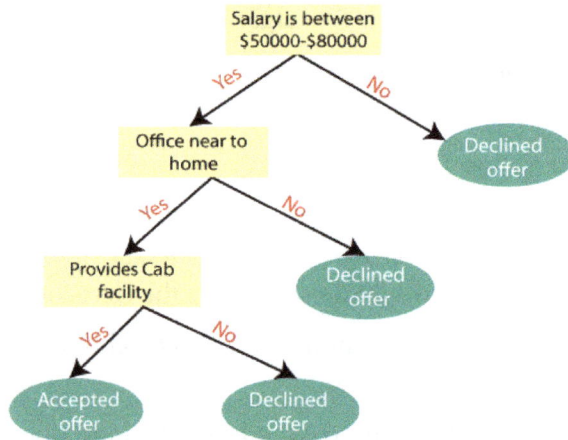

Fig. 3.3 Working of Decision Tree Algorithm

Attribute Selection Measures

While implementing a Decision tree, the main issue arises that how to select the best attribute for the root node and for sub-nodes. So, to solve such problems there is a technique which is called as Attribute selection measure or ASM. By this measurement, we can easily select the best attribute for the nodes of the tree. There are two popular techniques for ASM, which are:

- ⦿ Information Gain
- ⦿ Gini Index

Information Gain

- ⦿ Information gain is the measurement of changes in entropy after the segmentation of a dataset based on an attribute.
- ⦿ It calculates how much information a feature provides us about a class.
- ⦿ According to the value of information gain, we split the node and build the decision tree.
- ⦿ A decision tree algorithm always tries to maximize the value of information gain, and a node/attribute having the highest information gain is split first. It can be calculated using the below formula:

1. **Information Gain** = Entropy(S)- [(Weighted Avg) *Entropy(each feature)

Entropy: Entropy is a metric to measure the impurity in a given attribute. It specifies randomness in data. Entropy can be calculated as:

$$\text{Entropy(s)= -P(yes)log2 P(yes)- P(no) log2 P(no)}$$

Where,

- ⦿ **S = Total number of samples**
- ⦿ **P(yes) = probability of yes**
- ⦿ **P(no) = probability of no**

2. Gini Index:

- ⦿ Gini index is a measure of impurity or purity used while creating a decision tree in the CART(Classification and Regression Tree) algorithm.
- ⦿ An attribute with the low Gini index should be preferred as compared to the high Gini index.
- ⦿ It only creates binary splits, and the CART algorithm uses the Gini index to create binary splits.
- ⦿ Gini index can be calculated using the below formula:

Gini Index= 1- $S_j P_j^2$

Pruning: Getting an Optimal Decision tree

Pruning is a process of deleting the unnecessary nodes from a tree in order to get the optimal decision tree.

A too-large tree increases the risk of overfitting, and a small tree may not capture all the important features of the dataset. Therefore, a technique that decreases the size of the learning tree without reducing accuracy is known as Pruning. There are mainly two types of tree pruning technology used:

- Cost Complexity Pruning
- Reduced Error Pruning.

Advantages of the Decision Tree

- It is simple to understand as it follows the same process which a human follow while making any decision in real-life.
- It can be very useful for solving decision-related problems.
- It helps to think about all the possible outcomes for a problem.
- There is less requirement of data cleaning compared to other algorithms.

Disadvantages of the Decision Tree

- The decision tree contains lots of layers, which makes it complex.
- It may have an overfitting issue, which can be resolved using the Random Forest algorithm.
- For more class labels, the computational complexity of the decision tree may increase.

Python Implementation of Decision Tree

Now we will implement the Decision tree using Python. For this, we will use the dataset "user_data.csv," which we have used in previous classification models. By using the same dataset, we can compare the Decision tree classifier with other classification models such as KNN SVM, LogisticRegression, etc.

Steps will also remain the same, which are given below:

- Data Pre-processing step
- Fitting a Decision-Tree algorithm to the Training set
- Predicting the test result
- Test accuracy of the result(Creation of Confusion matrix)
- Visualizing the test set result.

1. Data Pre-Processing Step:

Below is the code for the pre-processing step:

```
1.   # importing libraries
2.   import numpy as nm
3.   import matplotlib.pyplot as mtp
4.   import pandas as pd
5.
6.   #importing datasets
7.   data_set= pd.read_csv('user_data.csv')
8.
9.   #Extracting Independent and dependent Variable
10.  x= data_set.iloc[:, [2,3]].values
11.  y= data_set.iloc[:, 4].values
12.
13.  # Splitting the dataset into training and test set.
14.  from sklearn.model_selection import train_test_split
15.  x_train, x_test, y_train, y_test= train_test_split(x, y, test_size= 0.25, random_state=0)
16.
17.  #feature Scaling
18.  from sklearn.preprocessing import StandardScaler
19.  st_x= StandardScaler()
20.  x_train= st_x.fit_transform(x_train)
21.  x_test= st_x.transform(x_test)
```

In the above code, we have pre-processed the data. Where we have loaded the dataset, which is given in Fig. 3.4 as:

2. Fitting a Decision-Tree algorithm to the Training set

Now we will fit the model to the training set. For this, we will import the DecisionTreeClassifier class from sklearn.tree library. Below is the code for it:

Index	User ID	Gender	Age	EstimatedSalary	Purchased
0	15624510	Male	19	19000	0
1	15810944	Male	35	20000	0
2	15668575	Female	26	43000	0
3	15603246	Female	27	57000	0
4	15804002	Male	19	76000	0
5	15728773	Male	27	58000	0
6	15598044	Female	27	84000	0
7	15694829	Female	32	150000	1
8	15600575	Male	25	33000	0
9	15727311	Female	35	65000	0
10	15570769	Female	26	80000	0
11	15606274	Female	26	52000	0
12	15746139	Male	20	86000	0
13	15704987	Male	32	18000	0
14	15628972	Male	18	82000	0
15	15697686	Male	29	80000	0

Fig. 3.4 code for the pre-processing

1. #Fitting Decision Tree classifier to the training set

2. From sklearn.tree **import** DecisionTreeClassifier

3. classifier= DecisionTreeClassifier(criterion='entropy', random_state=0)

4. classifier.fit(x_train, y_train)

In the above code, we have created a classifier object, in which we have passed two main parameters;

- ⊙ **"criterion='entropy':** Criterion is used to measure the quality of split, which is calculated by information gain given by entropy.

- ⊙ **random_state=0":** For generating the random states.

Below is the output for this:

Out[8]:

DecisionTreeClassifier(class_weight=None, criterion='entropy', max_depth=None,

max_features=None, max_leaf_nodes=None,

min_impurity_decrease=0.0, min_impurity_split=None,

min_samples_leaf=1, min_samples_split=2,

min_weight_fraction_leaf=0.0, presort=False,

  random_state=0, splitter='best')

3. Predicting the test result

Now we will predict the test set result. We will create a new prediction vector **y_pred.** Below is the code for it:

- ⦿ #Predicting the test set result
- ⦿ y_pred= classifier.predict(x_test)

Output

Figure 3.5 below output image, the predicted output and real test output are given. We can clearly see that there are some values in the prediction vector, which are different from the real vector values. These are prediction errors.

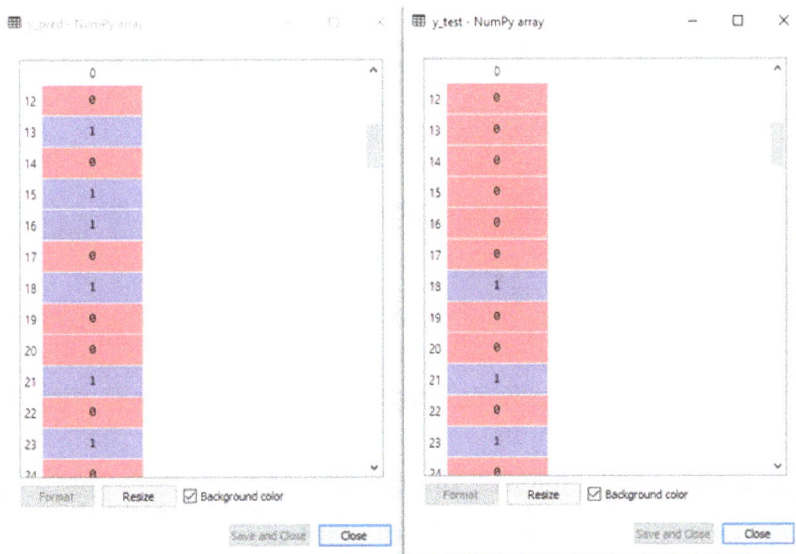

Fig. 3.5 The predicted output and real test output

4. Test accuracy of the result (Creation of Confusion matrix)

In the above output, we have seen that there were some incorrect predictions, so if we want to know the number of correct and incorrect predictions, we need to use the confusion matrix. Below is the code for it:

- ⦿ #Creating the Confusion matrix
- ⦿ from sklearn.metrics **import** confusion_matrix
- ⦿ cm= confusion_matrix(y_test, y_pred)

Output

In Fig. 3.6 - output image, we can see the confusion matrix, which has 6+3= 9 incorrect predictions and62+29=91 correct predictions. Therefore, we can say that compared to other classification models, the Decision Tree classifier made a good prediction.

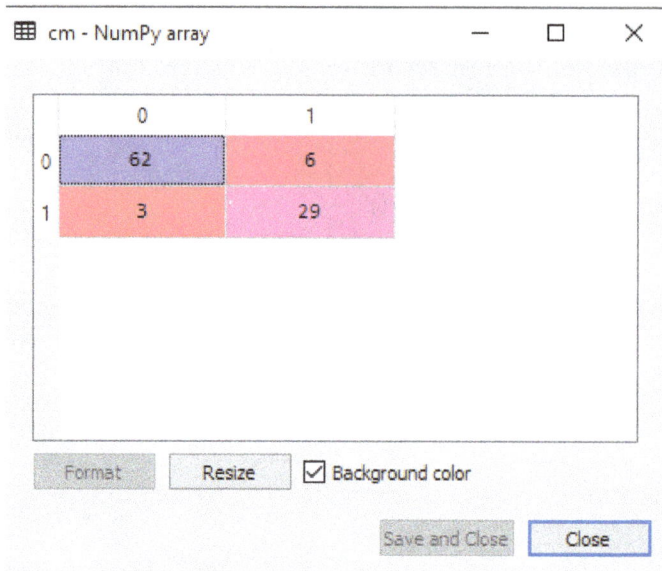

Fig. 3.6 Output image

5. Visualizing the training set result

Here we will visualize the training set result. To visualize the training set result we will plot a graph for the decision tree classifier. The classifier will predict yes or No for the users who have either Purchased or Not purchased the SUV car as we did in Logistic Regression. Below is the code for it:

- #Visulaizing the trianing set result
- from matplotlib.colors **import** ListedColormap
- x_set, y_set = x_train, y_train
- x1, x2 = nm.meshgrid(nm.arange(start = x_set[:, 0].min() - 1, stop = x_set[:, 0].max() + 1, step =0.01),
- nm.arange(start = x_set[:, 1].min() - 1, stop = x_set[:, 1].max() + 1, step = 0.01))
- mtp.contourf(x1, x2, classifier.predict(nm.array([x1.ravel(), x2.ravel()]).T).reshape(x1.shape),
- alpha = 0.75, cmap = ListedColormap(('purple','green')))
- mtp.xlim(x1.min(), x1.max())
- mtp.ylim(x2.min(), x2.max())
- fori, j in enumerate(nm.unique(y_set)):
- mtp.scatter(x_set[y_set == j, 0], x_set[y_set == j, 1],
- c = ListedColormap(('purple', 'green'))(i), label = j)
- mtp.title('Decision Tree Algorithm (Training set)')

- ⊙ mtp.xlabel('Age')
- ⊙ mtp.ylabel('Estimated Salary')
- ⊙ mtp.legend()
- ⊙ mtp.show()

Output:

The above output (Fig. 3.7) is completely different from the rest classification models. It has both vertical and horizontal lines that are splitting the dataset according to the age and estimated salary variable.

As we can see, the tree is trying to capture each dataset, which is the case of overfitting.

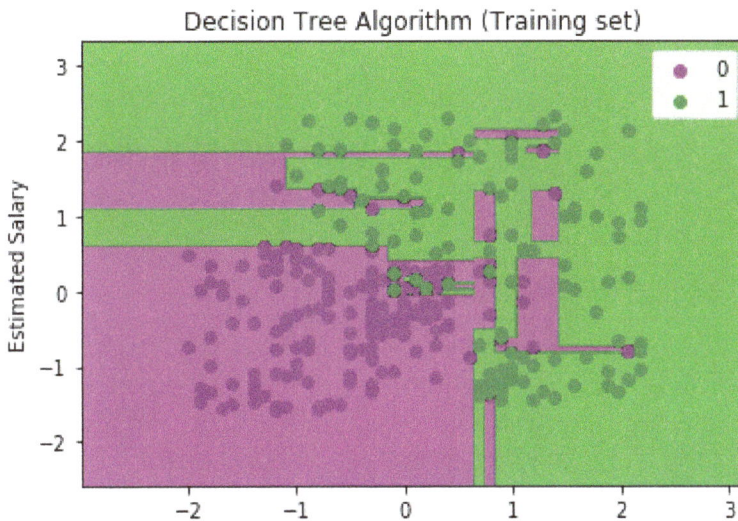

Fig. 3.7 **Visualizing the training set result**

6. Visualizing the test set result

Visualization of test set result will be similar to the visualization of the training set except that the training set will be replaced with the test set.

- ⊙ #Visulaizing the test set result
- ⊙ from matplotlib.colors **import** ListedColormap
- ⊙ x_set, y_set = x_test, y_test
- ⊙ x1, x2 = nm.meshgrid(nm.arange(start = x_set[:, 0].min() - 1, stop = x_set[:, 0].max() + 1, step =0.01),
- ⊙ nm.arange(start = x_set[:, 1].min() - 1, stop = x_set[:, 1].max() + 1, step = 0.01))
- ⊙ mtp.contourf(x1, x2, classifier.predict(nm.array([x1.ravel(), x2.ravel()]).T).reshape(x1.shape),

- alpha = 0.75, cmap = ListedColormap(('purple','green')))
- mtp.xlim(x1.min(), x1.max())
- mtp.ylim(x2.min(), x2.max())
- fori, j in enumerate(nm.unique(y_set)):
- mtp.scatter(x_set[y_set == j, 0], x_set[y_set == j, 1],
- c = ListedColormap(('purple', 'green'))(i), label = j)
- mtp.title('Decision Tree Algorithm(Test set)')
- mtp.xlabel('Age')
- mtp.ylabel('Estimated Salary')
- mtp.legend()
- mtp.show()

Output

As we can see in Fig. 3.8 that there are some green data points within the purple region and *vice versa*. So, these are the incorrect predictions which we have discussed in the confusion matrix.

SUPPORT VECTOR MACHINES (SVM)

Support Vector Machine or SVM is one of the most popular Supervised Learning algorithms, which is used for Classification as well as Regression problems. However, primarily, it is used for Classification problems in Machine Learning.

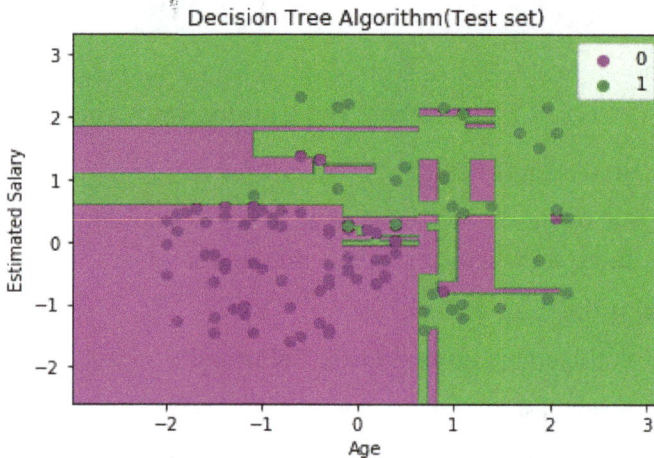

Fig. 3.8 Visualization of test set result

The goal of the SVM algorithm is to create the best line or decision boundary that can segregate n-dimensional space into classes so that we can easily put the new data point in the correct category in the future. This best decision boundary is called a hyperplane.

SVM chooses the extreme points/vectors that help in creating the hyperplane. These extreme cases are called as support vectors, and hence algorithm is termed as Support Vector Machine. Consider diagram (Fig. 3.9) in which there are two different categories that are classified using a decision boundary or hyperplane:

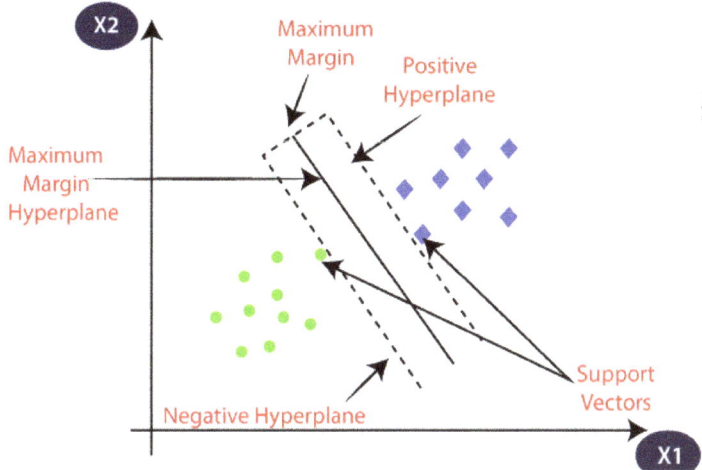

Fig. 3.9 Decision boundary or hyperplane

Example: SVM can be understood with the example that we have used in the KNN classifier. Suppose we see a strange cat that also has some features of dogs, so if we want a model that can accurately identify whether it is a cat or dog, so such a model can be created by using the SVM algorithm. We will first train our model with lots of images of cats and dogs so that it can learn about different features of cats and dogs, and then we test it with this strange creature. So as support vector creates a decision boundary between these two data (cat and dog) and choose extreme cases (support vectors), it will see the extreme case of cat and dog. On the basis of the support vectors, it will classify it as a cat (Fig. 3.10).

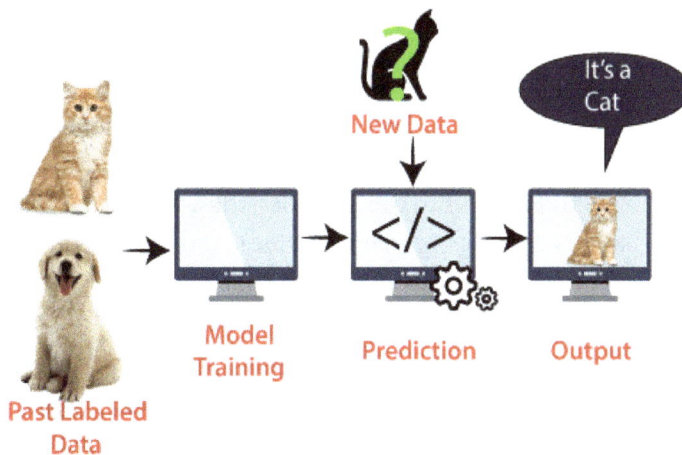

Fig. 3.10 the extreme case of cat and dog

SVM algorithm can be used for Face detection, image classification, text categorization, etc.

Types of SVM

SVM can be of two types:

- ◉ **Linear SVM:** Linear SVM is used for linearly separable data, which means if a dataset can be classified into two classes by using a single straight line, then such data is termed as linearly separable data, and classifier is used called as Linear SVM classifier.

- ◉ **Non-linear SVM:** Non-Linear SVM is used for non-linearly separated data, which means if a dataset cannot be classified by using a straight line, then such data is termed as non-linear data and classifier used is called as Non-linear SVM classifier.

Hyperplane and Support Vectors in the SVM algorithm

Hyperplane: There can be multiple lines/decision boundaries to segregate the classes in n-dimensional space, but we need to find out the best decision boundary that helps to classify the data points. This best boundary is known as the hyperplane of SVM.

The dimensions of the hyperplane depend on the features present in the dataset, which means if there are 2 features (as shown in image), then hyperplane will be a straight line. And if there are 3 features, then hyperplane will be a 2-dimension plane.

We always create a hyperplane that has a maximum margin, which means the maximum distance between the data points.

Support Vectors

The data points or vectors that are the closest to the hyperplane and which affect the position of the hyperplane are termed as Support Vector. Since these vectors support the hyperplane, hence called a Support vector.

How does SVM works?

Linear SVM

The working of the SVM algorithm can be understood by using an example. Suppose we have a dataset that has two tags (green and blue), and the dataset has two features x1 and x2. We want a classifier that can classify the pair(x1, x2) of coordinates in either green or blue. Consider Fig. 3.11:

So as it is 2-d space so by just using a straight line, we can easily separate these two classes. But there can be multiple lines that can separate these classes. Consider Fig. 3.12:

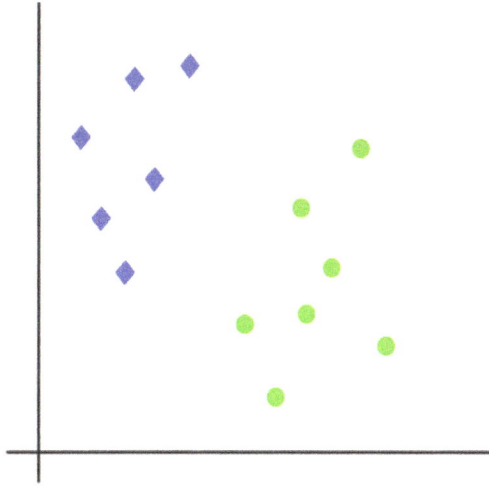

Fig. 3.11

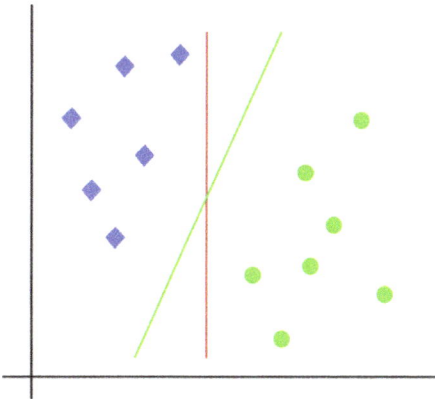

Fig. 3.12

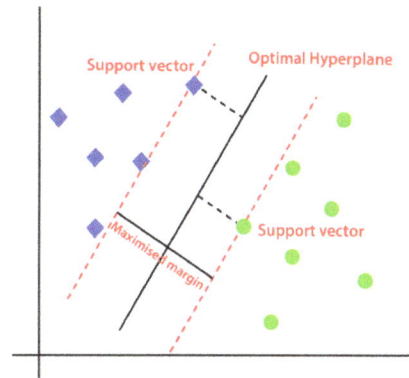

Fig. 3.13

Hence, the SVM algorithm helps to find the best line or decision boundary; this best boundary or region is called as a hyperplane. SVM algorithm finds the closest point of the lines from both the classes. These points are called support vectors. The distance between the vectors and the hyperplane is called as margin. And the goal of SVM is to maximize this margin. The hyperplane with maximum margin is called the optimal hyperplane (Fig. 3.13 above).

Non-Linear SVM

If data is linearly arranged, then we can separate it by using a straight line, but for non-linear data, we cannot draw a single straight line (Fig. 3.14):

So to separate these data points, we need to add one more dimension. For linear data, we have used two dimensions x and y, so for non-linear data, we will add a third dimension z. It can be calculated as:

$$z = x^2 + y^2$$

By adding the third dimension, the sample space will become as below (Fig. 3.15):

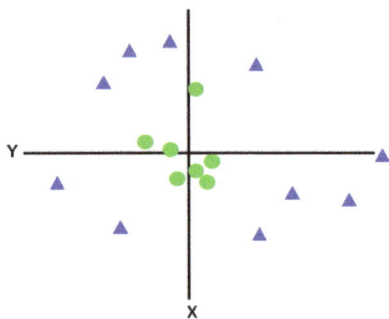

Fig. 3.14 Non-Linear SVM

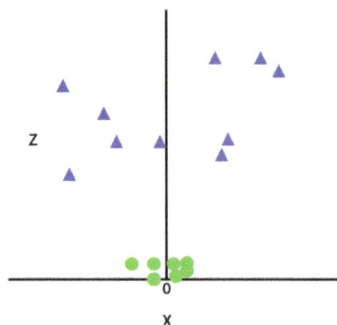

Fig. 3.15

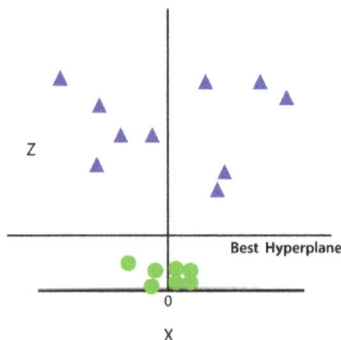

Fig. 3.16

So now, SVM will divide the datasets into classes in the following way. Consider Fig. 3.16 above.

Since we are in 3-d Space, hence it is looking like a plane parallel to the x-axis. If we convert it in 2d space with z=1, then it will become as Fig. 3.17:

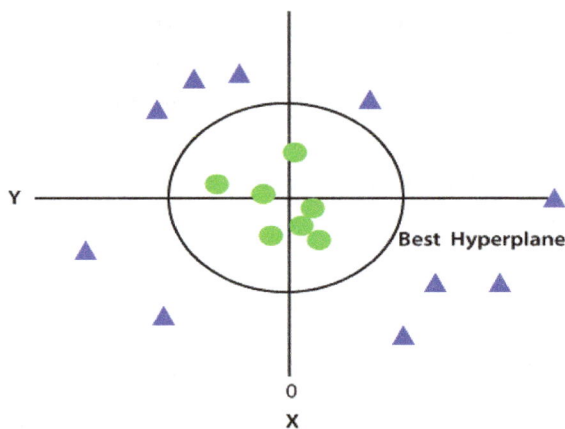

Fig. 3.17

Hence we get a circumference of radius 1 in case of non-linear data.

Python Implementation of Support Vector Machine

Now we will implement the SVM algorithm using Python. Here we will use the same dataset **user_data**, which we have used in Logistic regression and KNN classification.

Data Pre-processing step

Till the Data pre-processing step, the code will remain the same. Below is the code:

- ⊙ #Data Pre-processing Step
- ⊙ # importing libraries
- ⊙ **import** numpy as nm
- ⊙ **import** matplotlib.pyplot as mtp
- ⊙ **import** pandas as pd
- ⊙ #importing datasets
- ⊙ data_set= pd.read_csv('user_data.csv')
- ⊙ #Extracting Independent and dependent Variable
- ⊙ x= data_set.iloc[:, [2,3]].values
- ⊙ y= data_set.iloc[:, 4].values
- ⊙ # Splitting the dataset into training and test set.
- ⊙ from sklearn.model_selection **import** train_test_split
- ⊙ x_train, x_test, y_train, y_test= train_test_split(x, y, test_size= 0.25, random_state=0)
- ⊙ #feature Scaling
- ⊙ from sklearn.preprocessing **import** StandardScaler
- ⊙ st_x= StandardScaler()
- ⊙ x_train= st_x.fit_transform(x_train)
- ⊙ x_test= st_x.transform(x_test)

After executing the above code, we will pre-process the data. The code will give the dataset as (Fig. 3.18):

data_set - DataFrame

Index	User ID	Gender	Age	EstimatedSalary	Purchased
0	15624510	Male	19	19000	0
1	15810944	Male	35	20000	0
2	15668575	Female	26	43000	0
3	15603246	Female	27	57000	0
4	15804002	Male	19	76000	0
5	15728773	Male	27	58000	0
6	15598044	Female	27	84000	0
7	15694829	Female	32	150000	1
8	15600575	Male	25	33000	0
9	15727311	Female	35	65000	0
10	15570769	Female	26	80000	0
11	15606274	Female	26	52000	0
12	15746139	Male	20	86000	0
13	15704987	Male	32	18000	0
14	15628972	Male	18	82000	0

Format Resize ☑ Background color ☑ Column min/max Save and Close Close

Fig. 3.18 Data Pre-processing Step

The scaled output for the test set will be:

x_test - NumPy array

	0	1
0	-0.804802	0.504964
1	-0.0125441	-0.567782
2	-0.309641	0.157046
3	-0.804802	0.273019
4	-0.309641	-0.567782
5	-1.1019	-1.43758
6	-0.70577	-1.58254
7	-0.210609	2.15757
8	-1.99319	-0.0459058
9	0.878746	-0.770734
10	-0.804802	-0.596776
11	-1.00287	-0.422817
12	-0.111576	-0.422817

Format Resize ☑ Background color Save and Close Close

y_test - NumPy array

	0
0	0
1	0
2	0
3	0
4	0
5	0
6	0
7	1
8	0
9	0
10	0
11	0
12	0

Format Resize ☑ Background color Save and Close Close

Fig. 3.19 The scaled output for the test set

Fitting the SVM classifier to the training set:

Now the training set will be fitted to the SVM classifier. To create the SVM classifier, we will import **SVC** class from **Sklearn.svm** library. Below is the code for it:

- from sklearn.svm **import** SVC # "Support vector classifier"
- classifier = SVC(kernel='linear', random_state=0)
- classifier.fit(x_train, y_train)

In the above code, we have used **kernel='linear'**, as here we are creating SVM for linearly separable data. However, we can change it for non-linear data. And then we fitted the classifier to the training dataset(x_train, y_train)

Output

Out[8]:

SVC(C=1.0, cache_size=200, class_weight=None, coef0=0.0,

  decision_function_shape='ovr', degree=3, gamma='auto_deprecated',

  kernel='linear', max_iter=-1, probability=False, random_state=0,

  shrinking=True, tol=0.001, verbose=False)

The model performance can be altered by changing the value of C(Regularization factor), gamma, and kernel.

Predicting the test set result:

Now, we will predict the output for test set. For this, we will create a new vector y_pred. Below is the code for it:

- ⦿ #Predicting the test set result
- ⦿ y_pred= classifier.predict(x_test)

After getting the y_pred vector, we can compare the result of **y_pred** and **y_test** to check the difference between the actual value and predicted value.

Output: Below is the output for the prediction of the test set (Fig. 3.20):

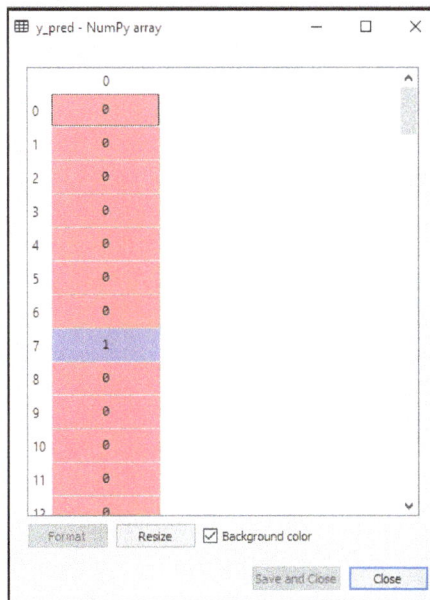

Fig. 3.20 The output for the prediction of the test set

Creating the confusion matrix

Now we will see the performance of the SVM classifier that how many incorrect predictions are there as compared to the Logistic regression classifier. To create the confusion matrix, we need to import the confusion_matrix function of the sklearn library. After importing the function, we will call it using a new variable cm. The function takes two parameters, mainly y_true(the actual values) and y_pred (the targeted value return by the classifier). Below is the code for it:

- #Creating the Confusion matrix
- from sklearn.metrics **import** confusion_matrix
- cm = confusion_matrix(y_test, y_ pred)

Output:

As we can see in Fig. 3.21, there are 66 + 24 = 90 correct predictions and 8 + 2 = 10 correct predictions. Therefore we can say that our SVM model improved as compared to the Logistic regression model.

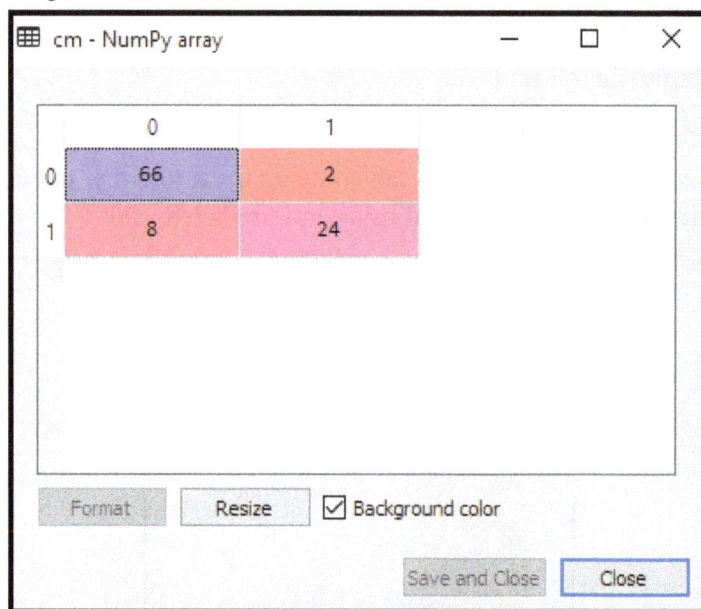

	0	1
0	66	2
1	8	24

Fig. 3.21

Visualizing the training set result:

Now we will visualize the training set result, below is the code for it:

- from matplotlib.colors **import** ListedColormap
- x_set, y_set = x_train, y_train
- x1, x2 = nm.meshgrid(nm.arange(start = x_set[:, 0].min() - 1, stop = x_set[:, 0].max() + 1, step =0.01),

- nm.arange(start = x_set[:, 1].min() - 1, stop = x_set[:, 1].max() + 1, step = 0.01))
- mtp.contourf(x1, x2, classifier.predict(nm.array([x1.ravel(), x2.ravel()]).T).reshape(x1.shape),
- alpha = 0.75, cmap = ListedColormap(('red', 'green')))
- mtp.xlim(x1.min(), x1.max())
- mtp.ylim(x2.min(), x2.max())
- **for** i, j in enumerate(nm.unique(y_set)):
- mtp.scatter(x_set[y_set == j, 0], x_set[y_set == j, 1],
- c = ListedColormap(('red', 'green'))(i), label = j)
- mtp.title('SVM classifier (Training set)')
- mtp.xlabel('Age')
- mtp.ylabel('Estimated Salary')
- mtp.legend()
- mtp.show()

Visualizing the test set result:

- #Visulaizing the test set result
- from matplotlib.colors **import** ListedColormap
- x_set, y_set = x_test, y_test
- x1, x2 = nm.meshgrid(nm.arange(start = x_set[:, 0].min() - 1, stop = x_set[:, 0].max() + 1, step =0.01),
- nm.arange(start = x_set[:, 1].min() - 1, stop = x_set[:, 1].max() + 1, step = 0.01))
- mtp.contourf(x1, x2, classifier.predict(nm.array([x1.ravel(), x2.ravel()]).T).reshape(x1.shape),
- alpha = 0.75, cmap = ListedColormap(('red','green')))
- mtp.xlim(x1.min(), x1.max())
- mtp.ylim(x2.min(), x2.max())
- **for** i, j in enumerate(nm.unique(y_set)):
- mtp.scatter(x_set[y_set == j, 0], x_set[y_set == j, 1],
- c = ListedColormap(('red', 'green'))(i), label = j)
- mtp.title('SVM classifier (Test set)')
- mtp.xlabel('Age')
- mtp.ylabel('Estimated Salary')

- mtp.legend()
- mtp.show()

NEURAL NETWORKS AND DEEP LEARNING

Neural Networks are computational models that mimic the complex functions of the human brain. The neural networks consist of interconnected nodes or neurons that process and learn from data, enabling tasks such as pattern recognition and decision making in machine learning. The article explores more about neural networks, their working, architecture and more.

Evolution of Neural Networks

Since the 1940s, there have been a number of noteworthy advancements in the field of neural networks:

- **1940s-1950s: Early Concepts**: Neural networks began with the introduction of the first mathematical model of artificial neurons by McCulloch and Pitts. But computational constraints made progress difficult.

- **1960s-1970s: Perceptrons**: This era is defined by the work of Rosenblatt on perceptrons. Perceptrons are single-layer networks whose applicability was limited to issues that could be solved linearly separately.

- **1980s: Backpropagation and Connectionism**: Multi-layer network training was made possible by Rumelhart, Hinton, and Williams' invention of the backpropagation method. With its emphasis on learning through interconnected nodes, connectionism gained appeal.

- **1990s: Boom and Winter**; With applications in image identification, finance, and other fields, neural networks saw a boom. Neural network research did, however, experience a "winter" due to exorbitant computational costs and inflated expectations.

- **2000s: Resurgence and Deep Learning**: Larger datasets, innovative structures, and enhanced processing capability spurred a comeback. Deep learning has shown amazing effectiveness in a number of disciplines by utilizing numerous layers.

- **2010s-Present: Deep Learning Dominance**: Convolutional neural networks (CNNs) and recurrent neural networks (RNNs), two deep learning architectures, dominated machine learning. Their power was demonstrated by innovations in gaming, picture recognition, and natural language processing.

Neural networks extract identifying features from data, lacking pre-programmed understanding. Network components include neurons, connections, weights, biases, propagation functions, and a learning rule. Neurons receive inputs, governed by thresholds and activation functions. Connections involve weights and biases regulating information transfer. Learning, adjusting weights and biases, occurs in three stages: input computation, output generation, and iterative refinement enhancing the network's proficiency in diverse tasks.

These include:

- The neural network is simulated by a new environment.
- Then the free parameters of the neural network are changed as a result of this simulation.
- The neural network then responds in a new way to the environment because of the changes in its free parameters.

Importance of Neural Networks

The ability of neural networks to identify patterns, solve intricate puzzles, and adjust to changing surroundings is essential. Their capacity to learn from data has far-reaching effects, ranging from revolutionizing technology like natural language processing and self-driving automobiles to automating decision-making processes and increasing efficiency in numerous industries. The development of artificial intelligence is largely dependent on neural networks, which also drive innovation and influence the direction of technology.

Working of a Neural Network

Neural networks are complex systems that mimic some features of the functioning of the human brain. It is composed of an input layer, one or more hidden layers, and an output layer made up of layers of artificial neurons that are coupled. The two stages of the basic process are called backpropagation and forward propagation (Fig. 3.22).

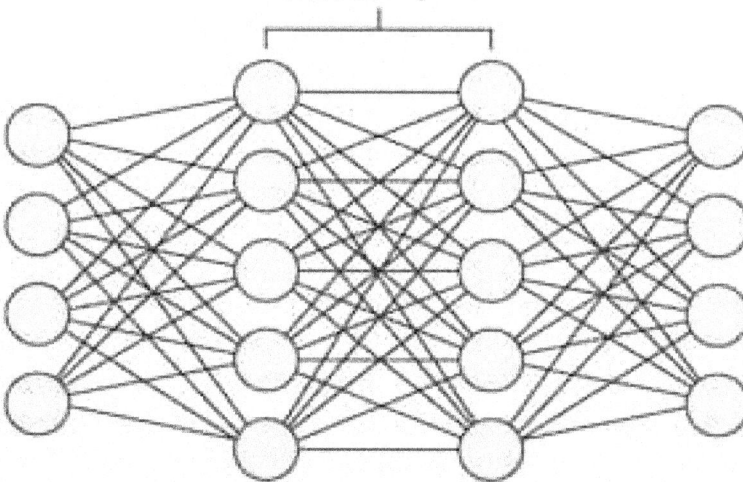

Fig. 3.22 Working of a Neural Network

Forward Propagation

- ◉ **Input Layer:** Each feature in the input layer is represented by a node on the network, which receives input data.

- ◉ **Weights and Connections:** The weight of each neuronal connection indicates how strong the connection is. Throughout training, these weights are changed.

- ◉ **Hidden Layers:** Each hidden layer neuron processes inputs by multiplying them by weights, adding them up, and then passing them through an activation function. By doing this, non-linearity is introduced, enabling the network to recognize intricate patterns.

- ◉ **Output:** The final result is produced by repeating the process until the output layer is reached.

Backpropagation

Loss Calculation: The network's output is evaluated against the real goal values, and a loss function is used to compute the difference. For a regression problem, the Mean Squared Error (MSE) is commonly used as the cost function.

Loss Function

- ◉ **Gradient Descent:** Gradient descent is then used by the network to reduce the loss. To lower the inaccuracy, weights are changed based on the derivative of the loss with respect to each weight.

- ◉ **Adjusting weights:** The weights are adjusted at each connection by applying this iterative process, or backpropagation, backward across the network.

- ◉ **Training:** During training with different data samples, the entire process of forward propagation, loss calculation, and backpropagation is done iteratively, enabling the network to adapt and learn patterns from the data.

- ◉ **Actvation Functions:** Model non-linearity is introduced by activation functions like the rectified linear unit (ReLU) or sigmoid. Their decision on whether to "fire" a neuron is based on the whole weighted input.

Learning of a Neural Network

- ◉ **Learning with supervised learning:** In supervised learning, the neural network is guided by a teacher who has access to both input-output pairs. The network creates outputs based on inputs without taking into account the surroundings. By comparing these outputs to the teacher-known desired outputs, an error signal is generated. In order to reduce errors, the network's parameters are changed iteratively and stop when performance is at an acceptable level.

- ◉ **Learning with Unsupervised learning:** Equivalent output variables are absent in unsupervised learning. Its main goal is to comprehend incoming data's

(X) underlying structure. No instructor is present to offer advice. Modeling data patterns and relationships is the intended outcome instead. Words like regression and classification are related to supervised learning, whereas unsupervised learning is associated with clustering and association.

- ◉ **Learning with Reinforcement Learning**: Through interaction with the environment and feedback in the form of rewards or penalties, the network gains knowledge. Finding a policy or strategy that optimizes cumulative rewards over time is the goal for the network. This kind is frequently utilized in gaming and decision-making applications.

Types of Neural Networks

There are seven types of neural networks that can be used.

- ◉ **Feedforward Neteworks:** A feedforward neural network is a simple artificial neural network architecture in which data moves from input to output in a single direction. It has input, hidden, and output layers; feedback loops are absent. Its straightforward architecture makes it appropriate for a number of applications, such as regression and pattern recognition.

- ◉ **Multilayer Perceptron (MLP):** MLP is a type of feedforward neural network with three or more layers, including an input layer, one or more hidden layers, and an output layer. It uses nonlinear activation functions.

- ◉ **Convolutional Neural Network (CNN):** A Convolutional Neural Network (CNN) is a specialized artificial neural network designed for image processing. It employs convolutional layers to automatically learn hierarchical features from input images, enabling effective image recognition and classification. CNNs have revolutionized computer vision and are pivotal in tasks like object detection and image analysis.

- ◉ **Recurrent Neural Network (RNN):** An artificial neural network type intended for sequential data processing is called a Recurrent Neural Network (RNN). It is appropriate for applications where contextual dependencies are critical, such as time series prediction and natural language processing, since it makes use of feedback loops, which enable information to survive within the network.

- ◉ **Long Short-Term Memory (LSTM):** LSTM is a type of RNN that is designed to overcome the vanishing gradient problem in training RNNs. It uses memory cells and gates to selectively read, write, and erase information.

- ◉ In **artificial neural networks (ANNs)**, Convolution is a crucial mathematical procedure.

- ◉ **Convolutional neural networks (CNNs)** can categorize data using image frames and learn features. There are numerous varieties of CNNs. Depth-wise separable convolutional neural networks are one type of CNN.

Convolutional neural networks: These CNNs are frequently utilized for the two reasons listed below:

- Compared to standard CNNs, they have fewer parameters to change, which lessens overfitting.
- Because they use less computations and are hence more affordable computationally, they are appropriate for mobile vision applications.

Convolutional neural networks (CNN most)'s widely used convolutional layer is 2D Convolution. A novel type of convolutional layer known as Depth wise Separable convolution is used in the considerably quicker and smaller CNN architecture known as Mobile Net. Due to their compact size, these models are regarded as being extremely beneficial for implementation on embedded and mobile devices. Hence the moniker Mobile Net.

Depth-wise Convolutions

Differences

The primary distinction between Depth wise Convolution and 2D Convolution is that Depth wise Convolution keeps each input channel independent, while 2D Convolution performs convolutions overall or multiple input channels.

Method

- The three-dimensional input tensor is divided into distinct channels.
- The input is convolved using a filter for each channel (2D)
- Each channel's output is combined to provide the output for the complete 3D tensor.

Convolutions that can be Separated in Depth

Usually, Depthwise Separable Convolution is used in conjunction with Depthwise Convolutions. This consists of two parts: 1. Filtering (all the prior processes) and 2. Combining (combining the three color channels to create as many channels as needed; in the example below, we can see how the three channels can be combined to create a single output channel).

Why is Depthwise Separable Convolution so efficient?

- Convolutions are performed at a depth of -1x1 for all channels.
- Assume we have an input tensor with the dimensions 8x8x3.
- The size of the required output tensor is 8x8x256.

2D Convolutions

- The required multiplications are (8x8) x (5x5x3) x (256) for a total of 1,228,800.

Convolutions that can be Separable in Depth

⊙ The required number of multiplications is:

Filtering: Due to the split into single channels, a 5x5x1 filter is needed instead of a 5x5x3 filter, and since there are three channels, a total of three 5x5x1 filters are needed.

$$(8x8) \times (5x5x1) \times (3) = 3,800$$

Combining: A total of 256 channels are needed, hence,

$$(8x8) \times (1x1x3) \times (256) = 49,152$$

3,800 + 49,152 multiplied together equals 53,952 in total.

Thus, a Depthwise Separable convolution will only need 53,952 multiplications to get the same output as a 2D convolution, which will require 1,228,800.

Finally,

1,228,800/53,952 equals 23 times fewer multiplications needed.

Because of this, Depthwise Separable convolutions have very high efficiency. These are the layers that the Mobile Net architecture has incorporated to reduce the number of computations and make them less power-hungry so that they can be used on mobile and embedded devices that lack potent graphical processing units.

How Normal Convolution works

Consider the following input data dimensions: Df x Df x M, where M is the number of channels and Df x Df may be the size of the image (3 for an RGB image). Assume that there are N filters or kernels with Dk x Dk x M dimensions. A typical convolution operation will have an output size of Dp x Dp x N (Fig. 3.23)

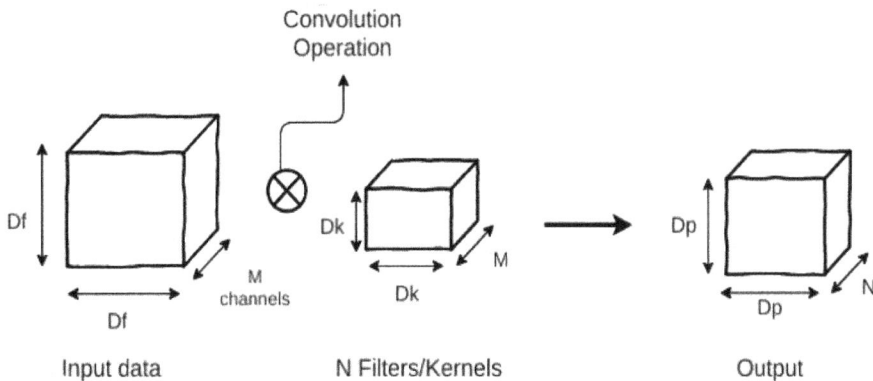

Fig. 3.23 Working of Normal Convolution

For the number of multiplications in a single convolution operation, the filter size is equal to Dk x Dk x M.

Each of the N filters slides Dp times in both the vertical and horizontal directions.

The total number of multiplications (Multiplications per Convolution) required to carry out a convolution is N x Dp x Dp x.

The total number of multiplications is N x Dp2 x Dk2 x M.

Convolutions that can be Divided by Depth

Look at separable convolutions based on Depth now. There are two operations in this process:

- ◉ Convolutions based on Depth.
- ◉ Convolutions are based on points.

1. Convolutions based on Depth.

Contrary to normal CNNs, where Convolution is applied to all M channels simultaneously, the depth-wise operation only applies Convolution to one channel simultaneously. The filters/kernels used here will therefore be Dk x Dk x 1. Given that the input data has M channels, M such filters are necessary. The output will be Dp x Dp x M in size (Fig. 3.24).

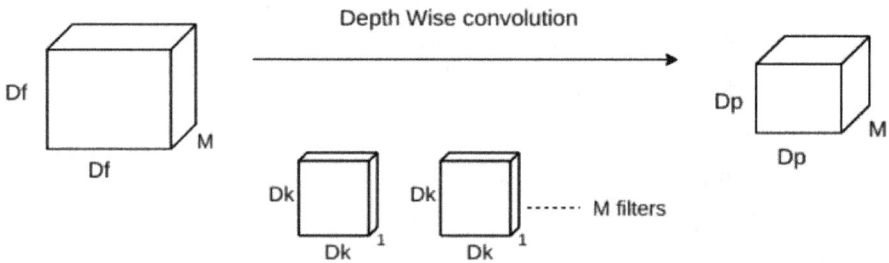

Fig. 3.24 Convolutions based on Depth.

Cost of the Procedure:

Dk x Dk multiplications are necessary for a single convolution operation.

Since all M channels have the filter slid by DpxDp times, MxDpxDpxDkxDk is the total number of multiplications to perform depth-wise Convolution,

Multiplications total = M x Dk2 x Dp2

2. Convolutions based on points.

A 1 x 1 convolution procedure is used on the M channels during point-wise operation. Therefore, 1 x 1 x M will be the filter size for this operation. If N of these filters is used, the output size is Dp x Dp x N (Fig. 3.25).

Cost of the Procedure:

1 x M multiplications are needed for each convolution operation.

Given that the filter is being moved by Dp times Dp,

M x Dp x Dp x is the total number of multiplications (no. of filters)

To perform point-wise Convolution,

M x Dp2 x N is the total number of multiplications.

Consequently, for optimal operation:

Total multiplications equal the sum of the depth-wise and point-wise conversions.

Total multiplications are calculated as follows:

$$M*Dk2*Dp2+M*Dp2*N=M*Dp2*(Dk2 + n)$$

To perform depth-wise separable Convolution,

The total number of multiplications equals M x (Dk2 + N) x Dp2.

Advantages of Neural Networks

Neural networks are widely used in many different applications because of their many benefits:

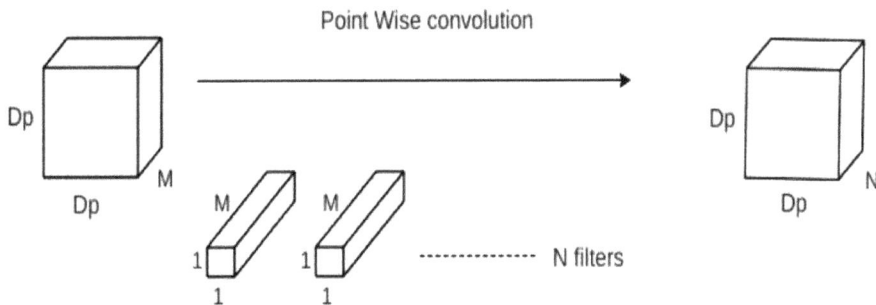

Fig. 3.25 Convolutions based on points

- ◉ **Adaptability:** Neural networks are useful for activities where the link between inputs and outputs is complex or not well defined because they can adapt to new situations and learn from data.

- ◉ **Pattern Recognition:** Their proficiency in pattern recognition renders them efficacious in tasks like as audio and image identification, natural language processing, and other intricate data patterns.

- ◉ **Parallel Processing:** Because neural networks are capable of parallel processing by nature, they can process numerous jobs at once, which speeds up and improves the efficiency of computations.

- ◉ **Non-Linearity:** Neural networks are able to model and comprehend complicated relationships in data by virtue of the non-linear activation functions found in neurons, which overcome the drawbacks of linear models.

Disadvantages of Neural Networks

Neural networks, while powerful, are not without drawbacks and difficulties:

- ⦿ **Computational Intensity:** Large neural network training can be a laborious and computationally demanding process that demands a lot of computing power.

- ⦿ **Black box Nature:** As "black box" models, neural networks pose a problem in important applications since it is difficult to understand how they make decisions.

- ⦿ **Overfitting:** Overfitting is a phenomenon in which neural networks commit training material to memory rather than identifying patterns in the data. Although regularization approaches help to alleviate this, the problem still exists.

- ⦿ **Need for Large datasets:** For efficient training, neural networks frequently need sizable, labeled datasets; otherwise, their performance may suffer from incomplete or skewed data.

Deep Learning

Deep learning is the branch of machine learning which is based on artificial neural network architecture. An artificial neural network or ANN uses layers of interconnected nodes called neurons that work together to process and learn from the input data.

In a fully connected Deep neural network, there is an input layer and one or more hidden layers connected one after the other. Each neuron receives input from the previous layer neurons or the input layer. The output of one neuron becomes the input to other neurons in the next layer of the network, and this process continues until the final layer produces the output of the network. The layers of the neural network transform the input data through a series of nonlinear transformations, allowing the network to learn complex representations of the input data (Fig. 3.26).

Today Deep learning has become one of the most popular and visible areas of machine learning, due to its success in a variety of applications, such as computer vision, natural language processing, and Reinforcement learning.

Deep learning can be used for supervised, unsupervised as well as reinforcement machine learning. it uses a variety of ways to process these.

- ⦿ **Supervised Machine Learning:** Supervised machine learning is the machine learning technique in which the neural network learns to make predictions or classify data based on the labeled datasets. Here we input both input features along with the target variables. the neural network learns to make predictions based on the cost or error that comes from the difference between the predicted and the actual target, this process is known as backpropagation. Deep learning algorithms like Convolutional neural networks, Recurrent neural networks are used for many supervised tasks like image classifications and recognition, sentiment analysis, language translations, etc.

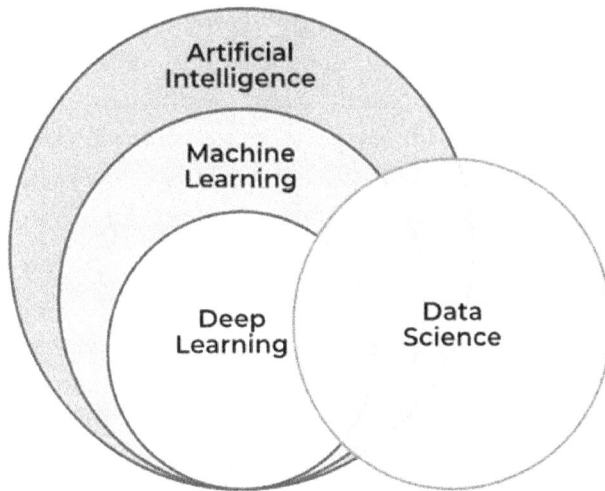

Fig. 3.26 Deep Learning

◉ **Unsupervised Machine Learning:** Unsupervised machine learning is the machine learning technique in which the neural network learns to discover the patterns or to cluster the dataset based on unlabeled datasets. Here there are no target variables. while the machine has to self-determined the hidden patterns or relationships within the datasets. Deep learning algorithms like autoencoders and generative models are used for unsupervised tasks like clustering, dimensionality reduction, and anomaly detection.

◉ **Reinforcement Machine Learning:** Reinforcement Machine Learning is the machine learning technique in which an agent learns to make decisions in an environment to maximize a reward signal. The agent interacts with the environment by taking action and observing the resulting rewards. Deep learning can be used to learn policies, or a set of actions, that maximizes the cumulative reward over time. Deep reinforcement learning algorithms like Deep Q networks and Deep Deterministic Policy Gradient (DDPG) are used to reinforce tasks like robotics and game playing etc.

Artificial neural networks

Artificial neural networks are built on the principles of the structure and operation of human neurons. It is also known as neural networks or neural nets. An artificial neural network's input layer, which is the first layer, receives input from external sources and passes it on to the hidden layer, which is the second layer. Each neuron in the hidden layer gets information from the neurons in the previous layer, computes the weighted total, and then transfers it to the neurons in the next layer. These connections are weighted, which means that the impacts of the inputs from the preceding layer are more or less optimized by giving each input a distinct weight. These weights are then adjusted during the training process to enhance the performance of the model.

Artificial neurons, also known as units, are found in artificial neural networks. The whole Artificial Neural Network is composed of these artificial neurons, which are arranged in a series of layers. The complexities of neural networks will depend on the complexities of the underlying patterns in the dataset whether a layer has a dozen units or millions of units. Commonly, Artificial Neural Network has an input layer, an output layer as well as hidden layers. The input layer receives data from the outside world which the neural network needs to analyze or learn about.

In a fully connected artificial neural network, there is an input layer and one or more hidden layers connected one after the other. Each neuron receives input from the previous layer neurons or the input layer. The output of one neuron becomes the input to other neurons in the next layer of the network, and this process continues until the final layer produces the output of the network. Then, after passing through one or more hidden layers, this data is transformed into valuable data for the output layer. Finally, the output layer provides an output in the form of an artificial neural network's response to the data that comes in. Units are linked to one another from one layer to another in the bulk of neural networks. Each of these links has weights that control how much one unit influences another. The neural network learns more and more about the data as it moves from one unit to another, ultimately producing an output from the output layer.

Applications of Deep Learning

The main applications of deep learning can be divided into computer vision, natural language processing (NLP), and reinforcement learning.

Computer vision

In computer vision, Deep learning models can enable machines to identify and understand visual data. Some of the main applications of deep learning in computer vision include:

- ◉ **Object detection and recognition:** Deep learning model can be used to identify and locate objects within images and videos, making it possible for machines to perform tasks such as self-driving cars, surveillance, and robotics.

- ◉ **Image classification:** Deep learning models can be used to classify images into categories such as animals, plants, and buildings. This is used in applications such as medical imaging, quality control, and image retrieval.

- ◉ **Image segmentation:** Deep learning models can be used for image segmentation into different regions, making it possible to identify specific features within images.

Natural language processing (NLP):

In NLP, the Deep learning model can enable machines to understand and generate human language. Some of the main applications of deep learning in NLP include:

- ◎ **Automatic Text Generation** – Deep learning model can learn the corpus of text and new text like summaries, essays can be automatically generated using these trained models.

- ◎ **Language translation:** Deep learning models can translate text from one language to another, making it possible to communicate with people from different linguistic backgrounds.

- ◎ **Sentiment analysis:** Deep learning models can analyze the sentiment of a piece of text, making it possible to determine whether the text is positive, negative, or neutral. This is used in applications such as customer service, social media monitoring, and political analysis.

- ◎ **Speech recognition:** Deep learning models can recognize and transcribe spoken words, making it possible to perform tasks such as speech-to-text conversion, voice search, and voice-controlled devices.

Reinforcement learning:

In reinforcement learning, deep learning works as training agents to take action in an environment to maximize a reward. Some of the main applications of deep learning in reinforcement learning include:

- ◎ **Game playing:** Deep reinforcement learning models have been able to beat human experts at games such as Go, Chess, and Atari.

- ◎ **Robotics:** Deep reinforcement learning models can be used to train robots to perform complex tasks such as grasping objects, navigation, and manipulation.

- ◎ **Control systems:** Deep reinforcement learning models can be used to control complex systems such as power grids, traffic management, and supply chain optimization.

Challenges in Deep Learning

Deep learning has made significant advancements in various fields, but there are still some challenges that need to be addressed. Here are some of the main challenges in deep learning:

- ◎ **Data availability**: It requires large amounts of data to learn from. For using deep learning it's a big concern to gather as much data for training.

- ◎ **Computational Resources**: For training the deep learning model, it is computationally expensive because it requires specialized hardware like GPUs and TPUs.

- **Time-consuming**: While working on sequential data depending on the computational resource it can take very large even in days or months.

- **Interpretability**: Deep learning models are complex, it works like a black box. it is very difficult to interpret the result.

- **Overfitting**: when the model is trained again and again, it becomes too specialized for the training data, leading to overfitting and poor performance on new data.

Advantages of Deep Learning:

- **High accuracy**: Deep Learning algorithms can achieve state-of-the-art performance in various tasks, such as image recognition and natural language processing.

- **Automated feature engineering**: Deep Learning algorithms can automatically discover and learn relevant features from data without the need for manual feature engineering.

- **Scalability**: Deep Learning models can scale to handle large and complex datasets, and can learn from massive amounts of data.

- **Flexibility**: Deep Learning models can be applied to a wide range of tasks and can handle various types of data, such as images, text, and speech.

- **Continual improvement**: Deep Learning models can continually improve their performance as more data becomes available.

Disadvantages of Deep Learning:

- **High computational requirements**: Deep Learning models require large amounts of data and computational resources to train and optimize.

- **Requires large amounts of labeled data**: Deep Learning models often require a large amount of labeled data for training, which can be expensive and time- consuming to acquire.

- **Interpretability**: Deep Learning models can be challenging to interpret, making it difficult to understand how they make decisions.

- **Overfitting**: Deep Learning models can sometimes overfit to the training data, resulting in poor performance on new and unseen data.

- **Black-box nature**: Deep Learning models are often treated as black boxes, making it difficult to understand how they work and how they arrived at their predictions.

In summary, while Deep Learning offers many advantages, including high accuracy and scalability, it also has some disadvantages, such as high computational requirements, the need for large amounts of labeled data, and interpretability challenges.

These limitations need to be carefully considered when deciding whether to use Deep Learning for a specific task.

Bayesian Deep Learning

Bayesian deep learning is shortly represented as BDL. It is dependent on deep learning theory and Bayesian probability theory. Meanwhile, Bayesian inference is important to statistics and probabilistic distribution machine learning. Probability is used mainly for model learning, uncertainty, and observable states. The main aim of Bayesian deep learning (BDL) is to provide an uncertainty estimate for deep learning.

Bayesian deep learning is an emerging field that combines uncertainty modelling of Bayesian methods with the presentation and representation of deep learning. Bayesian deep learning has always been fascinating and frightening. Uncertainty in neural networks is used to measure the accuracy of the prediction model. There are mainly two types of uncertainty in Bayesian modelling, which are discussed below:

- ⊙ **Aleatoric uncertainty:** Aleatoric uncertainty is a part of uncertainty in the Bayesian modelling. It mainly used to measure the noise which is inherit in the time of observation. Example of it is sensor noise. The noise sensor can uniform in the data set. This uncertainty cannot be reduced even by collecting more data.

- ⊙ **Epistemic uncertainty:** Epistemic uncertainty is another part of the uncertainty in the Bayesian modelling. This uncertainty is caused by the model itself, also known as model uncertainty. It captures our need for understanding about our collected data, which the model generated. By collecting more data, we can reduce this uncertainty.

So, the BDL models often estimate uncertainty by locating the distribution of sample weights or learning a direct probability map. Epistemic uncertainty is modelled by performing a preliminary distribution on the sample weights. It also can capture how much those weights vary with the data. On the other hand, arbitrary uncertainty is modelled by providing an output distribution, and it is also used to measure the noise of the given data set.

Many data scientists consider combining machine learning, Bayesian learning, and neural networks a successful application. However, the Bayesian neural networks are often very difficult to train. By using the backdrop method, we can easily train any neural network. We usually use Bayesian with Backprop for training BNN, which means Bayesian Neural Network.

Bayesian Inference and Marginalization

The Bayesian interface is the learning process. It is used to find out the posterior distribution. This is the opposite of finding the best by optimizing the variance. On the other hand, to calculate the total final value, we need to marginalize the entire parameter space. But this is often impossible because we can have an infinite number of such data sets. Therefore, the Bayesian method used marginalization rather than an optimization technique.

Complex integration in the posterior leads to many variables for run parameter values. Bayesian interface often uses sampling methods such as Markov Chain Monte Carlo (MCMC) or differential equations instead of gradient descent. These strategies try to model after the use of simpler classification. VAEs are a new method for approximating complex distributions to normalize flows.

Advantage of Bayesian Deep Learning?

Recently, many people have tried to combine the advantages of neural networks with the Bayesian methods. There are various advantages of Bayesian Deep Learning, which are discussed below:

- ◉ **Interpolation:** Interpolation is an important advantage of Bayesian Learning. Bayesian learning work includes pure architecture. When faced with a learning problem, a choice must be made between how much time and effort humans and computers should devote. When you build a designed machine, you create a model of the earth and find a good controller in that model.

- ◉ The Bayesian method interpolates this extreme position because it may be a function of the Bayesian premise global model. This means that "thinking well" (referring to teaching patterns before the world) and "thinking hard" (as next) will be described. Many other machine learning methods still need this guarantee.

- ◉ **Intuition:** Intuition is another advantage of Bayesian Deep Learning. Bayesian learning involves two operations, which are prioritization and integration. These operations are often useful.

- ◉ **Language:** Language is another advantage of Bayesian Deep Learning. Bayesian and near Bayesian learning techniques have an associated language for the before and after expression. This is useful when dealing with "thinking hard" about a solution.

Disadvantage of Bayesian Deep Learning?

Uncertainty estimation, especially for medical care, automobiles, etc., is important to the decision-making process. In Bayesian Deep Learning, there are various disadvantages, which are discussed below:

- ◉ **Computational infeasibility:** The Computational infeasibility is a disadvantage of the Bayesian Deep Learning (BDL). Suppose you can accurately predict every air molecule in the room. But, calculate the posterior can take a lot of time. This difficulty means that there is a need to make computational predictions.

- ⊙ **Theoretical infeasibility:** The theoretical infeasibility is another disadvantage of Bayesian Deep Learning. It turned out to take a lot of work to prior specifications. Here, we need to specify the real number for each setting of the model parameters. Many people knowledgeable in Bayesian learning do not see this difficulty for some reasons, which are given below -

  - They know the language that allows prior specification. Obtaining this information requires great effort.

  - They are lying. Their actual prior is not specified earlier.

- ⊙ **Unautomated:** Unautomated is another disadvantage of Bayesian Deep Learning. "Critical thinking" is a part of Bayesian research in the "Bayes employment" rule. As new learning problems arise, Bayesian assures that engineers must solve them.

CLUSTERING ALGORITHMS: K-MEANS, HIERARCHICAL, DBSCAN

K-Means Clustering Algorithm

K-Means Clustering is an unsupervised learning algorithm that is used to solve the clustering problems in machine learning or data science. In this topic, we will learn what is K-means clustering algorithm, how the algorithm works, along with the Python implementation of k-means clustering.

K-Means Clustering is an Unsupervised Learning algorithm, which groups the unlabeled dataset into different clusters. Here K defines the number of pre-defined clusters that need to be created in the process, as if K=2, there will be two clusters, and for K=3, there will be three clusters, and so on.

It allows us to cluster the data into different groups and a convenient way to discover the categories of groups in the unlabeled dataset on its own without the need for any training.

It is a centroid-based algorithm, where each cluster is associated with a centroid. The main aim of this algorithm is to minimize the sum of distances between the data point and their corresponding clusters.

The algorithm takes the unlabeled dataset as input, divides the dataset into k-number of clusters, and repeats the process until it does not find the best clusters. The value of k should be predetermined in this algorithm.

The k-means clustering algorithm mainly performs two tasks:

- ⊙ Determines the best value for K center points or centroids by an iterative process.

- ⊙ Assigns each data point to its closest k-center. Those data points which are near to the particular k-center, create a cluster.

Hence each cluster has datapoints with some commonalities, and it is away from other clusters.

Figure 3.27 explains the working of the K-means Clustering Algorithm:

Working of the K-Means Algorithm

The working of the K-Means algorithm is explained in the below steps:

Step-1: Select the number K to decide the number of clusters.

Step-2: Select random K points or centroids. (It can be other from the input dataset).

Step-3: Assign each data point to their closest centroid, which will form the predefined K clusters.

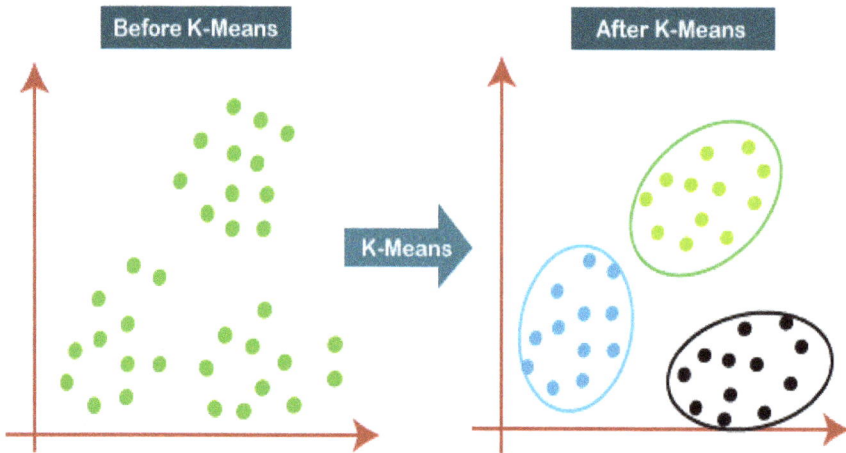

Fig. 3.27 Working of the K-means Clustering Algorithm

Step-4: Calculate the variance and place a new centroid of each cluster.

Step-5: Repeat the third steps, which means reassign each datapoint to the new closest centroid of each cluster.

Step-6: If any reassignment occurs, then go to step-4 else go to FINISH.

Step-7: The model is ready.

Let's understand the above steps by considering the visual plots:

Suppose we have two variables M1 and M2. The x-y axis scatter plot of these two variables is given below (Fig. 3.28):

⊙ Let's take number k of clusters, i.e., K=2, to identify the dataset and to put them into different clusters. It means here we will try to group these datasets into two different clusters.

⊙ We need to choose some random k points or centroid to form the cluster. These points can be either the points from the dataset or any other point. So, here we are selecting the below two points as k points, which are not the part of our dataset. Consider the below image (Fig. 3.29):

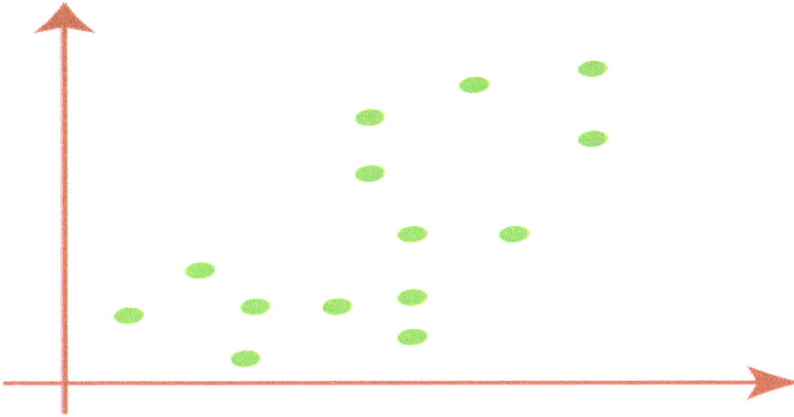

- Now we will assign each data point of the scatter plot to its closest K-point or centroid. We will compute it by applying some mathematics that we have studied to calculate the distance between two points. So, we will draw a median between both the centroids. Consider Fig. 3.30:

From Fig. 3.30, it is clear that points left side of the line is near to the K1 or blue centroid, and points to the right of the line are close to the yellow centroid. Let's color them as blue and yellow for clear visualization (Fig. 3.31).

- As we need to find the closest cluster, so we will repeat the process by choosing **a new centroid**. To choose the new centroids, we will compute the center of gravity of these centroids, and will find new centroids as below (Fig. 3.32):

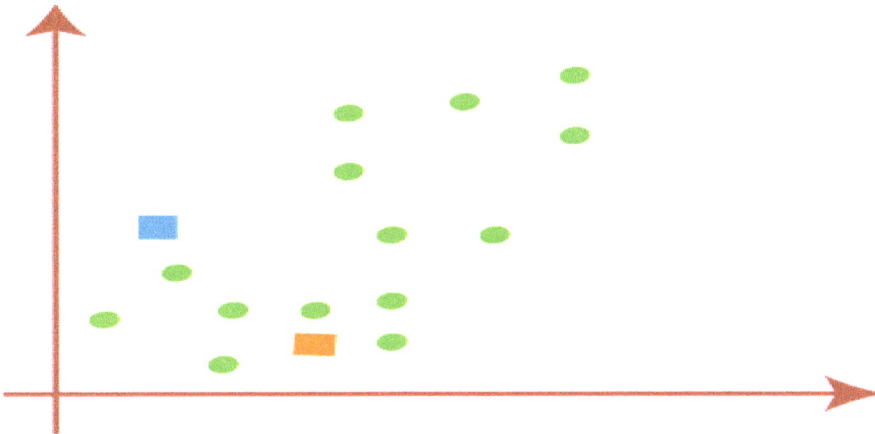

- Next, we will reassign each datapoint to the new centroid. For this, we will repeat the same process of finding a median line. The median will be like as in above image (Fig. 3.33).

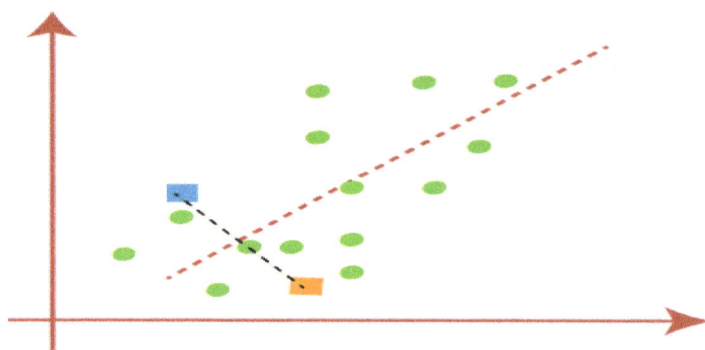

From the above image, we can see, one yellow point is on the left side of the line, and two blue points are right to the line.

Python Implementation of K-means Clustering Algorithm

In the above section, we have discussed the K-means algorithm, now let's see how it can be implemented using Python.

Before implementation, let's understand what type of problem we will solve here. So, we have a dataset of Mall_Customers, which is the data of customers who visit the mall and spend there.

In the given dataset, we have Customer_Id, Gender, Age, Annual Income ($), and Spending Score (which is the calculated value of how much a customer has spent in the mall, the more the value, the more he has spent). From this dataset, we need to calculate some patterns, as it is an unsupervised method, so we don't know what to calculate exactly.

The steps to be followed for the implementation are given below:

- ⊙ Data Pre-processing
- ⊙ Finding the optimal number of clusters using the elbow method
- ⊙ Training the K-means algorithm on the training dataset
- ⊙ Visualizing the clusters

Step-1: Data pre-processing Step

The first step will be the data pre-processing, as we did in our earlier topics of Regression and Classification. But for the clustering problem, it will be different from other models. Let's discuss it:

- ⊙ **Importing Libraries**: As we did in previous topics, firstly, we will import the libraries for our model, which is part of data pre-processing. The code is given below:

  - ● # importing libraries
  - ● **import** numpy as nm

- **import** matplotlib.pyplot as mtp
- **import** pandas as pd

In the above code, the **numpy** we have imported for the performing mathematics calculation, **matplotlib** is for plotting the graph, and **pandas** are for managing the dataset.

- ◉ **Importing the Dataset:** Next, we will import the dataset that we need to use. So here, we are using the Mall_Customer_data.csv dataset. It can be imported using the below code:

- # Importing the dataset
- dataset = pd.read_csv('Mall_Customers_data.csv')

By executing the above lines of code, we will get our dataset in the Spyder IDE. The dataset looks like Fig. 3.34 below:

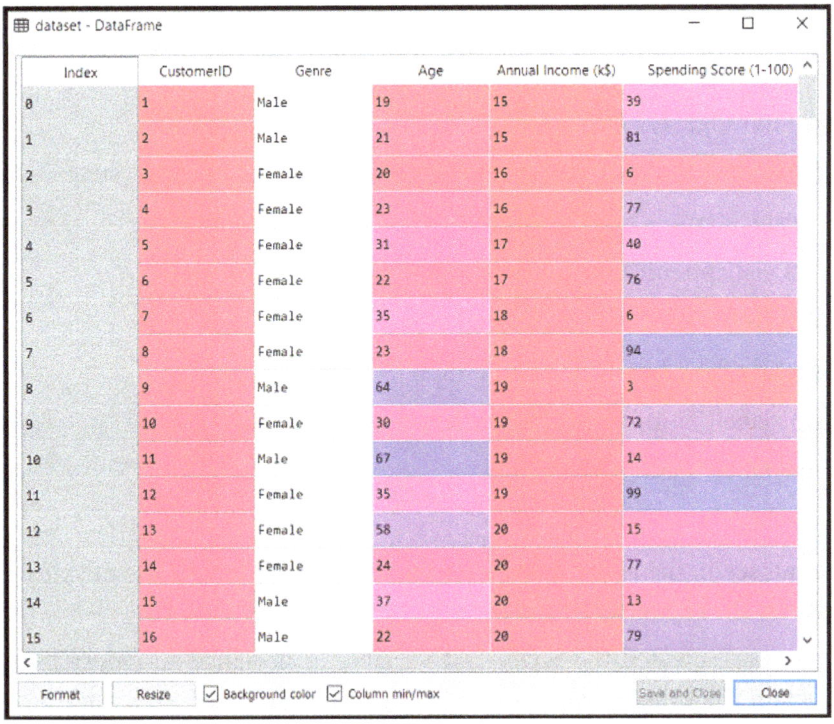

Index	CustomerID	Genre	Age	Annual Income (k$)	Spending Score (1-100)
0	1	Male	19	15	39
1	2	Male	21	15	81
2	3	Female	20	16	6
3	4	Female	23	16	77
4	5	Female	31	17	40
5	6	Female	22	17	76
6	7	Female	35	18	6
7	8	Female	23	18	94
8	9	Male	64	19	3
9	10	Female	30	19	72
10	11	Male	67	19	14
11	12	Female	35	19	99
12	13	Female	58	20	15
13	14	Female	24	20	77
14	15	Male	37	20	13
15	16	Male	22	20	79

Fig. 3.34 Dataset in the Spyder IDE.

From the below dataset, we need to find some patterns in it.

- ◉ **Extracting Independent Variables**: Here we don't need any dependent variable for data pre-processing step as it is a clustering problem, and we have no idea about what to determine. So we will just add a line of code for the matrix of features.

$$x = dataset.iloc[:, [3, 4]].values$$

As we can see, we are extracting only 3rd and 4th feature. It is because we need a 2d plot to visualize the model, and some features are not required, such as customer_id.

Step-2: Finding the optimal number of clusters using the elbow method

In the second step, we will try to find the optimal number of clusters for our clustering problem. So, as discussed above, here we are going to use the elbow method for this purpose.

As we know, the elbow method uses the WCSS concept to draw the plot by plotting WCSS values on the Y-axis and the number of clusters on the X-axis. So we are going to calculate the value for WCSS for different k values ranging from 1 to 10. Below is the code for it:

- #finding optimal number of clusters using the elbow method
- from sklearn.cluster **import** KMeans
- wcss_list= [] #Initializing the list **for** the values of WCSS
- #Using **for** loop **for** iterations from 1 to 10.
- **for** i in range(1, 11):
- kmeans = KMeans(n_clusters=i, init='k-means++', random_state= 42)
- kmeans.fit(x)
- wcss_list.append(kmeans.inertia_)
- mtp.plot(range(1, 11), wcss_list)
- mtp.title('The Elobw Method Graph')
- mtp.xlabel('Number of clusters(k)')
- mtp.ylabel('wcss_list')
- mtp.show()

As we can see in the above code, we have used the KMeans class of sklearn. cluster library to form the clusters.

Next, we have created the **wcss_list** variable to initialize an empty list, which is used to contain the value of wcss computed for different values of k ranging from 1 to 10.

After that, we have initialized the for loop for the iteration on a different value of k ranging from 1 to 10; since for loop in Python, exclude the outbound limit, so it is taken as 11 to include 10th value.

The rest part of the code is similar as we did in earlier topics, as we have fitted the model on a matrix of features and then plotted the graph between the number of clusters and WCSS.

Output: After executing the above code, we will get the below output (Fig. 3.35):

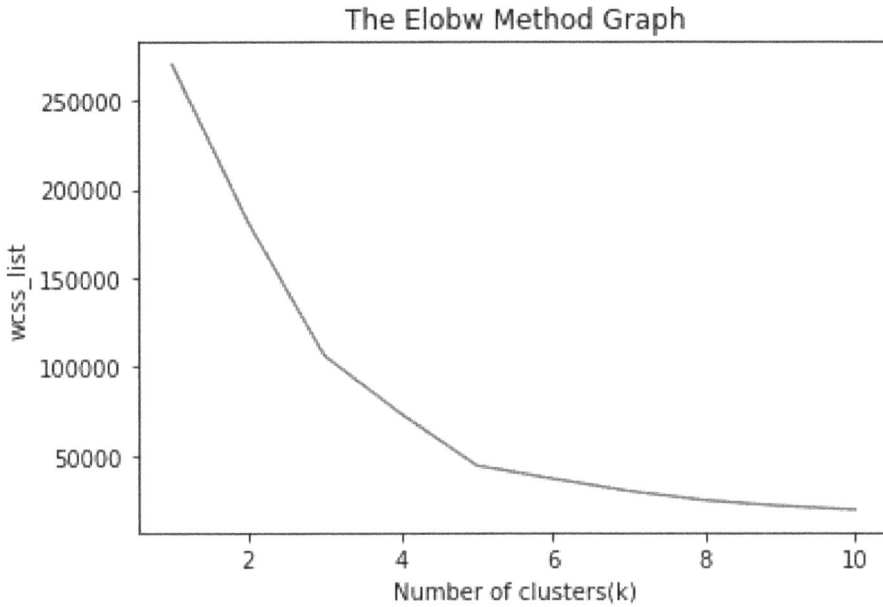

Fig. 3.35 Finding the optimal number of clusters using the elbow method

From the above plot, we can see the elbow point is at 5. So the number of clusters here will be 5.

Step- 3: Training the K-means algorithm on the training dataset

As we have got the number of clusters, so we can now train the model on the dataset.

To train the model, we will use the same two lines of code as we have used in the above section, but here instead of using i, we will use 5, as we know there are 5 clusters that need to be formed. The code is given below:

- #training the K-means model on a dataset
- kmeans = KMeans(n_clusters=5, init='k-means++', random_state= 42)
- y_predict= kmeans.fit_predict(x)

The first line is the same as above for creating the object of KMeans class.

In the second line of code, we have created the dependent variable y_predict to train the model.

By executing the above lines of code, we will get the y_predict variable. We can check it under the variable explorer option in the Spyder IDE. We can now compare the values of y_predict with our original dataset (Fig. 3.36).

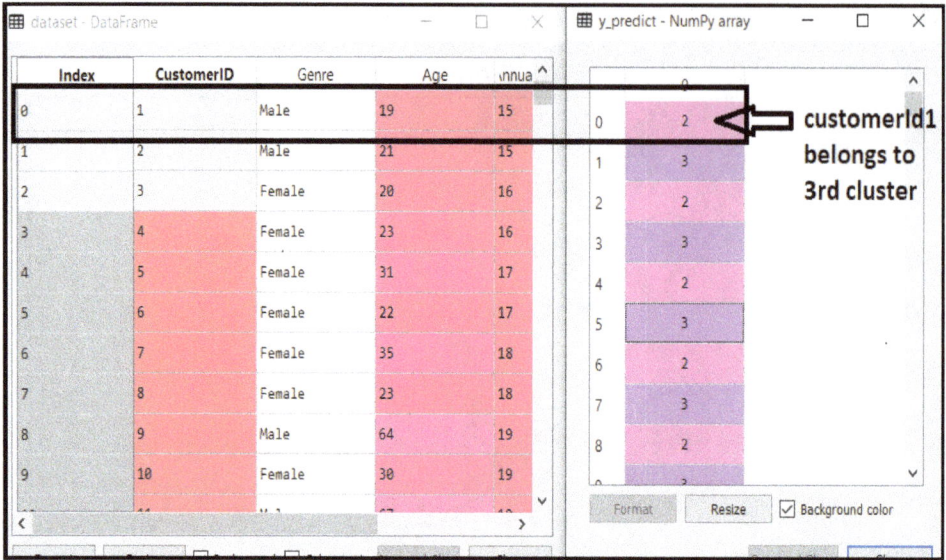

From Fig. 3.36, we can now relate that the CustomerID 1 belongs to a cluster 3 (as index starts from 0, hence 2 will be considered as 3), and 2 belongs to cluster 4, and so on.

Step-4: Visualizing the Clusters

The last step is to visualize the clusters. As we have 5 clusters for our model, so we will visualize each cluster one by one.

To visualize the clusters will use scatter plot using mtp.scatter() function of matplotlib.

- #visulaizing the clusters
- mtp.scatter(x[y_predict == 0, 0], x[y_predict == 0, 1], s = 100, c = 'blue', label = 'Cluster 1') #for first cluster
- mtp.scatter(x[y_predict == 1, 0], x[y_predict == 1, 1], s = 100, c = 'green', label = 'Cluster 2') #for second cluster
- mtp.scatter(x[y_predict== 2, 0], x[y_predict == 2, 1], s = 100, c = 'red', label = 'Cluster 3') #for third cluster
- mtp.scatter(x[y_predict == 3, 0], x[y_predict == 3, 1], s = 100, c = 'cyan', label = 'Cluster 4') #for fourth cluster
- mtp.scatter(x[y_predict == 4, 0], x[y_predict == 4, 1], s = 100, c = 'magenta', label = 'Cluster 5') #for fifth cluster
- mtp.scatter(kmeans.cluster_centers_[:, 0], kmeans.cluster_centers_[:, 1], s = 300, c = 'yellow', label = 'Centroid')
- mtp.title('Clusters of customers')

- ⊙ mtp.xlabel('Annual Income (k$)')

- ⊙ mtp.ylabel('Spending Score (1-100)')

- ⊙ mtp.legend()

- ⊙ mtp.show()

In above lines of code, we have written code for each clusters, ranging from 1 to 5. The first coordinate of the mtp.scatter, i.e., x[y_predict == 0, 0] containing the x value for the showing the matrix of features values, and the y_predict is ranging from 0 to 1.

Hierarchical Clustering

Hierarchical clustering is another unsupervised machine learning algorithm, which is used to group the unlabeled datasets into a cluster and also known as hierarchical cluster analysis or HCA.

In this algorithm, we develop the hierarchy of clusters in the form of a tree, and this tree-shaped structure is known as the dendrogram.

Sometimes the results of K-means clustering and hierarchical clustering may look similar, but they both differ depending on how they work. As there is no requirement to predetermine the number of clusters as we did in the K-Means algorithm.

The hierarchical clustering technique has two approaches:

- ⊙ **Agglomerative:** Agglomerative is a bottom-up approach, in which the algorithm starts with taking all data points as single clusters and merging them until one cluster is left.

- ⊙ **Divisive:** Divisive algorithm is the reverse of the agglomerative algorithm as it is a **to**p-down approach.

As we already have other clustering algorithms such as K-Means Clustering, then why we need hierarchical clustering? So, as we have seen in the K-means clustering that there are some challenges with this algorithm, which are a predetermined number of clusters, and it always tries to create the clusters of the same size. To solve these two challenges, we can opt for the hierarchical clustering algorithm because, in this algorithm, we don't need to have knowledge about the predefined number of clusters.

In this topic, we will discuss the Agglomerative Hierarchical clustering algorithm.

Agglomerative Hierarchical clustering

The agglomerative hierarchical clustering algorithm is a popular example of HCA. To group the datasets into clusters, it follows the **bottom-up approach**. It means, this algorithm considers each dataset as a single cluster at the beginning, and then start combining the closest pair of clusters together. It does this until all the clusters are merged into a single cluster that contains all the datasets.

This hierarchy of clusters is represented in the form of the dendrogram.

The Working of Agglomerative Hierarchical clustering

The working of the AHC algorithm can be explained using the below steps:

- ⊙ **Step-1:** Create each data point as a single cluster. Let's say there are N data points, so the number of clusters will also be N (Fig. 3.37).

- ⊙ **Step-2:** Take two closest data points or clusters and merge them to form one cluster. So, there will now be N-1 clusters (Fig. 3.38).

- ⊙ **Step-3:** Again, take the two closest clusters and merge them together to form one cluster. There will be N-2 clusters (Fig. 3.39).

- ⊙ **Step-4:** Repeat Step 3 until only one cluster left. So, we will get the following clusters. Consider the below image (Fig. 3.40):

- ⊙ **Step-5:** Once all the clusters are combined into one big cluster, develop the dendrogram to divide the clusters as per the problem.

Python Implementation of Agglomerative Hierarchical Clustering

Now we will see the practical implementation of the agglomerative hierarchical clustering algorithm using Python. To implement this, we will use the same dataset problem that we have used in the previous topic of K-means clustering so that we can compare both concepts easily.

The dataset is containing the information of customers that have visited a mall for shopping. So, the mall owner wants to find some patterns or some particular behavior of his customers using the dataset information.

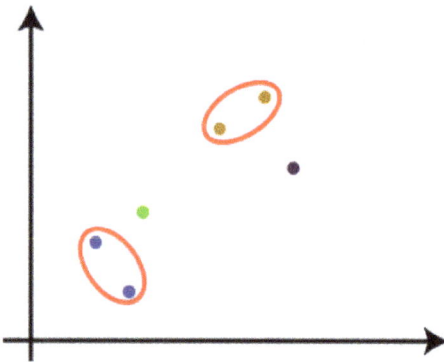

Fig. 3.39

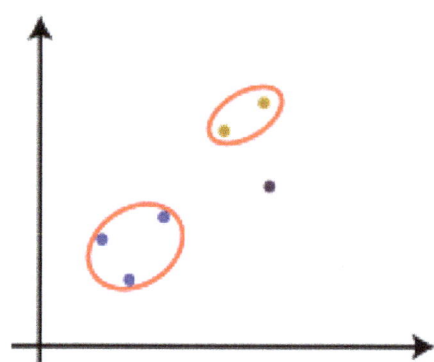

Fig. 3.40

Steps for implementation of AHC using Python:

The steps for implementation will be the same as the k-means clustering, except for some changes such as the method to find the number of clusters. Below are the steps:

- ⊙ Data Pre-processing

- ⊙ Finding the optimal number of clusters using the Dendrogram

- ⊙ Training the hierarchical clustering model
- ⊙ Visualizing the clusters

Data Pre-processing Steps:

In this step, we will import the libraries and datasets for our model.

- ⊙ **Importing the libraries**
  - # Importing the libraries
  - **import** numpy as nm
  - **import** matplotlib.pyplot as mtp
  - **import** pandas as pd

The above lines of code are used to import the libraries to perform specific tasks, such as **numpy** for the Mathematical operations, **matplotlib** for drawing the graphs or scatter plot, and **pandas** for importing the dataset.

- ⊙ **Importing the dataset**
  - # Importing the dataset
  - dataset = pd.read_csv('Mall_Customers_data.csv')
  - **Extracting the matrix of features**

Here we will extract only the matrix of features as we don't have any further information about the dependent variable. Code is given below:

$$x = dataset.iloc[:, [3, 4]].values$$

Here we have extracted only 3 and 4 columns as we will use a 2D plot to see the clusters. So, we are considering the Annual income and spending score as the matrix of features.

Step-2: Finding the optimal number of clusters using the Dendrogram

Now we will find the optimal number of clusters using the Dendrogram for our model. For this, we are going to use **scipy** library as it provides a function that will directly return the dendrogram for our code. Consider the below lines of code:

- ⊙ #Finding the optimal number of clusters using the dendrogram
- ⊙ **import** scipy.cluster.hierarchy as shc
- ⊙ dendro = shc.dendrogram(shc.linkage(x, method="ward"))
- ⊙ mtp.title("Dendrogrma Plot")
- ⊙ mtp.ylabel("Euclidean Distances")
- ⊙ mtp.xlabel("Customers")
- ⊙ mtp.show()

In the above lines of code, we have imported the hierarchy module of scipy library. This module provides us a method shc.denrogram(), which takes the linkage() as a parameter. The linkage function is used to define the distance between two clusters, so here we have passed the x(matrix of features), and method "ward," the popular method of linkage in hierarchical clustering.

Step-3: Training the hierarchical clustering model

As we know the required optimal number of clusters, we can now train our model. The code is given below:

- #training the hierarchical model on dataset
- from sklearn.cluster **import** AgglomerativeClustering
- hc= AgglomerativeClustering(n_clusters=5, affinity='euclidean', linkage='ward')
- y_pred= hc.fit_predict(x)

In the above code, we have imported the AgglomerativeClustering class of cluster module of scikit learn library.

Then we have created the object of this class named as hc. The Agglomerative Clustering class takes the following parameters:

- **n_clusters=5**: It defines the number of clusters, and we have taken here 5 because it is the optimal number of clusters.
- **affinity='euclidean'**: It is a metric used to compute the linkage.
- **linkage='ward'**: It defines the linkage criteria, here we have used the "ward" linkage. This method is the popular linkage method that we have already used for creating the Dendrogram. It reduces the variance in each cluster.

In the last line, we have created the dependent variable y_pred to fit or train the model. It does train not only the model but also returns the clusters to which each data point belongs.

Step-4: Visualizing the clusters

As we have trained our model successfully, now we can visualize the clusters corresponding to the dataset.

Here we will use the same lines of code as we did in k-means clustering, except one change. Here we will not plot the centroid that we did in k-means, because here we have used dendrogram to determine the optimal number of clusters. The code is given below:

- #visulaizing the clusters
- mtp.scatter(x[y_pred == 0, 0], x[y_pred == 0, 1], s = 100, c = 'blue', label = 'Cluster 1')

- ◉ mtp.scatter(x[y_pred == 1, 0], x[y_pred == 1, 1], s = 100, c = 'green', label = 'Cluster 2')
- ◉ mtp.scatter(x[y_pred== 2, 0], x[y_pred == 2, 1], s = 100, c = 'red', label = 'Cluster 3')
- ◉ mtp.scatter(x[y_pred == 3, 0], x[y_pred == 3, 1], s = 100, c = 'cyan', label = 'Cluster 4')
- ◉ mtp.scatter(x[y_pred == 4, 0], x[y_pred == 4, 1], s = 100, c = 'magenta', label = 'Cluster 5')
- ◉ mtp.title('Clusters of customers')
- ◉ mtp.xlabel('Annual Income (k$)')
- ◉ mtp.ylabel('Spending Score (1-100)')
- ◉ mtp.legend()
- ◉ mtp.show()

DBSCAN (Density based clustering) Clustering

Clustering analysis or simply Clustering is basically an Unsupervised learning method that divides the data points into a number of specific batches or groups, such that the data points in the same groups have similar properties and data points in different groups have different properties in some sense. It comprises many different methods based on differential evolution, e.g. K-Means (distance between points), Affinity propagation (graph distance), Mean-shift (distance between points), DBSCAN (distance between nearest points), Gaussian mixtures (Mahalanobis distance to centers), Spectral clustering (graph distance), etc.

Fundamentally, all clustering methods use the same approach i.e. first we calculate similarities and then we use it to cluster the data points into groups or batches. Here we will focus on the **Density-based spatial clustering of applications with noise** (DBSCAN) clustering method.

Density-Based Spatial Clustering of Applications With Noise (DBSCAN)

Clusters are dense regions in the data space, separated by regions of the lower density of points. The DBSCAN algorithm is based on this intuitive notion of "clusters" and "noise". The key idea is that for each point of a cluster, the neighborhood of a given radius has to contain at least a minimum number of points.

Why DBSCAN?

Partitioning methods (K-means, PAM clustering) and hierarchical clustering work for finding spherical-shaped clusters or convex clusters. In other words, they are suitable only for compact and well-separated clusters. Moreover, they are also severely affected by the presence of noise and outliers in the data.

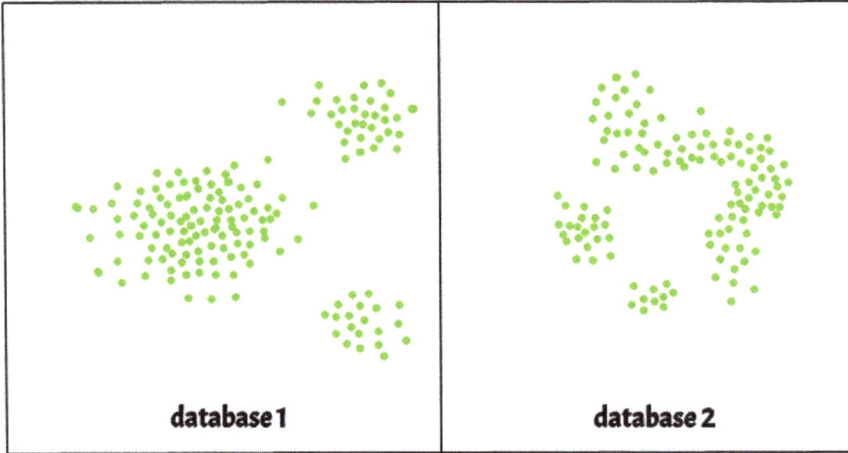

Fig. 3.41

Real-life data may contain irregularities, like:

⊙ Clusters can be of arbitrary shape such as those shown in the figure below.

⊙ Data may contain noise.

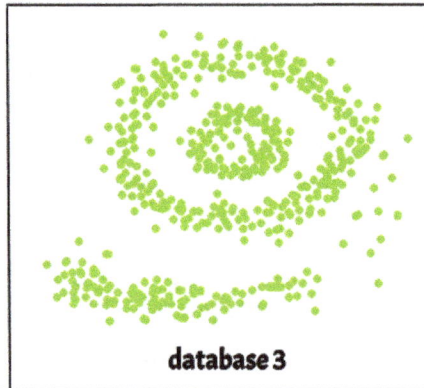

Fig. 3.42 Data set containing non-convex shape clusters and outliers

Figure 3.42 shows a data set containing non-convex shape clusters and outliers. Given such data, the k-means algorithm has difficulties in identifying these clusters with arbitrary shapes.

Parameters Required For DBSCAN Algorithm

⊙ **eps**: It defines the neighborhood around a data point i.e. if the distance between two points is lower or equal to 'eps' then they are considered neighbors. If the eps value is chosen too small then a large part of the data will be considered as an outlier. If it is chosen very large then the clusters will merge and the majority of the data points will be in the same clusters. One way to find the eps value is based on the k-distance graph.

- **MinPts**: Minimum number of neighbors (data points) within eps radius. The larger the dataset, the larger value of MinPts must be chosen. As a general rule, the minimum MinPts can be derived from the number of dimensions D in the dataset as, MinPts >= D+1. The minimum value of MinPts must be chosen at least 3.

In this algorithm, we have 3 types of data points.

- **Core Point**: A point is a core point if it has more than MinPts points within eps.
- **Border Point**: A point which has fewer than MinPts within eps but it is in the neighborhood of a core point.
- **Noise or outlier**: A point which is not a core point or border point.

Steps Used In DBSCAN Algorithm

- Find all the neighbor points within eps and identify the core points or visited with more than MinPts neighbors.
- For each core point if it is not already assigned to a cluster, create a new cluster.
- Find recursively all its density-connected points and assign them to the same cluster as the core point.

A point a and b are said to be density connected if there exists a point c which has a sufficient number of points in its neighbors and both points a and b are within the *eps distance*. This is a chaining process. So, if b is a neighbor of c, c is a neighbor of d, and d is a neighbor of e, which in turn is neighbor of a implying that b is a neighbor of a.

- Iterate through the remaining unvisited points in the dataset. Those points that do not belong to any cluster are noise.

Pseudocode For DBSCAN Clustering Algorithm

```
DBSCAN(dataset, eps, MinPts){
# cluster index
C = 1
for each unvisited point p in dataset {
    mark p as visited
    # find neighbors
    Neighbors N = find the neighboring points of p
    if |N|>=MinPts:
        N = N U N'
        if p' is not a member of any cluster:
        add p' to cluster C
```

}Implementation Of DBSCAN Algorithm Using Machine Learning In Python

Here, we'll use the Python library sklearn to compute DBSCAN. We'll also use the matplotlib.pyplot library for visualizing clusters.

Import Libraries

⊙ **Python3**:

```
import matplotlib.pyplot as plt

import numpy as np

from sklearn.cluster import DBSCAN

from sklearn import metrics

from sklearn.datasets import make_blobs

from sklearn.preprocessing import StandardScaler

from sklearn import datasets
```

Prepare dataset : We will create a dataset using sklearn for modeling. We make_ blob for creating the dataset

⊙ **Python3**

```
# Load data in X

X, y_true = make_blobs(n_samples=300, centers=4,

                cluster_std=0.50, random_state=0)
```

Modeling the Data Using DBSCAN

```
Python3

db = DBSCAN(eps=0.3, min_samples=10).fit(X)

core_samples_mask = np.zeros_like(db.labels_, dtype=bool)

core_samples_mask[db.core_sample_indices_] = True

labels = db.labels_

 # Number of clusters in labels, ignoring noise if present.

n_clusters_ = len(set(labels)) - (1 if -1 in labels else 0)

# Plot result

# Black removed and is used for noise instead.

unique_labels = set(labels)

colors = ['y', 'b', 'g', 'r']

print(colors)
```

```
for k, col in zip(unique_labels, colors):
if k == -1:
# Black used for noise.
col = 'k'
class_member_mask = (labels == k)
xy = X[class_member_mask & core_samples_mask]
plt.plot(xy[:, 0], xy[:, 1], 'o', markerfacecolor=col,
markeredgecolor='k',
markersize=6)
xy = X[class_member_mask & ~core_samples_mask]
plt.plot(xy[:, 0], xy[:, 1], 'o', markerfacecolor=col,
markeredgecolor='k',
markersize=6)
plt.title('number of clusters: %d' % n_clusters_)
plt.show()
```

Cluster of dataset

Evaluation Metrics For DBSCAN Algorithm In Machine Learning

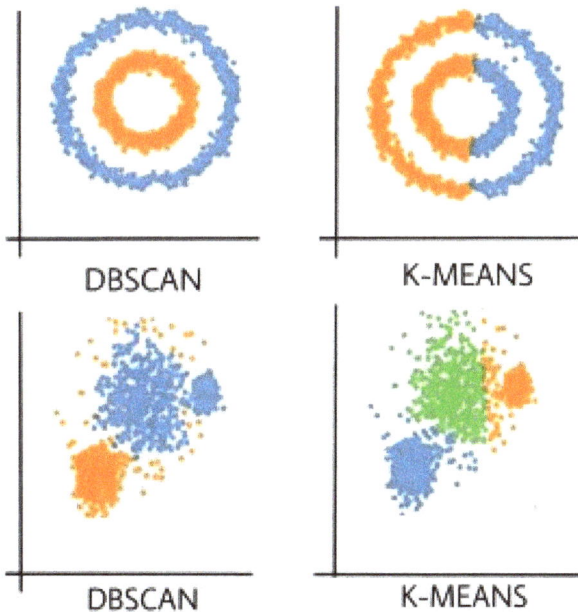

Fig. 3.43 Clusters formed in K-means and DBSCAN

We will use the Silhouette score and Adjusted rand score for evaluating clustering algorithms. Silhouette's score is in the range of -1 to 1. A score near 1 denotes the best meaning that the data point i is very compact within the cluster to which it belongs and far away from the other clusters. The worst value is -1. Values near 0 denote overlapping clusters.

Absolute Rand Score is in the range of 0 to 1. More than 0.9 denotes excellent cluster recovery, and above 0.8 is a good recovery. Less than 0.5 is considered to be poor recovery.

⦿ Python3

```
# evaluation metrics
sc = metrics.silhouette_score(X, labels)
print("Silhouette Coefficient:%0.2f" % sc)
ari = adjusted_rand_score(y_true, labels)
print("Adjusted Rand Index: %0.2f" % ari)
```

Output:

Coefficient:0.13

Adjusted Rand Index: 0.31

Black points represent outliers. By changing the *eps* and the *MinPts*, we can change the cluster configuration.

Now the question that should be raised is –

When Should We Use DBSCAN Over K-Means In Clustering Analysis?

DBSCAN(*Density-Based Spatial Clustering of Applications with Noise*) and K-Means are both clustering algorithms that group together data that have the same characteristic. However, They work on different principles and are suitable for different types of data. We prefer to use DBSCAN when the data is not spherical in shape or the number of classes is not known beforehand.

ENSEMBLE LEARNING AND MODEL EVALUATION

Ensemble learning is based on the idea that a group of models can produce better outcomes than a single model. This is because different models may have different strengths and weaknesses, and by combining them, you can reduce the errors and biases that affect each model. Ensemble learning can also increase the diversity and complexity of the features and hypotheses that are considered by the models, leading to more expressive and flexible solutions.

Create an ensemble

There are many ways to create an ensemble, but they can be broadly classified into two categories: parallel and sequential. In parallel ensembles, the models are trained independently and then combined using some aggregation method, such as voting, averaging, or weighting. In sequential ensembles, the models are trained iteratively and depend on the outputs of the previous models, such as in boosting or stacking. The choice of the ensemble method depends on the type and size of the data, the complexity and diversity of the models, and the desired trade-off between accuracy and efficiency.

Validating an ensemble

Validating an ensemble is similar to validating a single model, but it requires some additional considerations. One of the main challenges is to avoid over-fitting, which can occur when the ensemble is too complex or too specific to the training data. To prevent overfitting, you can use techniques such as cross-validation, regularization, pruning, or bagging. Another challenge is to measure the performance and contribution of each model in the ensemble, which can be done using techniques such as error analysis, feature importance, or model selection.

Evaluating an ensemble

Evaluating an ensemble is the process of comparing its performance with other models or benchmarks, and analyzing its strengths and weaknesses. There are many metrics and criteria that can be used to evaluate an ensemble, such as accuracy, precision, recall, F1-score, ROC curve, AUC, or R-squared. However, these metrics may not capture the full picture of the ensemble's behavior, especially when dealing with complex or imbalanced data. Therefore, you should also use techniques such as confusion matrix, learning curve, or error distribution to gain more insights into the ensemble's performance.

Benefits of ensemble learning

Ensemble learning can provide many advantages for model validation and evaluation, such as improving accuracy and reducing variance by averaging out errors and noises of individual models, enhancing stability and robustness by reducing sensitivity to outliers, missing values, or data changes, increasing generalization and scalability by adapting to different data domains, distributions, or dimensions, exploiting diversity and complementarity by leveraging different features, algorithms, or parameters of individual models, and facilitating interpretation and explanation by providing multiple perspectives, evidences, or explanations for the predictions.

Model Evaluation

Model evaluation is the process that uses some metrics which help us to analyze the performance of the model. As we all know that model development is a multi-step process and a check should be kept on how well the model generalizes future predictions. Therefore evaluating a model plays a vital role so that we can judge the performance of our model. The evaluation also helps to analyze a model's key weaknesses. There are many metrics like Accuracy, Precision, Recall, F1 score, Area under Curve, Confusion Matrix, and Mean Square Error. Cross Validation is one technique that is followed during the training phase and it is a model evaluation technique as well.

Cross Validation and Holdout

Cross Validation is a method in which we do not use the whole dataset for training. In this technique, some part of the dataset is reserved for testing the model. There are many types of Cross-Validation out of which K Fold Cross Validation is mostly used. In K Fold Cross Validation the original dataset is divided into k subsets. The subsets are known as folds. This is repeated k times where 1 fold is used for testing purposes. Rest k-1 folds are used for training the model. So each data point acts as a test subject for the model as well as acts as the training subject. It is seen that this technique generalizes the model well and reduces the error rate

CHAPTER-4

DATA SCIENCE AND AL PIPELINES

The field encompasses analysis, preparing data for analysis, and presenting findings to inform high-level decisions in an organization. As such, it incorporates skills from computer science, mathematics, statistics, information visualization, graphic, and business.

But besides storage and analysis, it is important to formulate the questions that we will solve using our data. And these questions would yield the hidden information which will give us the power to predict results, just like a wizard.

After getting hold of our questions, now we are ready to see what lies inside the data science pipeline. When the raw data enters a pipeline, it's unsure of how much potential it holds within. It is we data scientists, waiting eagerly inside the pipeline, who bring out its worth by cleaning it, exploring it, and finally utilizing it in the best way possible. So, to understand its journey let's jump into the pipeline.

EXTRACT, TRANSFORM, LOAD (ETL) PROCESSES

Introduction

ETL stands for Extract, Transform, Load and it is a process used in data warehousing to extract data from various sources, transform it into a format suitable for loading into a data warehouse, and then load it into the warehouse. The process of ETL can be broken down into the following three stages:

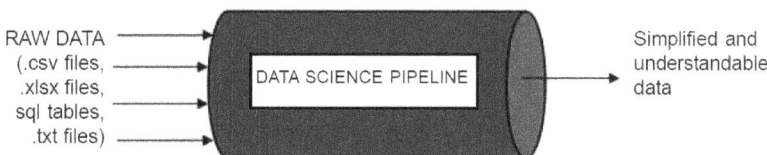

Fig. 4.1 Data science pipeline in a simplified way

Extract: The first stage in the ETL process is to extract data from various sources such as transactional systems, spreadsheets, and flat files. This step involves reading data from the source systems and storing it in a staging area.

⊙ **Transform**: In this stage, the extracted data is transformed into a format that is suitable for loading into the data warehouse. This may involve cleaning and validating the data, converting data types, combining data from multiple sources, and creating new data fields.

⊙ **Load**: After the data is transformed, it is loaded into the data warehouse. This step involves creating the physical data structures and loading the data into the warehouse.

The ETL process is an iterative process that is repeated as new data is added to the warehouse. The process is important because it ensures that the data in the data warehouse is accurate, complete, and up-to-date. It also helps to ensure that the data is in the format required for data mining and reporting.

Additionally, there are many different ETL tools and technologies available, such as Informatica, Talend, DataStage, and others, that can automate and simplify the ETL process.

ETL is a process in Data Warehousing and it stands for Extract, Transform and Load. It is a process in which an ETL tool extracts the data from various data source systems, transforms it in the staging area, and then finally, loads it into the Data Warehouse system.

Let us understand each step of the ETL process in-depth:

Extraction:

The first step of the ETL process is extraction. In this step, data from various source systems is extracted which can be in various formats like relational databases, No SQL, XML, and flat files into the staging area. It is important to extract the data from various source systems and store it into the staging area first and not directly into the data warehouse because the extracted data is in various formats and can be corrupted also. Hence loading it directly into the data warehouse may damage it and rollback will be much more difficult. Therefore, this is one of the most important steps of ETL process.

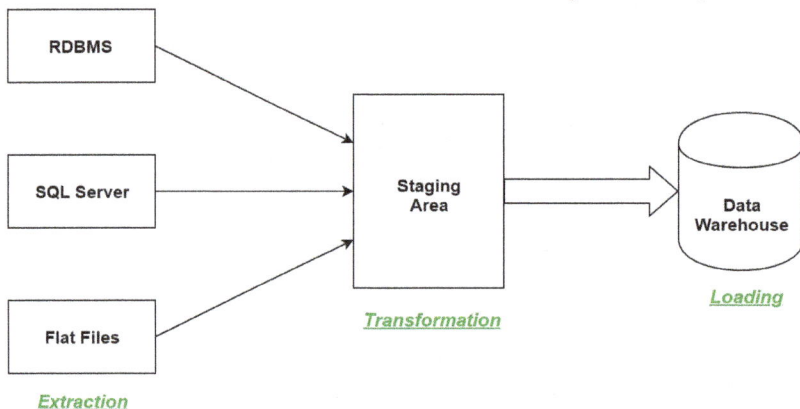

Fig. 4.3 Data Warehouse system

Transformation:

The second step of the ETL process is transformation. In this step, a set of rules or functions are applied on the extracted data to convert it into a single standard format. It may involve following processes/tasks:

- ⊙ Filtering – loading only certain attributes into the data warehouse.
- ⊙ Cleaning – filling up the NULL values with some default values, mapping U.S.A, United States, and America into USA, etc.
- ⊙ Joining – joining multiple attributes into one.
- ⊙ Splitting – splitting a single attribute into multiple attributes.
- ⊙ Sorting – sorting tuples on the basis of some attribute (generally key-attribute).

Loading:

The third and final step of the ETL process is loading. In this step, the transformed data is finally loaded into the data warehouse. Sometimes the data is updated by loading into the data warehouse very frequently and sometimes it is done after longer but regular intervals. The rate and period of loading solely depends on the requirements and varies from system to system.

ETL process can also use the pipelining concept i.e. as soon as some data is extracted, it can transformed and during that period some new data can be extracted. And while the transformed data is being loaded into the data warehouse, the already extracted data can be transformed. The block diagram of the pipelining of ETL process is shown in Fig. 4.4.

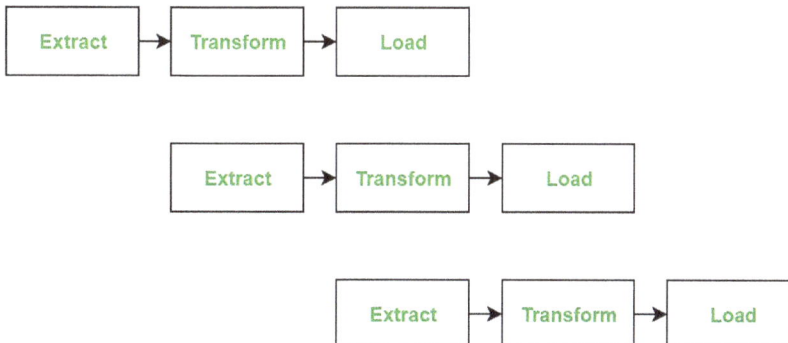

Fig. 4.4 Pipelining of ETL process

ETL Tools: Most commonly used ETL tools are Hevo, Sybase, Oracle Warehouse builder, CloverETL, and MarkLogic.

Data Warehouses: Most commonly used Data Warehouses are Snowflake, Redshift, BigQuery, and Firebolt.

Advantages or Disadvantages:

Advantages of ETL process in data warehousing:

- ⊙ **Improved data quality:** ETL process ensures that the data in the data warehouse is accurate, complete, and up-to-date.

- ⊙ **Better data integration:** ETL process helps to integrate data from multiple sources and systems, making it more accessible and usable.

- ⊙ **Increased data security:** ETL process can help to improve data security by controlling access to the data warehouse and ensuring that only authorized users can access the data.

- ⊙ **Improved scalability:** ETL process can help to improve scalability by providing a way to manage and analyze large amounts of data.

- ⊙ **Increased automation:** ETL tools and technologies can automate and simplify the ETL process, reducing the time and effort required to load and update data in the warehouse.

Disadvantages of ETL process in data warehousing:

- ⊙ **High cost:** ETL process can be expensive to implement and maintain, especially for organizations with limited resources.

- ⊙ **Complexity:** ETL process can be complex and difficult to implement, especially for organizations that lack the necessary expertise or resources.

- ⊙ **Limited flexibility:** ETL process can be limited in terms of flexibility, as it may not be able to handle unstructured data or real-time data streams.

- ⊙ **Limited scalability:** ETL process can be limited in terms of scalability, as it may not be able to handle very large amounts of data.

- ⊙ **Data privacy concerns:** ETL process can raise concerns about data privacy, as large amounts of data are collected, stored, and analyzed.

Overall, ETL process is an essential process in data warehousing that helps to ensure that the data in the data warehouse is accurate, complete, and up-to-date. However, it also comes with its own set of challenges and limitations, and organizations need to carefully consider the costs and benefits before implementing them.

FEATURE SCALING AND SELECTION

Feature Scaling is a technique to standardize the independent features present in the data in a fixed range. It is performed during the data pre-processing to handle highly varying magnitudes or values or units. If feature scaling is not done, then a machine learning algorithm tends to weigh greater values, higher and consider smaller values as the lower values, regardless of the unit of the values.

Why use Feature Scaling?

In machine learning, feature scaling is employed for a number of purposes:

- **Scaling guarantees** that all features are on a comparable scale and have comparable ranges. This process is known as feature normalisation. This is significant because the magnitude of the features has an impact on many machine learning techniques. Larger scale features may dominate the learning process and have an excessive impact on the outcomes. You can avoid this problem and make sure that each feature contributes equally to the learning process by scaling the features.

- **Algorithm performance improvement**: When the features are scaled, several machine learning methods, including gradient descent-based algorithms, distance-based algorithms (such k-nearest neighbours), and support vector machines, perform better or converge more quickly. The algorithm's performance can be enhanced by scaling the features, which can hasten the convergence of the algorithm to the ideal outcome.

- **Preventing numerical instability**: Numerical instability can be prevented by avoiding significant scale disparities between features. Examples include distance calculations or matrix operations, where having features with radically differing scales can result in numerical overflow or underflow problems. Stable computations are ensured and these issues are mitigated by scaling the features.

- **Scaling features** makes ensuring that each characteristic is given the same consideration during the learning process. Without scaling, bigger scale features could dominate the learning, producing skewed outcomes. This bias is removed through scaling, which also guarantees that each feature contributes fairly to model predictions.

Absolute Maximum Scaling

This method of scaling requires two-step:

- We should first select the maximum absolute value out of all the entries of a particular measure.

- Then after this, we divide each entry of the column by this maximum value.

$$X_{scaled} = X_i - max\ (|X|)/max(|X|)$$

After performing the above-mentioned two steps we will observe that each entry of the column lies in the range of -1 to 1. But this method is not used that often the reason behind this is that it is too sensitive to the outliers. And while dealing with the real-world data presence of outliers is a very common thing.

For the demonstration purpose, we will use the dataset which you can download from here. This dataset is a simpler version of the original house price prediction dataset having only two columns from the original dataset. The first five rows of the original data are shown below:

◉ **Python3**

```
import pandas as pd

df = pd.read_csv('SampleFile.csv')
```

print(df.head())

Output:

LotArea MSSubClass

0	8450	60
1	9600	20
2	11250	60
3	9550	70
4	14260	60

Now let's apply the first method which is of the absolute maximum scaling. For this first, we are supposed to evaluate the absolute maximum values of the columns.

◉ Python3

import numpy as np

max_vals = np.max(np.abs(df))

max_vals

Output:

LotArea   215245

MSSubClass   190

dtype: int64

Now we are supposed to subtract these values from the data and then divide the results from the maximum values as well.

◉ Python3

print((df - max_vals) / max_vals)

Output:

	LotArea	MSSubClass
0	-0.960742	-0.684211
1	-0.955400	-0.894737
2	-0.947734	-0.684211
3	-0.955632	-0.631579
4	-0.933750	-0.684211
...	...	...
1455	-0.963219	-0.684211
1456	-0.938791	-0.894737
1457	-0.957992	-0.631579
1458	-0.954856	-0.894737
1459	-0.953834	-0.894737

[1460 rows x 2 columns]

Min-Max Scaling

This method of scaling requires below two-step:

⦿ First, we are supposed to find the minimum and the maximum value of the column.

⦿ Then we will subtract the minimum value from the entry and divide the result by the difference between the maximum and the minimum value.

This method is more or less

$$X_{scaled} = X_i - X_{min}/X_{max} - X_{min}$$

As we are using the maximum and the minimum value this method is also prone to outliers but the range in which the data will range after performing the above two steps is between 0 to 1.

⦿ Python3

```
from sklearn.preprocessing import MinMaxScaler
scaler = MinMaxScaler()
scaled_data = scaler.fit_transform(df)
scaled_df = pd.DataFrame(scaled_data,
          columns=df.columns)
scaled_df.head()
```

Output:

LotArea MSSubClass

0 0.033420   0.235294

1 0.038795   0.000000

2 0.046507   0.235294

3 0.038561   0.294118

4 0.060576   0.235294

Normalization

This method is more or less the same as the previous method but here instead of the minimum value, we subtract each entry by the mean value of the whole data and then divide the results by the difference between the minimum and the maximum value.

$$X_{scaled} = X_i - X_{min}/X_{max} - X_{min}$$

⊙ Python3

```
from sklearn.preprocessing import Normalizer
scaler = Normalizer()
scaled_data = scaler.fit_transform(df)
scaled_df = pd.DataFrame(scaled_data,
              columns=df.columns)
print(scaled_df.head())
```

Output:

   LotArea MSSubClass

0 0.999975   0.007100

1 0.999998   0.002083

2 0.999986   0.005333

3 0.999973   0.007330

4 0.999991   0.004208

Standardization

This method of scaling is basically based on the central tendencies and variance of the data.

⊙ First, we should calculate the mean and standard deviation of the data we would like to normalize.

⊙ Then we are supposed to subtract the mean value from each entry and then divide the result by the standard deviation.

This helps us achieve a normal distribution(if it is already normal but skewed) of the data with a mean equal to zero and a standard deviation equal to 1.

$$X_{scaled} = X_i - X_{max} \backslash d$$

⦿ **Python3**

from sklearn.preprocessing import StandardScaler

scaler = StandardScaler()

scaled_data = scaler.fit_transform(df)

scaled_df = pd.DataFrame(scaled_data,

columns=df.columns)

print(scaled_df.head())

Output:

```
   LotArea  MSSubClass
0 -0.207142   0.073375
1 -0.091886  -0.872563
2  0.073480   0.073375
3 -0.096897   0.309859
4  0.375148   0.073375
```

Robust Scaling

In this method of scaling, we use two main statistical measures of the data.

⦿ Median

⦿ Inter-Quartile Range

After calculating these two values we are supposed to subtract the median from each entry and then divide the result by the interquartile range.

$$X_{scaled} = X_i - X_{median}/IQR$$

⦿ Python3

from sklearn.preprocessing import RobustScaler

scaler = RobustScaler()

scaled_data = scaler.fit_transform(df)

scaled_df = pd.DataFrame(scaled_data,

columns=df.columns)

print(scaled_df.head())

Output:

```
   LotArea  MSSubClass
0 -0.254076      0.2
1  0.030015     -0.6
```

2 0.437624   0.2

3 0.017663   0.4

4 1.181201   0.2

MODEL TRAINING AND HYPERPARAMETER TUNING

Model Parameter

Model parameters are configuration variables that are internal to the model, and a model learns them on its own. For example, W Weights or Coefficients of independent variables in the Linear regression model. Weights or Coefficients of independent variables SVM, weight, and biases of a neural network, cluster centroid in clustering.

We can understand model parameters using the below image (Fig. 4.5). Fig. 4.5 shows the model representation of Simple Linear Regression. Here, x is an independent variable, y is the dependent variable, and the goal is to fit the best regression line for the given data to define a relationship between x and y. The regression line can be given by the equation: $y = mx+c$

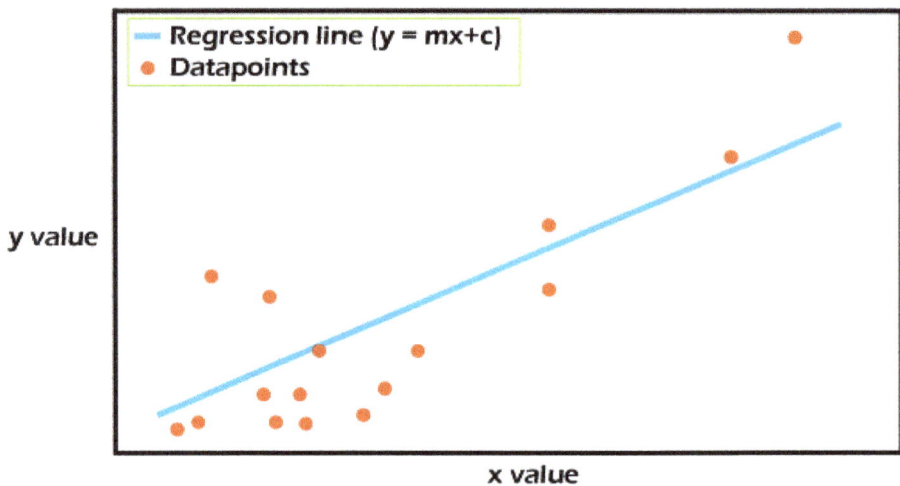

Fig. 4.5 The model representation of Simple Linear Regression

Where m is the slope of the line, and c is the intercept of the line. These two parameters are calculated by fitting the line by minimizing RMSE, and these are known as model parameters.

Some key points for model parameters are as follows:

◉ The model uses them for making predictions.

◉ They are learned by the model from the data itself

◉ These are usually not set manually.

◉ These are the part of the model and key to Machine Learning Algorithms.

Model Hyperparameter

Hyperparameters are those parameters that are explicitly defined by the user to control the learning process.

- ⊙ These are usually defined manually by the machine learning engineer.
- ⊙ One cannot know the exact best value for hyperparameters for the given problem. The best value can be determined either by the rule of thumb or by trial and error.

Comparison table between Parameters and Hyperparameters

Parameters	Hyperparameters
Parameters are the configuration model, which are internal to the model.	Hyperparameters are the explicitly specified parameters that control the training process.
Parameters are essential for making predictions.	Hyperparameters are essential for optimizing the model.
These are specified or estimated while training the model.	These are set before the beginning of the training of the model.
It is internal to the model.	These are external to the model.
These are learned & set by the model by itself.	These are set manually by a machine learning engineer/practitioner.
These are dependent on the dataset, which is used for training.	These are independent of the dataset.
The values of parameters can be estimated by the optimization algorithms, such as Gradient Descent.	The values of hyperparameters can be estimated by hyperparameter tuning.
The final parameters estimated after training decide the model performance on unseen data.	The selected or fine-tuned hyperparameters decide the quality of the model.
Some examples of model parameters are Weights in an ANN, Support vectors in SVM, Coefficients in Linear Regression or Logistic Regression.	Some examples of model hyperparameters are the learning rate for training a neural network, K in the KNN algorithm, etc.

Hyperparameters in Machine Learning

Some examples of Hyperparameters in Machine Learning

- ⊙ The k in kNN or K-Nearest Neighbour algorithm
- ⊙ Learning rate for training a neural network
- ⊙ Train-test split ratio
- ⊙ Batch Size
- ⊙ Number of Epochs
- ⊙ Branches in Decision Tree
- ⊙ Number of clusters in Clustering Algorithm

Categories of Hyperparameters

Broadly hyperparameters can be divided into two categories, which are given below:

◉ Hyperparameter for Optimization

◉ Hyperparameter for Specific Models

Hyperparameter for Optimization

The process of selecting the best hyperparameters to use is known as hyperparameter tuning, and the tuning process is also known as hyperparameter optimization. Optimization parameters are used for optimizing the model.

Some of the popular optimization parameters are given below:

◉ **Learning Rate:** The learning rate is the hyperparameter in optimization algorithms that controls how much the model needs to change in response to the estimated error for each time when the model's weights are updated. It is one of the crucial parameters while building a neural network, and also it determines the frequency of cross-checking with model parameters. Selecting the optimized learning rate is a challenging task because if the learning rate is very less, then it may slow down the training process. On the other hand, if the learning rate is too large, then it may not optimize the model properly.

◉ **Batch Size:** To enhance the speed of the learning process, the training set is divided into different subsets, which are known as a batch. **Number of Epochs:** An epoch can be defined as the complete cycle for training the machine learning model. Epoch represents an iterative learning process. The number of epochs varies from model to model, and various models are created with more than one epoch. To determine the right number of epochs, a validation error is taken into account. The number of epochs is increased until there is a reduction in a validation error. If there is no improvement in reduction error for the consecutive epochs, then it indicates to stop increasing the number of epochs.

Hyperparameter for Specific Models

Hyperparameters that are involved in the structure of the model are known as hyperparameters for specific models. These are given below:

◉ **A number of Hidden Units:** Hidden units are part of neural networks, which refer to the components comprising the layers of processors between input and output units in a neural network.

It is important to specify the number of hidden units hyperparameter for the neural network. It should be between the size of the input layer and the size of the output layer. More specifically, the number of hidden units should be 2/3 of the size of the input layer, plus the size of the output layer.

For complex functions, it is necessary to specify the number of hidden units, but it should not overfit the model.

⦿ **Number of Layers:** A neural network is made up of vertically arranged components, which are called layers. There are mainly **input layers, hidden layers, and output layers**. A 3-layered neural network gives a better performance than a 2-layered network. For a Convolutional Neural network, a greater number of layers make a better model.

MODEL DEPLOYMENT AND MONITORING

Deploy MLOps Module

It enables operationalizing the ML models we developed in the previous module(Build). In this "deploy module", we test our model performance in a production or production-like environment to ensure the robustness and scalability of the ML model for production use.

Model Deployment

Types of Deployment

One way to conceptualize different approaches to deploy ML models is to think about where to deploy them in your application's overall architecture.

⦿ The client-side runs locally on the user machine (web browser, mobile devices, etc..)

⦿ It connects to the server-side that runs your code remotely.

⦿ The server connects with a database to pull data out, render the data, and show the data to the user.

Batch Prediction

Batch prediction (Fig. 4.7) means that you train the models offline, dump the results into a database, then run the rest of the application normally. You periodically run your model on new data coming in and cache the results in a database. Batch prediction is commonly used in production when the universe of inputs is relatively small (e.g., one prediction per user per day).

The pros of batch prediction:

⦿ It is simple to implement.

⦿ It requires relatively low latency to the user.

The cons of batch prediction:

⦿ It does not scale to complex input types.

⦿ Users do not get the most up-to-date predictions.

⦿ Models frequently become "stale" and hard to detect.

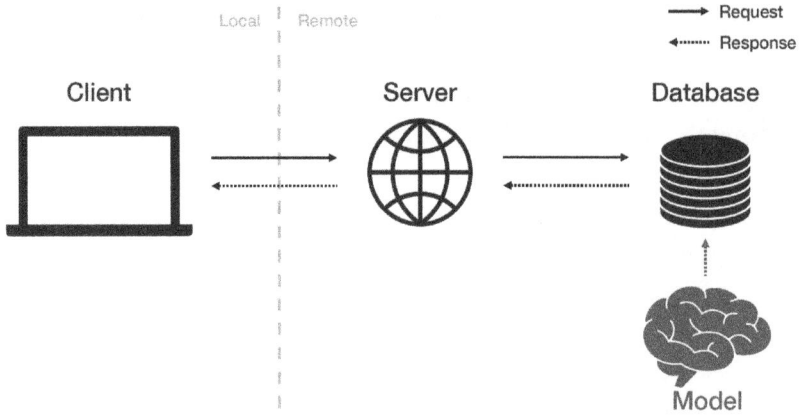

Fig. 4.7 Batch prediction

Model-in-service

Model-in-service means that you package up your model and include it in the deployed web server. Then, the web server loads the model and calls it to make predictions.

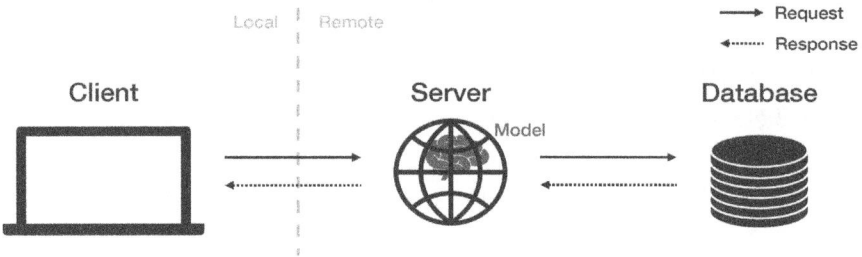

Fig. 4.8 Model-in-service

The pros of model-in-service prediction:

⊙ It reuses your existing infrastructure.

The cons of model-in-service prediction:

⊙ The web server may be written in a different language.

⊙ Models may change more frequently than the server code.

⊙ Large models can eat into the resources for your webserver.

⊙ Server hardware is not optimized for your model (e.g., no GPUs).

⊙ Model and server may scale differently.

Model-as-service

Model-as-service means that you deploy the model separately as its own service. The client and server can interact with the model by making requests to the model service and receiving responses.

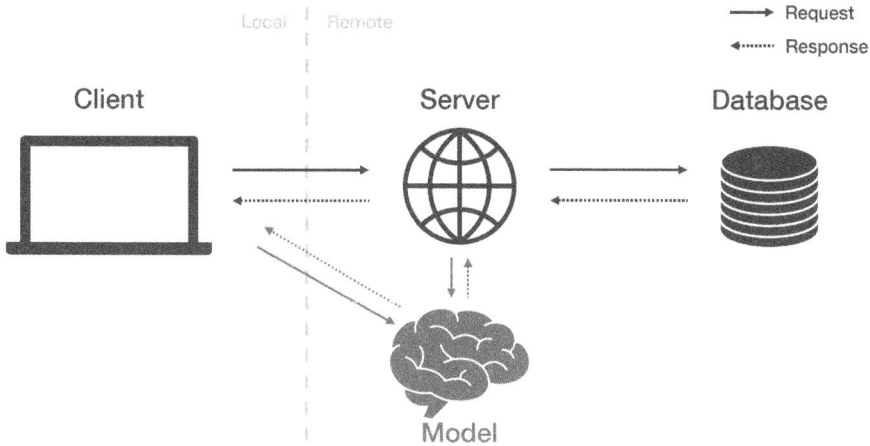

Local | Remote

→ Request
◄········ Response

Client   Server   Database

Model

Fig. 4.9 Model-as-service

The pros of model-as-service prediction:

◉ It is dependable, as model bugs are less likely to crash the web app.

◉ It is scalable, as you can choose the optimal hardware for the model and scale it appropriately.

◉ It is flexible, as you can easily reuse the model across multiple applications.

The cons of model-as-service prediction:

◉ It adds latency.

◉ It adds infrastructural complexity.

◉ Most importantly, you are now on the hook to run a model service...

2 - Building A Model Service

REST APIS

REST APIs represent a way of serving predictions in response to canonically formatted HTTP requests. There are alternatives such as gRPC and GraphQL. For instance, in your command line, you can use curl to post some data to an URL and get back JSON that contains the model predictions.

Sadly, there is no standard way of formatting the data that goes into an ML model.

Dependency Management

Model predictions depend on the code, the model weights, and the code dependencies. All three need to be present on your webserver. For code and model weights, you can simply copy them locally (or write a script to extract them if they are large). But dependencies are trickier because they cause troubles. As they are hard to make consistent and update, your model behavior might change accordingly.

There are two high-level strategies to manage code dependencies:

⊙ You constrain the dependencies of your model.

⊙ You use containers.

ONNX

If you go with the first strategy, you need a standard neural network format. The Open Neural Network Exchange (ONNX, for short) is designed to allow framework interoperability. The dream is to mix different frameworks, such that frameworks that are good for development (PyTorch) don't also have to be good at inference (Caffe2).

⊙ The promise is that you can train a model with one tool stack and then deploy it using another for inference/prediction. ONNX is a robust and open standard for preventing framework lock-in and ensuring that your models will be usable in the long run.

⊙ The reality is that since ML libraries change quickly, there are often bugs in the translation layer. Furthermore, how do you deal with non-library code (like feature transformations)?

Docker

If you go with the second strategy, you want to learn Docker. Docker is a computer program that performs operating-system-level virtualization, also known as containerization. What is a container, you might ask? It is a standardized unit of fully packaged software used for local development, shipping code, and deploying system.

The best way to describe it intuitively is to think of a process surrounded by its filesystem. You run one or a few related processes, and they see a whole filesystem, not shared by anyone.

⊙ This makes containers **extremely portable**, as they are detached from the underlying hardware and the platform that runs them.

⊙ They are very **lightweight**, as a minimal amount of data needs to be included.

⊙ They are **secure**, as the exposed attack surface of a container is extremely small.

⊙ Note here that containers are different from virtual machines.

⊙ Virtual machines require the hypervisor to virtualize a full hardware stack. There are also multiple guest operating systems, making them larger and more extended to boot. This is what AWS / GCP / Azure cloud instances are.

⊙ Containers, on the other hand, require no hypervisor/hardware virtualization. All containers share the same host kernel. There are dedicated isolated user-space environments, making them much smaller in size and faster to boot.

In brief, you should familiarize yourself with these basic concepts:

◉ **Dockerfile** defines how to build an image.

◉ **Image** is a built packaged environment.

◉ **Container** is where images are run inside.

◉ **Repository** hosts different versions of an image.

◉ **Registry** is a set of repositories.

Furthermore, Docker has a robust ecosystem. It has the **DockerHub** for community-contributed images. It's incredibly easy to search for images that meet your needs, ready to pull down and use with little-to-no modification.

Though Docker presents how to deal with each of the individual microservices, we also need an orchestrator to handle the whole cluster of services. Such an orchestrator distributes containers onto the underlying virtual machines or bare metal so that these containers talk to each other and coordinate to solve the task at hand. The standard container orchestration tool is Kubernetes.

Performance Optimization

We will talk mostly about how to run your model service faster on a single machine. Here are the key questions that you want to address:

◉ Do you want inference on a GPU or not?

◉ How can you run multiple copies of the model at the same time?

◉ How to make the model smaller?

◉ How to improve model performance via caching, batching, and GPU sharing?

GPU or no GPU?

Here are the pros of GPU inference:

◉ You use the same hardware that your model is trained on probably.

◉ If your model gets bigger and you want to limit model size or tune batch size, you will get high throughput.

Here are the cons of GPU inference:

◉ GPU is complex to set up.

◉ GPUs are expensive.

Concurrency

Instead of running a single model copy on your machine, you run multiple model copies on different CPUs or cores. In practice, you need to be careful about thread tuning - making sure that each model copy only uses the minimum number of threads required. Read this blog post from Roblox for the details.

Model distillation

Model distillation is a compression technique in which a small "student" model is trained to reproduce the behavior of a large "teacher" model. The method was first proposed by Bucila et al., 2006 and generalized by Hinton et al., 2015. In distillation, knowledge is transferred from the teacher model to the student by minimizing a loss function. The target is the distribution of class probabilities predicted by the teacher model. That is — the output of a softmax function on the teacher model's logits.

Distillation can be finicky to do yourself, so it is infrequently used in practice. Read this blog post from Derrick Mwiti for several model distillation techniques for deep learning.

Model quantization

Model quantization is a model compression technique that makes the model physically smaller to save disk space and require less memory during computation to run faster. It decreases the numerical precision of a model's weights. In other words, each weight is permanently encoded using fewer bits. Note here that there are tradeoffs with accuracy.

- A straightforward method is implemented in the TensorFlow Lite toolkit. It turns a matrix of 32-bit floats into 8-bit integers by applying a simple "center-and-scale" transform to it: $W\_8 = W\_32$ / scale + shift (scale and shift are determined individually for each weight matrix). This way, the 8-bit W is used in matrix multiplication, and only the result is then corrected by applying the "center-and-scale" operation in reverse.

- PyTorch also has quantization built-in that includes three techniques: dynamic quantization, post-training static quantization, and quantization-aware training.

Caching

For many ML models, the input distribution is non-uniform (some are more common than others). Caching takes advantage of that. Instead of constantly calling the model on every input no matter what, we first cache the model's frequently-used inputs. Before calling the model, we check the cache and only call it on the frequently-used inputs. Caching techniques can get very fancy, but the most basic way to get started is using Python's functools.

Batching

Typically, ML models achieve higher throughput when making predictions in parallel (especially true for GPU inference). At a high level, here's how batching works:

- You gather predictions that are coming in until you have a batch for your system. Then, you run the model on that batch and return predictions to those users who request them.

- You need to tune the batch size and address the tradeoff between throughput and latency.

- You need to have a way to shortcut the process if latency becomes too long.

- The last caveat is that you probably do not want to implement batching yourself.

Sharing The GPU

Your model may not take up all of the GPU memory with your inference batch size. Why not run multiple models on the same GPU? You probably want to use a model serving solution that supports this out of the box.

Model Serving Libraries

There are canonical open-source model serving libraries for both PyTorch (TorchServe) and TensorFlow (TensorFlow Serving). Ray Serve is another promising choice. Even NVIDIA has joined the game with Triton Inference Server.

Horizontal Scaling

If you have too much traffic for a single machine, let's split traffic among multiple machines. At a high level, you duplicate your prediction service, use a load balancer to split traffic, and send the traffic to the appropriate copy of your service. In practice, there are two common methods:

- Use a container orchestration toolkit like Kubernetes.

- Use a serverless option like AWS Lambda.

Container Orchestration

In this paradigm, your Docker containers are coordinated by Kubernetes. K8s provides a single service for you to send requests to. Then it divides up traffic that gets sent to that service to virtual copies of your containers (that are running on your infrastructure).

You can build a system like this yourself on top of K8s if you want to. But there are emerging frameworks that can handle all such infrastructure out of the box if you have a K8s cluster running. KFServing is a part of the Kubeflow package, a popular K8s-native ML infrastructure solution. Seldon provides a model serving stack on top of K8s.

Deploying Code as Serverless Functions

The idea here is that the app code and dependencies are packaged into .zip files (or Docker containers) with a single entry point function. All the major cloud providers such as AWS Lambda, Google Cloud Functions, or Azure Functions will manage everything else: instant scaling to 10,000+ requests per second, load balancing, etc.

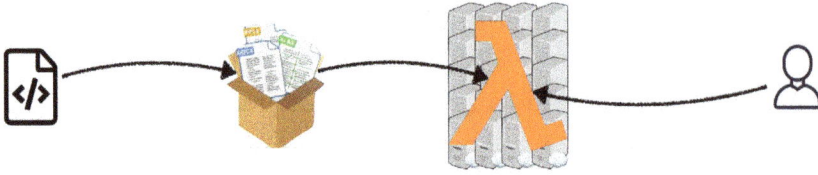

Fig. 4.10 Deploying Code as Serverless Functions

The good thing is that you only pay for compute-time. Furthermore, this approach lowers your DevOps load, as you do not own any servers.

The tradeoff is that you have to work with severe constraints:

◉ Your entire deployment package is quite limited.

◉ You can only do CPU execution.

◉ It can be challenging to build model pipelines.

◉ There are limited state management and deployment tooling.

MODEL DEPLOYMENT

If serving is how you turn a model into something that can respond to requests, deployment is how you roll out, manage, and update these services. You probably want to be able to roll out gradually, roll back instantly, and deploy pipelines of models. Many challenging infrastructure considerations go into this, but hopefully, your deployment library will take care of this for you.

Managed Options

If you do not want to deal with any of the things mentioned thus far, there are managed options in the market. All major cloud providers have ones that enable you to package your model in a predefined way and turn it into an API. Startups like Algorithmia and Cortex are some alternatives. The big drawback is that pricing tends to be high, so you pay a premium fee in exchange for convenience (Fig. 4.11).

Takeaways

◉ If you are making CPU inference, you can get away with scaling by launching more servers or going serverless.

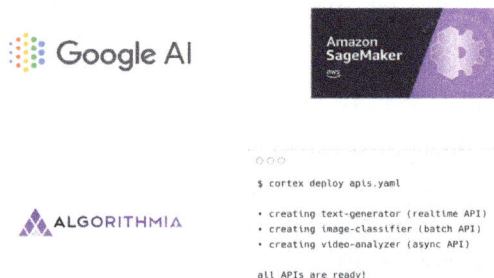

```
$ cortex deploy apis.yaml

• creating text-generator (realtime API)
• creating image-classifier (batch API)
• creating video-analyzer (async API)

all APIs are ready!
```

Fig. 4.11 Managed Options

- Serverless makes sense if you can get away with CPUs, and traffic is spiky or low-volume.
- If you are using GPU inference, serving tools will save you time.
- It's worth keeping an eye on startups in this space for GPU inference.

3 - Edge Deployment

Edge prediction means that you first send the model weights to the client edge device. Then, the client loads the model and interacts with it directly.

The pros of edge prediction:

- It has low latency.

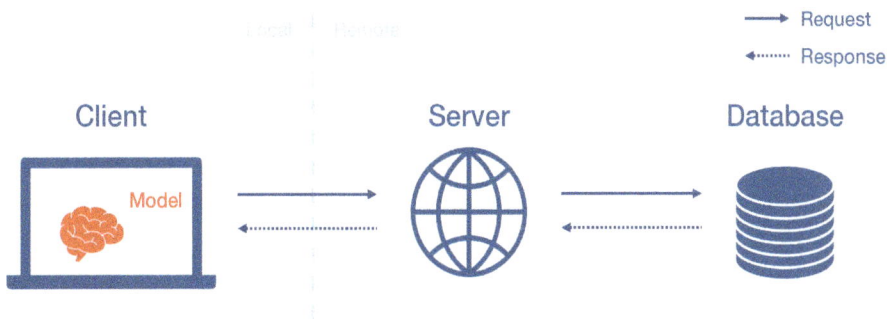

Fig. 4.12 3 - Edge Deployment

- It does not require an Internet connection.
- It satisfies data security requirements, as data does not need to leave the user's device.

The cons of edge prediction:

- The client often has limited hardware resources available.
- Embedded and mobile frameworks are less full-featured than TensorFlow and PyTorch.
- It is challenging to update models.
- It is difficult to monitor and debug when things go wrong.

Tools for edge deployment

TensorRT is NVIDIA's framework meant to help you optimize models for inference on NVIDIA devices in data centers and embedded/automotive environments. TensorRT is also integrated with application-specific SDKs to provide developers a unified path to deploy conversational AI, recommender, video conference, and streaming apps in production.

ApacheTVM is an open-source machine learning compiler framework for CPUs, GPUs, and ML accelerators. It aims to enable ML engineers to optimize and run computations efficiently on any hardware backend. In particular, it compiles ML models into minimum deployable modules and provides the infrastructure to automatically optimize models on more backends with better performance.

Tensorflow Lite provides a trained TensorFlow model framework to be compressed and deployed to a mobile or embedded application. TensorFlow's computationally expensive training process can still be performed in the environment that best suits it (personal server, cloud, overclocked computer). TensorFlow Lite then takes the resulting model (frozen graph, SavedModel, or HDF5 model) as input, packages, deploys, and then interprets it in the client application, handling the resource-conserving optimizations along the way.

PyTorch Mobile is a framework for helping mobile developers and machine learning engineers embed PyTorch models on-device. Currently, it allows any **TorchScript model** to run directly inside iOS and Android applications. PyTorch Mobile's initial release supports many different quantization techniques, which shrink model sizes without significantly affecting performance. PyTorch Mobile also allows developers to directly convert a PyTorch model to a mobile-ready format without needing to work through other tools/frameworks.

JavaScript is a portable way of running code on different devices. **Tensorflow.js** enables you to run TensorFlow code in JavaScript. You can use off-the-shelf JavaScript models or convert Python TensorFlow models to run in the browser or under Node.js, retrain pre-existing ML models using your data, and build/train models directly in JavaScript using flexible and intuitive APIs.

Core ML was released by Apple back in 2017. It is optimized for on-device performance, which minimizes a model's memory footprint and power consumption. Running strictly on the device also ensures that user data is kept secure. The app runs even in the absence of a network connection. Generally speaking, it is straightforward to use with just a few lines of code needed to integrate a complete ML model into your device. The downside is that you can only make the model inference, as no model training is possible.

ML Kit was announced by Google Firebase in 2018. It enables developers to utilize ML in mobile apps either with (1) inference in the cloud via API or (2) inference on-device (like Core ML). For the former option, ML Kit offers six base APIs with pertained models such as Image Labeling, Text Recognition, and Barcode Scanning. For the latter option, ML Kit offers lower accuracy but more security to user data, compared to the cloud version.

If you are interested in either of the above options, check out **this comparison** by the FritzAI team. Additionally, **FritzAI** is an ML platform for mobile developers that provide pre-trained models, developer tools, and SDKs for iOS, Android, and Unity.

More Efficient Models

Another thing to consider for edge deployment is to make the models more efficient. One way to do this is to use the same quantization and distillation techniques discussed above. Another way is to pick mobile-friendly model architectures. The first successful example is **MobileNet**, which performs various downsampling techniques to a traditional ConvNet architecture to maximize accuracy while being mindful of the restricted resources for a mobile or an embedded device. **This analysis** by Yusuke Uchida explains why MobileNet and its variants are fast.

A well-known case study of applying knowledge distillation in practice is Hugging Face's **DistilBERT**, a smaller language model derived from the supervision of the popular **BERT** language model. DistilBERT removes the toke-type embeddings and the pooler (used for the next sentence classification task) from BERT while keeping the rest of the architecture identical and reducing the number of layers by a factor of two. Overall, DistilBERT has about half the total number of parameters of the BERT base and retains 95% of BERT's performances on the language understanding benchmark GLUE.

MODEL MONITORING

Once you deploy models, how do you make sure they are staying healthy and working well? Enter model monitoring.

Many things can go wrong with a model once it's been trained. This can happen even if your model has been trained properly, with a reasonable validation and test loss, as well as robust performance across various slices and quality predictions. Even after you've troubleshot and tested a model, things can still go wrong!

Why Model Degrades Post-Deployment?

Model performance tends to degrade after you've deployed a model. Why does this occur? In supervised learning, we seek to fit a function f to approximate a posterior using the data available to us. If any component of this process changes (i.e., the data x), the deployed model can see an unexpectedly degraded performance. See the below chart for examples of how such post-deployment degradations can occur theoretically and in practice:

Data Drift

There are a few different types of data drift:

- ⊙ **Instantaneous drift**: In this situation, the paradigm of the draft dramatically shifts. Examples are deploying the model in a new domain (e.g., self-driving car model in a new city), a bug in the preprocessing pipeline, or even major external shifts like COVID.

◉ **Gradual drift**: In this situation, the value of data gradually changes with time. For example, users' preferences may change over time, or new concepts can get introduced to the domain.

◉ **Periodic drift**: Data can have fluctuating value due to underlying patterns like seasonality or time zones.

◉ **Temporary drift**: The most difficult to detect, drift can occur through a short-term change in the data that shifts back to normal. This could be via a short-lived malicious attack, or even simply because a user with different demographics or behaviors uses your product in a way that it's not designed to be used.

While these categories may seem like purely academic categories, the consequences of data shift are very real. This is a real problem that affects many companies and is only now starting to get the attention it merits.

What Should You Monitor?

There are four core types of signals to monitor for machine learning models.

These metrics trade off with another in terms of how informative they are and how easy they are to access. Put simply, the harder a metric may be to monitor, the more useful it likely is.

◉ The hardest and best metrics to monitor are model performance metrics, though these can be difficult to acquire in real-time (labels are hard to come by).

◉ Business metrics can be helpful signals of model degradation in monitoring but can easily be confounded by other impactful considerations.

◉ Model inputs and predictions are a simple way to identify high-level drift and are very easy to gather. Still, they can be difficult to assess in terms of actual performance impact, leaving it more of an art than science.

◉ Finally, system performance (e.g., GPU usage) can be a coarse method of catching serious bugs.

In considering which metrics to focus on, prioritize ground-truth metrics (model and business metrics), then approximate performance metrics (business and input/outputs), and finally, system health metrics.

How Do You Measure Distribution Changes?

Select a reference window

To measure distribution changes in metrics you're monitoring, start by picking a reference set of production data to compare new data to. There are a few different ways of picking this reference data (e.g., sliding window or fixed window of production data), but the most practical thing to do is to use your training or evaluation data as the reference. Data coming in looking different from what you developed your model using is an important signal to act on.

Select a measurement window

After picking a reference window, the next step is to choose a measurement window to compare, measure distance, and evaluate for drift. The challenge is that selecting a measurement window is highly problem-dependent. One solution is to pick one or several window sizes and slide them over the data. To avoid recomputing metrics over and over again, when you slide the window, it's worth looking into the literature on mergeable (quantile) sketching algorithms.

Compare Windows Using A Distance Metric

What distance metrics should we use to compare the reference window to the measurement window? Some 1-D metric categories are:

- ◎ **Rule-based distance metrics** (e.g., data quality): Summary statistics, the volume of data points, number of missing values, or more complex tests like overall comparisons are common data quality checks that can be applied. **Great Expectations** is a valuable library for this. **Definitely invest in simple rule-based metrics.** They catch a large number of bugs, as publications from Amazon and Google detail.

- ◎ **Statistical distance metrics** (e.g., KS statistics, KL divergence, D_1 distance, etc.)

  - • **KL Divergence**: Defined as the expectation of a ratio of logs of two different distributions, this commonly known metric is very sensitive to what happens in the tails of the distribution. It's not well-suited to data shift testing since it's easily disturbed, is not interpretable, and struggles with data in different ranges.

  - • **KS Statistic**: This metric is defined as the max distance between CDFs, which is easy to interpret and is thus used widely in practice. Say yes to the KS statistic!

  - • **D1 Distance**: Defined as the sum of distances between PDFs, this is a metric used at Google. Despite seeming less principled, it's easily interpretable and has the added benefit of knowing Google uses it (so why not you?).

An open area of research is understanding the impact of differing drift patterns on distance metrics and model performance. Another open area of research is high-dimensional distance metrics. Some options here are:

- ◎ Maximum mean discrepancy

- ◎ Performing multiple 1D comparisons across the data: While suffering from the multiple hypothesis testing problem, this is a practical approach.

- ◎ Prioritize some features for 1D comparisons: Another option is to avoid testing all the features and only focus on those that merit comparison; for example, those features you know may have shifted in the data.

◉ **Projections:** In this approach, large data points are put through a dimensionality reduction process and then subject to a two-sample statistical test. Reducing the dimensionality with a domain-specific approach (e.g., mean pixel value for images, length of sentence) is recommended.

At a high level, this entire distance metric work aims to identify not just a score for any data shift but also understand its impact on the model. While choosing a metric can be complicated with all the possible options, you should focus on understanding your model's robustness in a post-deployment scenario.

How Do You Tell If A Change Is Bad?

There's no hard and fast rule for finding if a change in the data is bad. An easy option is to set thresholds on the test values. Don't use a statistical test like the KS test, as they are too sensitive to small shifts. Other **options** include setting manual ranges, comparing values over time, or even applying an unsupervised model to detect outliers. In practice, fixed rules and specified ranges of test values are used most in practice.

Tools for Monitoring

There are three categories of tools useful for monitoring:

◉ System monitoring tools like AWS CloudWatch, Datadog, New Relic, and honeycomb test traditional performance metrics

◉ Data quality tools like Great Expectations, Anomalo, and Monte Carlo test if specific windows of data violate rules or assumptions.

◉ ML monitoring tools like Arize, Fiddler, and Arthur can also be useful, as they specifically test models.

Evaluation Store

Monitoring is more central to ML than for traditional software.

In traditional SWE, most bugs cause loud failures, and the data that is monitored is most valuable to detect and diagnose problems. If the system is working well, the data from these metrics and monitoring systems may not be useful.

◉ In machine learning, however, monitoring plays a different role. First off, bugs in ML systems often lead to silent degradations in performance. Furthermore, the data that is monitored in ML is literally the code used to train the next iteration of models.

Because monitoring is so essential to ML systems, tightly integrating it into the ML system architecture brings major benefits. In particular, better integrating and monitoring practices, or creating an evaluation store, can close the data flywheel loop, a concept we talked about earlier in the class.

As we build models, we create a mapping between data and model. As the data changes and we retrain models, monitoring these changes doesn't become an endpoint—it becomes a part of the entire model development process. Monitoring, via an evaluation store, should touch all parts of your stack. One challenge that this process helps solve is effectively choosing which data points to collect, store, and label.

CHAPTER-5

NATURAL LANGUAGE PROCESSING (NLP)

INTRODUCTION TO NLP

NLP stands for Natural Language Processing. It is the branch of Artificial Intelligence that gives the ability to machine understand and process human languages. Human languages can be in the form of text or audio format.

The essence of Natural Language Processing lies in making computers understand the natural language. That's not an easy task though. Computers can understand the structured form of data like spreadsheets and the tables in the database, but human languages, texts, and voices form an unstructured category of data, and it gets difficult for the computer to understand it, and there arises the need for Natural Language Processing. There's a lot of natural language data out there in various forms and it would get very easy if computers can understand and process that data.

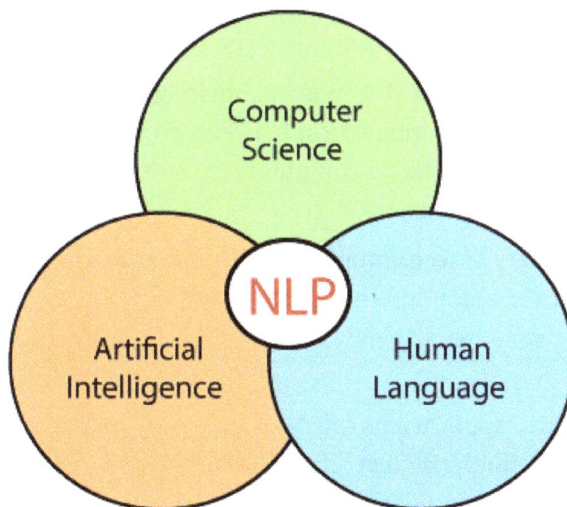

Fig. 5.1

We can train the models in accordance with expected output in different ways. Humans have been writing for thousands of years, there are a lot of literature pieces available, and it would be great if we make computers understand that. But the task is never going to be easy. There are various challenges floating out there like understanding the correct meaning of the sentence, correct Named-Entity Recognition(NER), correct prediction of various parts of speech, coreference resolution(the most challenging thing in my opinion).

Computers can't truly understand the human language. If we feed enough data and train a model properly, it can distinguish and try categorizing various parts of speech(noun, verb, adjective, supporter, etc...) based on previously fed data and experiences. If it encounters a new word it tried making the nearest guess which can be embarrassingly wrong few times. It's very difficult for a computer to extract the exact meaning from a sentence.

For example – The boy radiated fire like vibes. The boy had a very motivating personality or he actually radiated fire? As you see over here, parsing English with a computer is going to be complicated. There are various stages involved in training a model. Solving a complex problem in Machine Learning means building a pipeline. In simple terms, it means breaking a complex problem into a number of small problems, making models for each of them and then integrating these models.

A similar thing is done in NLP. We can break down the process of understanding English for a model into a number of small pieces. It would be really great if a computer could understand that San Pedro is an island in Belize district in Central America with a population of 16,444 and it is the second largest town in Belize.

But to make the computer understand this, we need to teach computer very basic concepts of written language. So let's start by creating an NLP pipeline. It has various steps which will give us the desired output(maybe not in a few rare cases) at the end.

Natural Language Processing (NLP) is a subfield of computer science and artificial intelligence that deals with the interaction between computers and human languages. The primary goal of NLP is to enable computers to understand, interpret, and generate natural language, the way humans do.

NLP involves a variety of techniques, including computational linguistics, machine learning, and statistical modeling. These techniques are used to analyze, understand, and manipulate human language data, including text, speech, and other forms of communication.

Some of the main applications of NLP include language translation, speech recognition, sentiment analysis, text classification, and information retrieval. NLP is used in a wide range of industries, including finance, healthcare, education, and entertainment, to name a few.

History of NLP

NLP stands for Natural Language Processing, which is a part of Computer Science, Human language, and Artificial Intelligence. It is the technology that is used by machines to understand, analyse, manipulate, and interpret human's languages. It helps developers to organize knowledge for performing tasks such as translation, automatic summarization, Named Entity Recognition (NER), speech recognition, relationship extraction, and topic segmentation.

Natural Language Processing started in 1950 When Alan Mathison Turing published an article in the name Computing Machinery and Intelligence. It is based on Artificial intelligence. It talks about automatic interpretation and generation of natural language. As the technology evolved, different approaches have come to deal with NLP tasks.

TEXT PREPROCESSING AND TOKENIZATION

Tokenization in natural language processing (NLP) is a technique that involves dividing a sentence or phrase into smaller units known as tokens. These tokens can encompass words, dates, punctuation marks, or even fragments of words. The article aims to cover the fundamentals of tokenization, it's types and use case.

Natural Language Processing (NLP) is a subfield of computer science, artificial intelligence, information engineering, and human-computer interaction. This field focuses on how to program computers to process and analyze large amounts of natural language data. It is difficult to perform as the process of reading and understanding languages is far more complex than it seems at first glance. Tokenization is a foundation step in NLP pipeline that shapes the entire workflow.

Tokenization is the process of dividing a text into smaller units known as tokens. Tokens are typically words or sub-words in the context of natural language processing. Tokenization is a critical step in many NLP tasks, including text processing, language modelling, and machine translation. The process involves splitting a string, or text into a list of tokens. One can think of tokens as parts like a word is a token in a sentence, and a sentence is a token in a paragraph.

Tokenization involves using a tokenizer to segment unstructured data and natural language text into distinct chunks of information, treating them as different elements. The tokens within a document can be used as vector, transforming an unstructured text document into a numerical data structure suitable for machine learning. This rapid conversion enables the immediate utilization of these tokenized elements by a computer to initiate practical actions and responses. Alternatively, they may serve as features within a machine learning pipeline, prompting more sophisticated decision-making processes or behaviors.

Types of Tokenization

Tokenization can be classified into several types based on how the text is segmented. Here are some types of tokenization:

Word Tokenization

Word tokenization divides the text into individual words. Many NLP tasks use this approach, in which words are treated as the basic units of meaning.

Example:

Input: "Tokenization is an important NLP task."

Output: ["Tokenization", "is", "an", "important", "NLP", "task", "."]

Sentence Tokenization:

The text is segmented into sentences during sentence tokenization. This is useful for tasks requiring individual sentence analysis or processing.

Example:

Input: "Tokenization is an important NLP task. It helps break down text into smaller units."

Output: ["Tokenization is an important NLP task.", "It helps break down text into smaller units."]

Subword Tokenization

Subword tokenization entails breaking down words into smaller units, which can be especially useful when dealing with morphologically rich languages or rare words.

Example:

Input: "tokenization"

Output: ["token", "ization"]

Character Tokenization

This process divides the text into individual characters. This can be useful for modelling character-level language.

Example:

Input: "Tokenization"

Output: ["T", "o", "k", "e", "n", "i", "z", "a", "t", "i", "o", "n"]

Need of Tokenization

Tokenization is a crucial step in text processing and natural language processing (NLP) for several reasons.

- **Effective Text Processing:** Tokenization reduces the size of raw text so that it can be handled more easily for processing and analysis.

- **Feature extraction:** Text data can be represented numerically for algorithmic comprehension by using tokens as features in machine learning models.

- **Language Modelling:** Tokenization in NLP facilitates the creation of organized representations of language, which is useful for tasks like text generation and language modelling.

- **Information Retrieval:** Tokenization is essential for indexing and searching in systems that store and retrieve information efficiently based on words or phrases.

- **Text Analysis:** Tokenization is used in many NLP tasks, including sentiment analysis and named entity recognition, to determine the function and context of individual words in a sentence.

- **Vocabulary Management:** By generating a list of distinct tokens that stand in for words in the dataset, tokenization helps manage a corpus's vocabulary.

- **Task-Specific Adaptation:** Tokenization can be customized to meet the needs of particular NLP tasks, meaning that it will work best in applications such as summarization and machine translation.

- **Preprocessing Step:** This essential preprocessing step transforms unprocessed text into a format appropriate for additional statistical and computational analysis.

Implementation for Tokenization

Sentence Tokenization using sent_tokenize

The code snippet uses **sent_tokenize** function from NLTK library. The sent_tokenize function is used to segment a given text into a list of sentences.

- Python3

```
from nltk.tokenize import sent_tokenize

text = "Hello everyone. Welcome to GeeksforGeeks. You are studying NLP article."

sent_tokenize(text)
```

Output:

['Hello everyone.',

 'Welcome to GeeksforGeeks.',

 'You are studying NLP article']

Sentence Tokenization using PunktSentenceTokenizer

When we have huge chunks of data then it is efficient to use 'PunktSentenceTokenizer' from the NLTK library. The Punkt tokenizer is a data-driven sentence tokenizer that comes with NLTK. It is trained on large corpus of text to identify sentence boundaries.

⦿ Python3

```
import nltk.data
# Loading PunktSentenceTokenizer using English pickle file
    tokenizer = nltk.data.load('tokenizers/punkt/PY3/english.pickle')
tokenizer.tokenize(text)
```

Output:

['Hello everyone.',

 'Welcome to GeeksforGeeks.',

 'You are studying NLP article']

Tokenize sentence of different language

One can also tokenize sentence from different languages using different pickle file other than English. In the following code snippet, we have used NLTK library to tokenize a Spanish text into sentences using pre-trained Punkt tokenizer for Spanish. The Punkt tokenizer is a data-driven tokenizer that uses machine learning techniques to identify sentence boundaries.

⦿ Python3

```
import nltk.data
spanish_tokenizer = nltk.data.load('tokenizers/punkt/PY3/spanish.pickle')
text = 'Hola amigo. Estoy bien.'
spanish_tokenizer.tokenize(text)
spanish.pickle') text = 'Hola amigo. Estoy bien.'spanish_tokenizer.tokenize(text)
```

Output:

['Hola amigo.',

 'Estoy bien.']

Word Tokenization using work_tokenize

The code snipped uses the word_tokenize function from NLTK library to tokenize a given text into individual words. The word_tokenize function is helpful for breaking down a sentence or text into its constituent words, facilitating further analysis or processing at the word level in natural language processing tasks.

⊙ Python3

from nltk.tokenize import word_tokenize

text = "Hello everyone. Welcome to GeeksforGeeks."

word_tokenize(text)

Output:

['Hello', 'everyone', '.', 'Welcome', 'to', 'GeeksforGeeks', '.']

How word_tokenize works?

word_tokenize() function is a wrapper function that calls tokenize() on an instance of the TreebankWordTokenizer class.

Word Tokenization Using TreebankWordTokenizer

The code snippet uses the TreebankWordTokenizer from the Natural Language Toolkit (NLTK) to tokenize a given text into individual words.

⊙ Python3

from nltk.tokenize import TreebankWordTokenizer

 tokenizer = TreebankWordTokenizer()

tokenizer.tokenize(text)

Output:

['Hello', 'everyone.', 'Welcome', 'to', 'GeeksforGeeks', '.']

These tokenizers work by separating the words using punctuation and spaces. And as mentioned in the code outputs above, it doesn't discard the punctuation, allowing a user to decide what to do with the punctuations at the time of pre-processing.

Word Tokenization using WordPunctTokenizer

The WordPunctTokenizer is one of the NLTK tokenizers that splits words based on punctuation boundaries. Each punctuation mark is treated as a separate token.

⊙ Python3

from nltk.tokenize import WordPunctTokenizer

 tokenizer = WordPunctTokenizer()

tokenizer.tokenize("Let's see how it's working.")

Output:

['Let', '"', 's', 'see', 'how', 'it', '"', 's', 'working', '.']

Word Tokenization using Regular Expression

The code snippet uses the RegexpTokenizer from the Natural Language Toolkit (NLTK) to tokenize a given text based on a regular expression pattern.

⦿ Python3

```
from nltk.tokenize import RegexpTokenizer
 tokenizer = RegexpTokenizer(r'\w+')
text = "Let's see how it's working."
tokenizer.tokenize(text)
```

Output:

['Let', 's', 'see', 'how', 'it', 's', 'working']

Using regular expressions allows for more fine-grained control over tokenization, and you can customize the pattern based on your specific requirements.

More Techniques for Tokenization

We have discussed the ways to implement how can we perform tokenization using NLTK library. We can also implement tokenization using following methods and libraries:

⦿ **Spacy:** Spacy is NLP library that provide robust tokenization capabilities.

⦿ **BERT tokenizer:** BERT uses WordPiece tokenizer is a type of subword tokenizer for tokenizing input text. Using regular expressions allows for more fine-grained control over tokenization, and you can customize the pattern based on your specific requirements.

⦿ **Byte-Pair Encoding:** Byte Pair Encoding (BPE) is a data compression algorithm that has also found applications in the field of natural language processing, specifically for tokenization. It is a subword tokenization technique that works by iteratively merging the most frequent pairs of consecutive bytes (or characters) in a given corpus.

⦿ **Sentence Piece:** SentencePiece is another subword tokenization algorithm commonly used for natural language processing tasks. It is designed to be language-agnostic and works by iteratively merging frequent sequences of characters or subwords in a given corpus.

Limitations of Tokenization

⦿ Tokenization is unable to capture the meaning of the sentence hence, results in **ambiguity**.

⦿ In certain languages like Chinese, Japanese, Arabic, lack distinct spaces between words. Hence, there is an **absence of clear boundaries** that complicates the process of tokenization.

◉ Text may also include more than one word, for example email address, URLs and **special symbols**, hence it is difficult to decide how to tokenize such elements.

SENTIMENT ANALYSIS

Sentiment analysis is the process of classifying whether a block of text is positive, negative, or neutral. The goal that Sentiment mining tries to gain is to be analysed people's opinions in a way that can help businesses expand. It focuses not only on polarity (positive, negative & neutral) but also on emotions (happy, sad, angry, etc.). It uses various Natural Language Processing algorithms such as Rule-based, Automatic, and Hybrid.

let's consider a scenario, if we want to analyze whether a product is satisfying customer requirements, or is there a need for this product in the market. We can use sentiment analysis to monitor that product's reviews. Sentiment analysis is also efficient to use when there is a large set of unstructured data, and we want to classify that data by automatically tagging it. Net Promoter Score (NPS) surveys are used extensively to gain knowledge of how a customer perceives a product or service. Sentiment analysis also gained popularity due to its feature to process large volumes of NPS responses and obtain consistent results quickly.

Importance of Sentiment Analysis

Sentiment analysis is the contextual meaning of words that indicates the social sentiment of a brand and also helps the business to determine whether the product they are manufacturing is going to make a demand in the market or not.

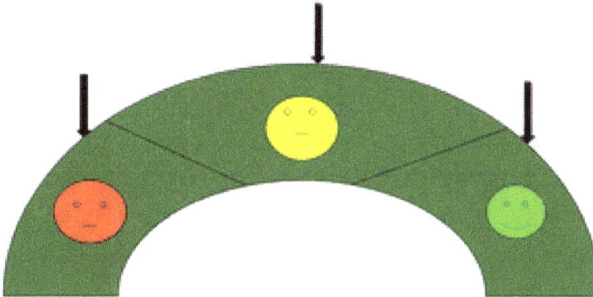

Fig. 5.2 Sentiment

According to the survey,80% of the world's data is unstructured. The data needs to be analyzed and be in a structured manner whether it is in the form of emails, texts, documents, articles, and many more.

◉ Sentiment Analysis is required as it stores data in an efficient, cost friendly.

◉ Sentiment analysis solves real-time issues and can help you solve all real-time scenarios.

Here are some key reasons why sentiment analysis is important for business:

- **Customer Feedback Analysis**: Businesses can analyze customer reviews, comments, and feedback to understand the sentiment behind them helping in identifying areas for improvement and addressing customer concerns, ultimately enhancing customer satisfaction.

- **Brand Reputation Management**: Sentiment analysis allows businesses to monitor their brand reputation in real-time.

By tracking mentions and sentiments on social media, review platforms, and other online channels, companies can respond promptly to both positive and negative sentiments, mitigating potential damage to their brand.

- **Product Development and Innovation**: Understanding customer sentiment helps identify features and aspects of their products or services that are well-received or need improvement. This information is invaluable for product development and innovation, enabling companies to align their offerings with customer preferences.

- **Competitor Analysis**: Sentiment Analysis can be used to compare the sentiment around a company's products or services with those of competitors.

- Businesses identify their strengths and weaknesses relative to competitors, allowing for strategic decision-making.

- **Marketing Campaign Effectiveness**: Businesses can evaluate the success of their marketing campaigns by analyzing the sentiment of online discussions and social media mentions.

Positive sentiment indicates that the campaign is resonating with the target audience, while negative sentiment may signal the need for adjustments.

Types of Sentiment Analysis

- **Fine-Grained Sentiment Analysis**: This depends on the polarity base. This category can be designed as very positive, positive, neutral, negative, or very negative. The rating is done on a scale of 1 to 5. If the rating is 5 then it is very positive, 2 then negative, and 3 then neutral.

- **Emotion detection**: The sentiments happy, sad, angry, upset, jolly, pleasant, and so on come under emotion detection. It is also known as a lexicon method of sentiment analysis.

- **Aspect-Based Sentiment Analysis**: It focuses on a particular aspect for instance if a person wants to check the feature of the cell phone then it checks the aspect such as the battery, screen, and camera quality then aspect based is used.

⊙ **Multilingual Sentiment Analysis** Multilingual consists of different languages where the classification needs to be done as positive, negative, and neutral. This is highly challenging and comparatively difficult.

Working of Sentiment Analysis

Sentiment Analysis in NLP, is used to determine the sentiment expressed in a piece of text, such as a review, comment, or social media post.

The goal is to identify whether the expressed sentiment is positive, negative, or neutral. let's understand the overview in general two steps:

Preprocessing

Starting with collecting the text data that needs to be analysed for sentiment like customer reviews, social media posts, news articles, or any other form of textual content. The collected text is pre-processed to clean and standardize the data with various tasks:

⊙ Removing irrelevant information (e.g., HTML tags, special characters).

⊙ Tokenization: Breaking the text into individual words or tokens.

⊙ Removing stop words (common words like "and," "the," etc. that don't contribute much to sentiment).

⊙ Stemming or Lemmatization: Reducing words to their root form.

Analysis

Text is converted for analysis using techniques like bag-of-words or word embeddings (e.g., Word2Vec, GloVe).Models are then trained with labeled datasets, associating text with sentiments (positive, negative, or neutral).

After training and validation, the model predicts sentiment on new data, assigning labels based on learned patterns.

Approaches to Sentiment Analysis

Following are the main approaches used:

⊙ **Rule-based**: Over here, the lexicon method, tokenization, and parsing come in the rule-based. The approach is that counts the number of positive and negative words in the given dataset. If the number of positive words is greater than the number of negative words then the sentiment is positive else vice-versa.

⊙ **Machine Learning**: This approach works on the machine learning technique. Firstly, the datasets are trained and predictive analysis is done. The next process is the extraction of words from the text is done. This text extraction can be done using different techniques such as Naive Bayes, Support Vector machines, hidden Markov model, and conditional random fields like this machine learning techniques are used.

- ⊙ **Neural Network**: In the last few years neural networks have evolved at a very rate. It involves using artificial neural networks, which are inspired by the structure of the human brain, to classify text into positive, negative, or neutral sentiments. it has Recurrent neural networks, Long short-term memory, Gated recurrent unit, etc to process sequential data like text.

- ⊙ **Hybrid Approach**: It is the combination of two or more approaches i.e. rule-based and Machine Learning approaches. The surplus is that the accuracy is high compared to the other two approaches.

Sentiment analysis Use Cases

Sentiment Analysis has a wide range of applications as:

Social Media

If for instance the comments on social media side as Instagram, over here all the reviews are analyzed and categorized as positive, negative, and neutral.

Nike Analyzing Instagram Sentiment for New Shoe Launch (Fig. 5.3)

Nike, a leading sportswear brand, launched a new line of running shoes with the goal of reaching a younger audience. To understand user perception and assess the campaign's effectiveness, Nike analyzed the sentiment of comments on its Instagram posts related to the new shoes.

- ⊙ Nike collected all comments from the past month on Instagram posts featuring the new shoes.

- ⊙ A sentiment analysis tool was used to categorize each comment as positive, negative, or neutral.

The analysis revealed that 60% of comments were positive, 30% were neutral, and 10% were negative. Positive comments praised the shoes' design, comfort, and performance. Negative comments expressed dissatisfaction with the price, fit, or availability.

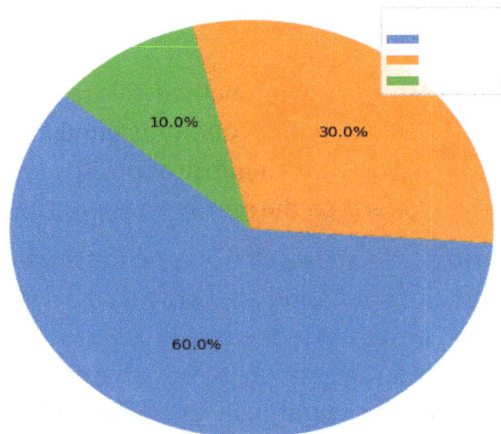

Fig. 5.3 Sentiment Distribution of Instagram Comments

Customer Service

In the play store, all the comments in the form of 1 to 5 are done with the help of sentiment analysis approaches. Play Store App Sentiment Analysis for Improved Customer Service (Fig. 5.4)

Duolingo, a popular language learning app, received a significant number of negative reviews on the Play Store citing app crashes and difficulty completing lessons. To understand the specific issues and improve customer service, Duolingo employed sentiment analysis on their Play Store reviews.

- ⊙ Duolingo collected all app reviews on the Play Store over a specific time period.
- ⊙ Each review's rating (1-5 stars) and text content were analyzed.
- ⊙ Sentiment analysis tools categorized the text content as positive, negative, or neutral.

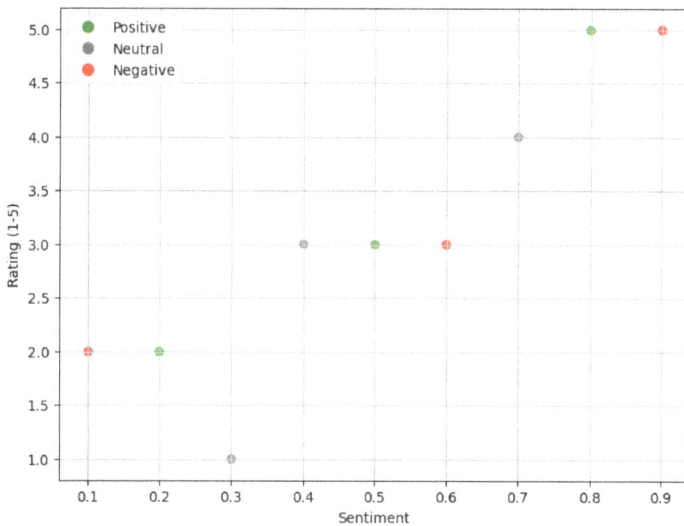

Fig. 5.4 Play Store App Sentiment Analysis for Improved Customer Service

The analysis revealed a correlation between lower star ratings and negative sentiment in the textual reviews. Common themes in negative reviews included app crashes, difficulty progressing through lessons, and lack of engaging content. Positive reviews praised the app's effectiveness, user interface, and variety of languages offered.

Marketing Sector

In the marketing area where a particular product needs to be reviewed as good or bad.

Analysing Consumer Sentiment for Product Review in the Marketing Sector

A company launching a new line of organic skincare products needed to gauge consumer opinion before a major marketing campaign. To understand the potential market and identify areas for improvement, they employed sentiment analysis on social media conversations and online reviews mentioning the products.

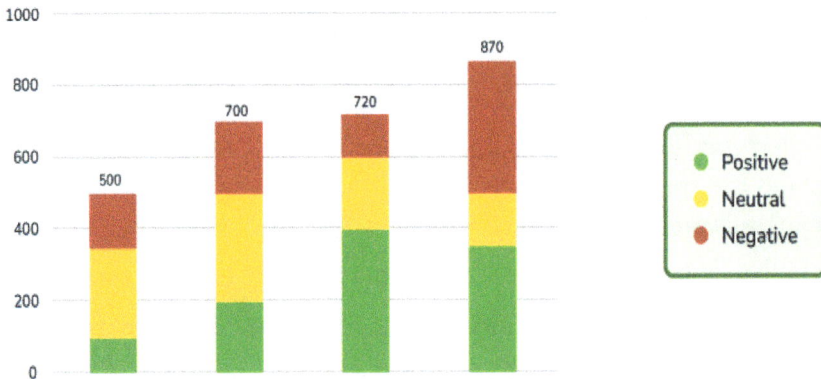

Fig. 5.5 Top Five words of Sentiments

◉ The company collected social media posts and online reviews mentioning the new skincare line using relevant keywords and hashtags.

◉ Text analysis tools were used to clean and pre-process the data.

◉ Sentiment analysis algorithms categorized each text snippet as positive, negative, or neutral towards the product.

The analysis revealed an overall positive sentiment towards the product, with 70% of mentions being positive, 20% neutral, and 10% negative. Positive comments praised the product's natural ingredients, effectiveness, and skin-friendly properties. Negative comments expressed dissatisfaction with the price, packaging, or fragrance.

The bar graph (Fig. 5.5) clearly shows the dominance of positive sentiment towards the new skincare line. This indicates a promising market reception and encourages further investment in marketing efforts.

What are the challenges in Sentiment Analysis?

There are major challenges in the sentiment analysis approach:

◉ If the data is in the form of a tone, then it becomes really difficult to detect whether the comment is pessimist or optimistic.

◉ If the data is in the form of emoji, then you need to detect whether it is good or bad.

◉ Even the ironic, sarcastic, comparing comments detection is really hard.

◉ Comparing a neutral statement is a big task.

Sentiment Analysis Vs Semantic Analysis

Sentiment analysis and Semantic analysis are both natural language processing techniques, but they serve distinct purposes in understanding textual content.

Sentiment Analysis

Sentiment analysis focuses on determining the emotional tone expressed in a piece of text. Its primary goal is to classify the sentiment as positive, negative, or neutral, especially valuable in understanding customer opinions, reviews, and social media comments. Sentiment analysis algorithms analyse the language used to identify the prevailing sentiment and gauge public or individual reactions to products, services, or events.

Semantic Analysis

Semantic analysis, on the other hand, goes beyond sentiment and aims to comprehend the meaning and context of the text. It seeks to understand the relationships between words, phrases, and concepts in a given piece of content. Semantic analysis considers the underlying meaning, intent, and the way different elements in a sentence relate to each other. This is crucial for tasks such as question answering, language translation, and content summarization, where a deeper understanding of context and semantics is required.

NAMED ENTITY RECOGNITION (NER) AND TEXT CLASSIFICATION

Name-entity recognition (NER) is also referred to as entity identification, entity chunking, and entity extraction. NER is the component of information extraction that aims to identify and categorize named entities within unstructured text. NER involves the identification of key information in the text and classification into a set of predefined categories. An entity is the thing that is consistently talked about or refer to in the text, such as person names, organizations, locations, time expressions, quantities, percentages and more predefined categories.

NER system fin applications across various domains, including question answering, information retrieval and machine translation. NER plays an important role in enhancing the precision of other NLP tasks like part-of-speech tagging and parsing. At its core, NLP is just a two-step process, below are the two steps that are involved:

- ◉ Detecting the entities from the text
- ◉ Classifying them into different categories

Ambiguity in NER

- ◉ For a person, the category definition is intuitively quite clear, but for computers, there is some ambiguity in classification. Let's look at some ambiguous examples:

England (Organization) won the 2019 world cup vs The 2019 world cup happened in England (Location).

- ◉ Washington (Location) is the capital of the US vs The first president of the US was Washington (Person).

Working of Entity Recognition (NER)

The working of Named Entity Recognition is discussed below:

◉ The NER system analyses the entire input text to identify and locate the named entities.

◉ The system then identifies the sentence boundaries by considering capitalization rules. It recognizes the end of the sentence when a word starts with a capital letter, assuming it could be the beginning of a new sentence. Knowing sentence boundaries aids in contextualizing entities within the text, allowing the model to understand relationships and meanings.

◉ NER can be trained to classify entire documents into different types, such as invoices, receipts, or passports. Document classification enhances the versatility of NER, allowing it to adapt its entity recognition based on the specific characteristics and context of different document types.

◉ NER employs machine learning algorithms, including supervised learning, to analyze labeled datasets. These datasets contain examples of annotated entities, guiding the model in recognizing similar entities in new, unseen data.

◉ Through multiple training iterations, the model refines its understanding of contextual features, syntactic structures, and entity patterns, continuously improving its accuracy over time.

◉ The model's ability to adapt to new data allows it to handle variations in language, context, and entity types, making it more robust and effective.

Named Entity Recognition (NER) Methods

Lexicon Based Method

The NER uses a dictionary with a list of words or terms. The process involves checking if any of these words are present in a given text. However, this approach isn't commonly used because it requires constant updating and careful maintenance of the dictionary to stay accurate and effective.

Rule Based Method

The Rule Based NER method uses a set of predefined rules guides the extraction of information. These rules are based on patterns and context. Pattern-based rules focus on the structure and form of words, looking at their morphological patterns. On the other hand, context-based rules consider the surrounding words or the context in which a word appears within the text document. This combination of pattern-based and context-based rules enhances the precision of information extraction in Named Entity Recognition (NER).

Machine Learning-Based Method

Multi-Class Classification with Machine Learning Algorithms

- One way is to train the model for multi-class classification using different machine learning algorithms, but it requires a lot of labelling. In addition to labelling the model also requires a deep understanding of context to deal with the ambiguity of the sentences. This makes it a challenging task for a simple machine learning algorithm.

Deep Learning Based Method

- Deep learning NER system is much more accurate than previous method, as it is capable to assemble words. This is due to the fact that it used a method called word embedding, that is capable of understanding the semantic and syntactic relationship between various words.

- It is also able to learn analyzes topic specific as well as high level words automatically.

- This makes deep learning NER applicable for performing multiple tasks. Deep learning can do most of the repetitive work itself, hence researchers for example can use their time more efficiently.

Use Cases of Name Entity Recognition

The use cases of Named entity recognition are many. Some of them are:

Customer support

Every company has its customer support systems available. Each day, they have to deal with a huge number of customer requests which may range from installation, maintenance, complaint, and troubleshooting of a particular product. NER helps in identifying and understanding the type of request that the customer makes. Further, this helps the company build an automated system that will identify incoming requests using NER and send them to the respective support desk.

Fig. 5.6 Customer support

Resume Filtering

Do you think that all the resumes that are sent while applying for a particular job role are read by the recruiting team? Well, the fact is that only 25 percent of the resumes are read by people. The rest are filtered out by an automated system.

Fig. 5.7 Resume Filtering

If you had previously attended a resume-building workshop, the mentor might have emphasized keeping the key skills as a separate section in the resume. Also, they might have advised you to add only the key skills that are related to the required job position. This is because the Named entity recognition in python (NER) model in the automated system might have been custom-trained to identify specific skill sets as entities. If a given resume has a required number of entities present, then it qualifies for the next stage. So, if you were not aware of this process, try to customize your resume accordingly while applying for the respective job.

Electronic Health Record (EHR) Entity Recognition

NER models can be used to build strong medical systems that are properly able to identify the symptoms present in the electronic healthcare data of patients and diagnose their disease depending on the symptoms. If you go through the above image, you can understand how perfectly the NER model was able to identify the symptoms, diseases, and chemicals that were present in the healthcare data of a particular person.

Those were some of the applications where NER was used in real-world scenarios. Next, we will check upon different types of NER systems.

Different Types of NER Systems

There are four different NER systems: rule-based, dictionary-based, machine learning (ML) based, and deep learning approaches. Let's look at them one by one.

Dictionary-based Systems

This is the simplest NER approach. Here we will be having a dictionary that contains a collection of vocabulary. In this approach, basic string matching algorithms are used to check whether the entity is occurring in the given text to the items in the vocabulary. The method has limitations as it is required to update and maintain the dictionary used for the system.

Rule-based Systems

Here, the model uses a pre-defined set of rules for information extraction. Mainly two types of rules are used, Pattern-based rules, which depend upon the morphological pattern of the words used, and context-based rules, which depend upon the context of the word used in the given text document. A simple example for a context-based rule is "If a person's title is followed by a proper noun, then that proper noun is the name of a person".

Machine Learning-based Systems

The ML-based systems use statistical-based models for detecting the entity names. These models try to make a feature-based representation of the observed data. By this approach, a lot of limitations of dictionary and rule-based approaches are solved by recognizing an existing entity name, even with small spelling variations.

There are mainly two phases when we use an ML-based solution for NER. The first phase involves training the ML model on the annotated documents. The time taken for the model to train will vary depending on the complexity of the model that we are building. In the next phase, the trained model can be used to annotate the raw documents.

Deep Learning Approaches

In recent years, deep learning-based models are being used for building state-of-the-art systems for NER. There are many advantages of using DL techniques over the previously discussed approaches. Using the DL approach, the input data is mapped to a non-linear representation. This approach helps to learn complex relations that are present in the input data. Another advantage is that we can avoid a lot of time and resources spent on feature engineering, which is required for the other traditional approaches.

CHAPTER-6
COMPUTER VISION

Computer vision is a field of computer science that focuses on enabling computers to identify and understand objects and people in images and videos. Like other types of AI, computer vision seeks to perform and automate tasks that replicate human capabilities. In this case, computer vision seeks to replicate both the way humans see, and the way humans make sense of what they see.

The range of practical applications for computer vision technology makes it a central component of many modern innovations and solutions. Computer vision can be run in the cloud or on premises.

Computer Vision Examples

Here are some examples of computer vision:

- Facial recognition: Identifying individuals through visual analysis.
- Self-driving cars: Using computer vision to navigate and avoid obstacles.
- Robotic automation: Enabling robots to perform tasks and make decisions based on visual input.
- Medical anomaly detection: Detecting abnormalities in medical images for improved diagnosis.
- Sports performance analysis: Tracking athlete movements to analyze and enhance performance.
- Manufacturing fault detection: Identifying defects in products during the manufacturing process.
- Agricultural monitoring: Monitoring crop growth, livestock health, and weather conditions through visual data.

These are just a few examples of the many ways that computer vision is used today. As the technology continues to develop, we can expect to see even more applications for computer vision in the future.

Applications of Computer Vision

- Healthcare: Computer vision is used in medical imaging to detect diseases and abnormalities. It helps in analyzing X-rays, MRIs, and other scans to provide accurate diagnoses.

- Automotive Industry: In self-driving cars, computer vision is used for object detection, lane keeping, and traffic sign recognition. It helps in making autonomous driving safe and efficient.

- Retail: Computer vision is used in retail for inventory management, theft prevention, and customer behaviour analysis. It can track products on shelves and monitor customer movements.

- Agriculture: In agriculture, computer vision is used for crop monitoring and disease detection. It helps in identifying unhealthy plants and areas that need more attention.

- Manufacturing: Computer vision is used in quality control in defect detect can It. manufacturing products that are hard to spot with the human eye.

- Security and Surveillance: Computer vision is used in security cameras to detect suspicious activities, recognize faces, and track objects. It can alert security personnel when it detects a threat.

- Augmented and Virtual Reality: In AR and VR, computer vision is used to track the user's movements and interact with the virtual environment. It helps in creating a more immersive experience.

- Social Media: Computer vision is used in social media for image recognition. It can identify objects, places, and people in images and provide relevant tags.

- Drones: In drones, computer vision is used for navigation and object tracking. It helps in avoiding obstacles and tracking targets.

- Sports: In sports, computer vision is used for player tracking, game analysis, and highlight generation. It can track the movements of players and the ball to provide insightful statistics.

IMAGE PROCESSING TECHNIQUES

Image Processing is the field of enhancing the images by tuning many parameter and features of the images. So Image Processing is the subset of Computer Vision. Here, transformations are applied to an input image and the resultant output image is returned. Some of these transformations are- sharpening, smoothing, stretching etc.

Now, as both the fields deal with working in visuals, i.e., images and videos, there seems to be lot of confusion about the difference about these fields of computer science. In this article we will discuss the difference between them.

Digital Image processing is the class of methods that deal with manipulating digital images through the use of computer algorithms. It is an essential preprocessing step in many applications, such as face recognition, object detection, and image compression.

Image processing is done to enhance an existing image or to sift out important information from it. This is important in several Deep Learning-based Computer Vision applications, where such preprocessing can dramatically boost the performance of a model. Manipulating images, for example, adding or removing objects to images, is another application, especially in the entertainment industry.

Importance of Image Processing

Image contains a lot of information that can be used for multiple application. By using image processing techniques, we can extract the valuable information from the images and videos. Here are some of them main reasons why image processing is important for computer vision.

1. Image enhancement and restoration

Image processing techniques help us to improve image quality, remove noise and improve visual clarity. This is especially useful when processing images has taken in difficult conditions (such as dark or noisy environments). Image restoration techniques can improve the overall interpretability of images by reducing noise and enhancing detail.

2. Feature Extraction and Object Recognition

Computer vision applications often involve detecting and identifying patterns in specific objects or images. Image processing techniques facilitate feature extraction, which involves identifying and extracting significant features such as edges, corners or textures. These extracted features are the building blocks for subsequent object recognition algorithms that allow machines to accurately identify and classify objects.

3. Image Segmentation

Image segmentation is the process of dividing an image into multiple regions or segments based on their visual characteristics. This technique enables the separation of foreground and background elements, which is crucial for various applications, including object tracking, medical image analysis, and autonomous navigation. By segmenting the images, we can select specific areas of our image and focus on those areas.

4. Image Classification and Pattern Recognition

Image processing plays a key role in image classification and pattern recognition tasks. By analyzing the statistical characteristics and visual patterns of images, machine learning algorithms can learn to distinguish between different classes or categories. It enables automatic classification of images according to their content, such as identifying specific objects, scenes or even emotions expressed by individuals in the images.

5. Medical Imaging and Diagnosis

Image processing is widely used in medical imaging to diagnose and treat various diseases. Techniques such as image segmentation, registration, and feature extraction allow physicians to analyze medical images, detect abnormalities, and monitor treatment progress. This helps with accurate diagnosis, minimally invasive procedures and personalized patient care.

Common Image Processing Techniques

To achieve the aforementioned goals, several techniques are generally used in image processing. Let's explore some basic computer techniques:

1. Filtering and Convolution

Filtering operations such as blurring, sharpening and noise reduction are applied to images using convolution. Convolution involves sliding a filter or kernel over an image and performing mathematical operations on each pixel. This process enables various improvements such as anti-aliasing, edge detection and texture removal.

2. Histogram Equalization

Histogram smoothing is a technique used to improve image contrast by redistributing pixel intensity values. Extending the histogram maximizes the dynamic range of the image, improving visual quality and detail visibility. This technique is particularly useful in scenarios where images suffer from poor lighting conditions or limited contrast.

3. Edge Detection

Edge detection algorithms identify image boundaries and important transitions. They emphasize areas where the intensity changes quickly, such as edges, curves or contours. Edge detection plays an important role in object detection, shape analysis and feature extraction. Popular edge detection algorithms are Canny edge detector and Sobel operator.

4. Image Transformation

Image transformation techniques involve manipulating the geometric properties of images to achieve specific goals. Common transformations include rotation, scaling, translation and displacement. These functions enable operations such as image alignment, image registration, and perspective correction. By transforming images, we can adjust their orientation, size and spatial relationships to facilitate later analysis and interpretation.

5. Feature Detection and Extraction

Feature recognition algorithms aim to identify certain visual patterns or structures in images. These features can be corners, edges, patches or textures. Once identified, these features are extracted and described using numerical representations such as histograms of oriented gradients (HOG) or scale transformations (SIFT). Feature detection and extraction are essential for many applications, including object recognition, image fusion, and image-based localization.

6. Image Segmentation

Image segmentation involves dividing an image into several distinct regions based on their visual characteristics. This technique allows you to separate objects from the background or divide the image into significant regions. Common segmentation methods include thresholding, region growing, clustering, and graph-based algorithms. Image segmentation is an essential step in many computer vision tasks, including object detection, image annotation, and semantic understanding.

7. Object Detection and Recognition

Object detection and recognition refers to the recognition and classification of certain patterns of objects or images. This task typically involves training machine learning models using identified datasets to learn the visual properties of target objects. Technologies such as convolutional neural networks (CNN) and deep learning architectures have revolutionized object detection, enabling robust and accurate recognition in various fields, including autonomous driving, surveillance systems and facial recognition.

Types of Images / How Machines "See" Images?

Digital images are interpreted as 2D or 3D matrices by a computer, where each value or pixel in the matrix represents the amplitude, known as the "intensity" of the pixel. Typically, we are used to dealing with 8-bit images, wherein the amplitude value ranges from 0 to 255 (Fig. 6.1).

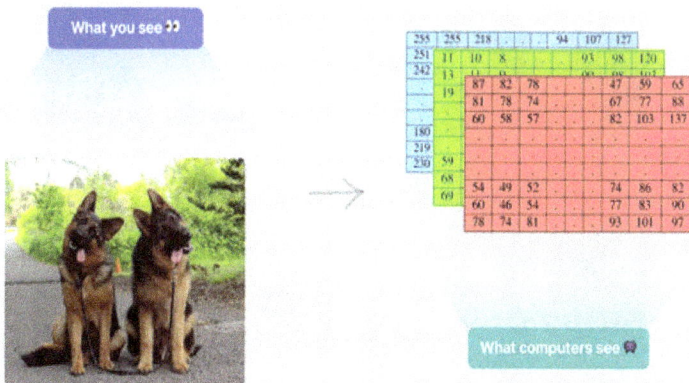

Fig. 6.1

Thus, a computer "sees" digital images as a function: $I(x, y)$ or $I(x, y, z)$, where "I" is the pixel intensity and (x, y) or (x, y, z) represent the coordinates (for binary/grayscale or RGB images respectively) of the pixel in the image (Fig. 6.2).

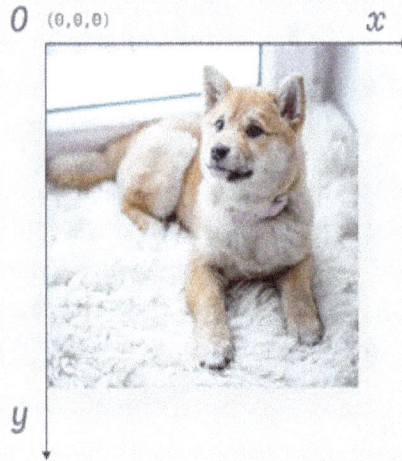

Fig. 6.2 Convention of the coordinate system used in an image

Computers deal with different "types" of images based on their function representations. Let us look into them next.

1. Binary Image

Images that have only two unique values of pixel intensity- 0 (representing black) and 1 (representing white) are called binary images. Such images are generally used to highlight a discriminating portion of a colored image. For example, it is commonly used for image segmentation, as shown below (Fig. 6.3).

Fig. 6.3 Image segmentation

2. Grayscale Image

Grayscale or 8-bit images are composed of 256 unique colors, where a pixel intensity of 0 represents the black color and pixel intensity of 255 represents the white color. All the other 254 values in between are the different shades of gray.

An example of an RGB image converted to its grayscale version is shown below. Notice that the shape of the histogram remains the same for the RGB and grayscale images (Fig. 6.4).

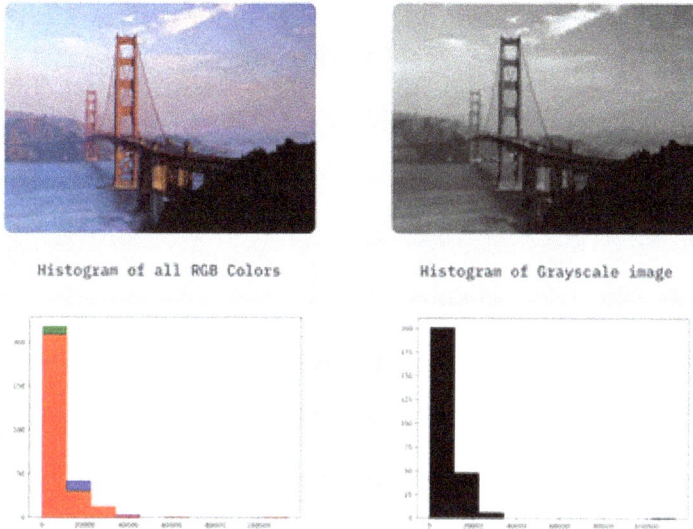

Fig. 6.4 Grayscale Image

3. RGB Color Image

The images we are used to in the modern world are RGB or colored images which are 16-bit matrices to computers. That is, 65,536 different colors are possible for each pixel. "RGB" represents the Red, Green, and Blue "channels" of an image.

Up until now, we had images with only one channel. That is, two coordinates could have defined the location of any value of a matrix. Now, three equal-sized matrices (called channels), each having values ranging from 0 to 255, are stacked on top of each other, and thus we require three unique coordinates to specify the value of a matrix element.

Thus, a pixel in an RGB image will be of color black when the pixel value is (0, 0, 0) and white when it is (255, 255, 255). Any combination of numbers in between gives rise to all the different colors existing in nature. For example, (255, 0, 0) is the color red (since only the red channel is activated for this pixel). Similarly, (0, 255, 0) is green and (0, 0, 255) is blue (Fig. 6.5).

Fig. 6.5 RGB Color Image

An example of an RGB image split into its channel components is shown below. Notice that the shapes of the histograms for each of the channels are different (Fig. 6.5).

4. RGBA Image

RGBA images are colored RGB images with an extra channel known as "alpha" that depicts the opacity of the RGB image. Opacity ranges from a value of 0% to 100% and is essentially a "see-through" property.

Opacity in physics depicts the amount of light that passes through an object. For instance, cellophane paper is transparent (100% opacity), frosted glass is translucent, and wood is opaque. The alpha channel in RGBA images tries to mimic this property. An example of this is shown in Fig. 6.6.

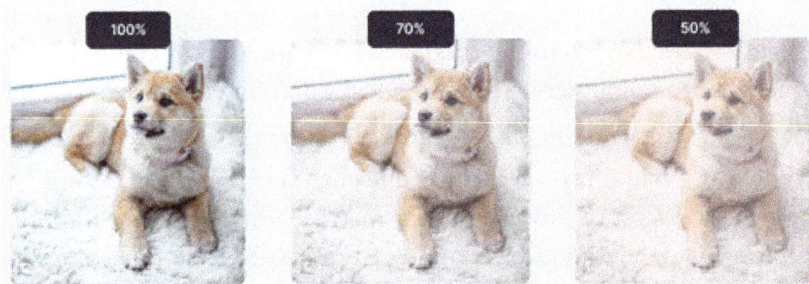

Fig. 6.6 Example of changing the "alpha"
parameter in RGBA images

Phases of Image Processing

The fundamental steps in any typical Digital Image Processing pipeline are as follows:

- **Image Acquisition:** The image is captured by a camera and digitized (if the camera output is not digitized automatically) using an analogue-to-digital converter for further processing in a computer.

- **Image Enhancement:** In this step, the acquired image is manipulated to meet the requirements of the specific task for which the image will be used. Such techniques are primarily aimed at highlighting the hidden or important details in an image, like contrast and brightness adjustment, etc. Image enhancement is highly subjective in nature.

- **Image Restoration:** This step deals with improving the appearance of an image and is an objective operation since the degradation of an image can be attributed to a mathematical or probabilistic model. For example, removing noise or blur from images.

- **Color Image Processing:** This step aims at handling the processing of colored images (16-bit RGB or RGBA images), for example, peforming color correction or color modeling in images.

- **Wavelets and Multi-Resolution Processing:** Wavelets are the building blocks for representing images in various degrees of resolution. Images subdivision successively into smaller regions for data compression and for pyramidal representation.

- **Image Compression:** For transferring images to other devices or due to computational storage constraints, images need to be compressed and cannot be kept at their original size. This is also important in displaying images over the internet; for example, on Google, a small thumbnail of an image is a highly compressed version of the original. Only when you click on the image is it shown in the original resolution. This process saves bandwidth on the servers.

- **Morphological Processing:** Image components that are useful in the representation and description of shape need to be extracted for further processing or downstream tasks. Morphological Processing provides the tools (which are essentially mathematical operations) to accomplish this. For example, erosion and dilation operations are used to sharpen and blur the edges of objects in an image, respectively.

- **Image Segmentation:** This step involves partitioning an image into different key parts to simplify and/or change the representation of an image into something that is more meaningful and easier to analyze. Image segmentation allows for computers to put attention on the more important parts of the image, discarding the rest, which enables automated systems to have improved performance.

- Representation and Description: Image segmentation procedures are generally followed by this step, where the task for representation is to decide whether the segmented region should be depicted as a boundary or a complete region. Description deals with extracting attributes that result in some quantitative information of interest or are basic for differentiating one class of objects from another.

- **Object Detection and Recognition:** After the objects are segmented from an image and the representation and description phases are complete, the automated system needs to assign a label to the object—to let the human users know what object has been detected, for example, "vehicle" or "person", etc.

- **Knowledge Base:** Knowledge may be as simple as the bounding box coordinates for an object of interest that has been found in the image, along with the object label assigned to it. Anything that will help in solving the problem for the specific task at hand can be encoded into the knowledge base.

CONVOLUTIONAL NEURAL NETWORKS (CNNS)

A Convolutional Neural Network (CNN) is a type of Deep Learning neural network architecture commonly used in Computer Vision. Computer vision is a field of Artificial Intelligence that enables a computer to understand and interpret the image or visual data.

When it comes to Machine Learning, Artificial Neural Networks perform really well. Neural Networks are used in various datasets like images, audio, and text. Different types of Neural Networks are used for different purposes, for example for predicting the sequence of words we use Recurrent Neural Networks more precisely an LSTM, similarly for image classification we use Convolution Neural networks. In this blog, we are going to build a basic building block for CNN.

In a regular Neural Network there are three types of layers:

- **Input Layers:** It's the layer in which we give input to our model. The number of neurons in this layer is equal to the total number of features in our data (number of pixels in the case of an image).

- **Hidden Layer:** The input from the Input layer is then fed into the hidden layer. There can be many hidden layers depending on our model and data size. Each hidden layer can have different numbers of neurons which are generally greater than the number of features. The output from each layer is computed by matrix multiplication of the output of the previous layer with learnable weights of that layer and then by the addition of learnable biases followed by activation function which makes the network nonlinear.

- **Output Layer:** The output from the hidden layer is then fed into a logistic function like sigmoid or softmax which converts the output of each class into the probability score of each class.

The data are fed into the model and output from each layer is obtained from the above step is called feedforward, we then calculate the error using an error function, some common error functions are cross-entropy, square loss error, etc. The error function measures how well the network is performing. After that, we backpropagate into the model by calculating the derivatives. This step is called Backpropagation which basically is used to minimize the loss.

Convolution Neural Network

Convolutional Neural Network (CNN) is the extended version of artificial neural networks (ANN) which is predominantly used to extract the feature from the grid-like matrix dataset. For example visual datasets like images or videos where data patterns play an extensive role.

CNN architecture

Convolutional Neural Network consists of multiple layers like the input layer, Convolutional layer, Pooling layer, and fully connected layers.

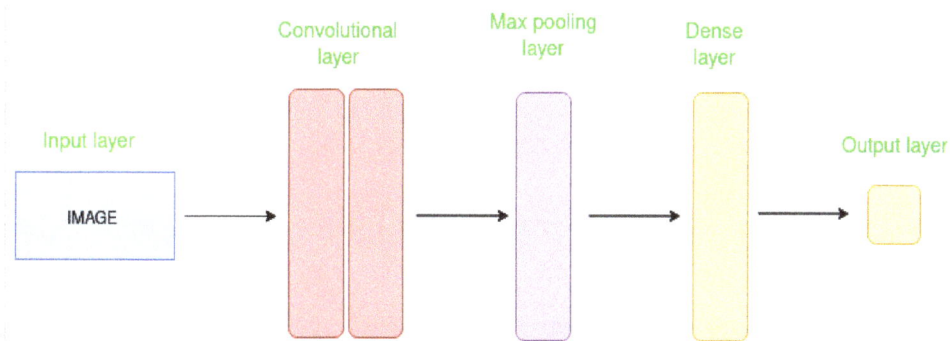

Fig. 6.7 Simple CNN architecture

The Convolutional layer applies filters to the input image to extract features, the Pooling layer downsamples the image to reduce computation, and the fully connected layer makes the final prediction. The network learns the optimal filters through backpropagation and gradient descent.

Working of Convolutional Layers

Convolution Neural Networks or covnets are neural networks that share their parameters. Imagine you have an image. It can be represented as a cuboid having its length, width (dimension of the image (Fig. 6.8)), and height (i.e the channel as images generally have red, green, and blue channels).

Now imagine taking a small patch of this image and running a small neural network, called a filter or kernel on it, with say, K outputs and representing them vertically. Now slide that neural network across the whole image, as a result, we will get another image with different widths, heights, and depths. Instead of just R, G, and B channels now we have more channels but lesser width and height. This operation is called Convolution. If the patch size is the same as that of the image it will be a regular neural network. Because of this small patch, we have fewer weights (Fig. 6.9).

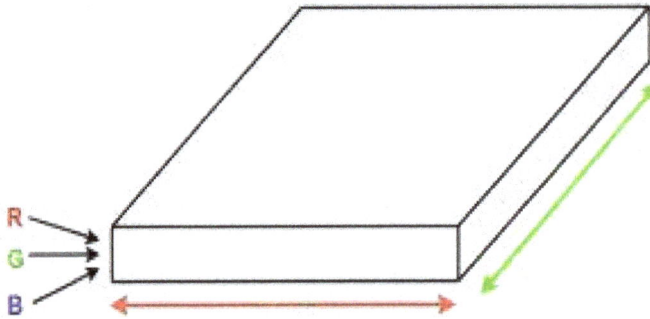

Fig. 6.8 Convolutional Layers

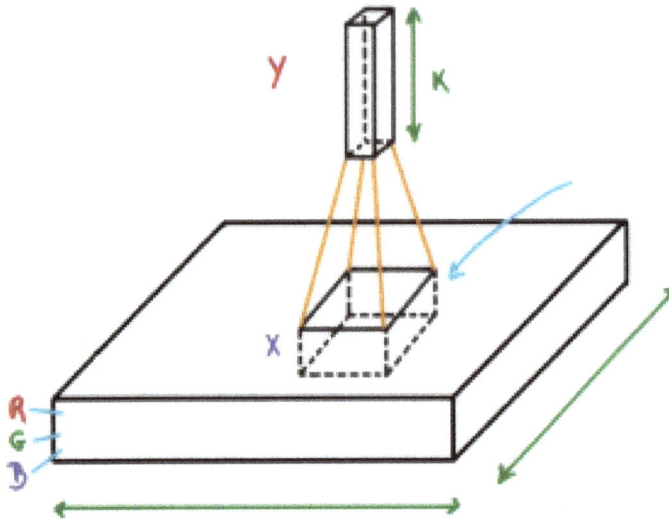

Fig. 6.9 Neural network

Now let's talk about a bit of mathematics that is involved in the whole convolution process.

- ◉ Convolution layers consist of a set of learnable filters (or kernels) having small widths and heights and the same depth as that of input volume (3 if the input layer is image input).

- ◉ For example, if we have to run convolution on an image with dimensions 34x34x3. The possible size of filters can be axax3, where 'a' can be anything like 3, 5, or 7 but smaller as compared to the image dimension.

- ◉ During the forward pass, we slide each filter across the whole input volume step by step where each step is called stride (which can have a value of 2, 3, or even 4 for high-dimensional images) and compute the dot product between the kernel weights and patch from input volume.

⊙ As we slide our filters we'll get a 2-D output for each filter and we'll stack them together as a result, we'll get output volume having a depth equal to the number of filters. The network will learn all the filters.

Layers used to build ConvNets

A complete Convolution Neural Networks architecture is also known as covnets. A covnets is a sequence of layers, and every layer transforms one volume to another through a differentiable function.

Types of layers: datasets

Let's take an example by running a covnets on of image of dimension 32 x 32 x 3.

⊙ **Input Layers:** It's the layer in which we give input to our model. In CNN, Generally, the input will be an image or a sequence of images. This layer holds the raw input of the image with width 32, height 32, and depth 3.

⊙ **Convolutional Layers:** This is the layer, which is used to extract the feature from the input dataset. It applies a set of learnable filters known as the kernels to the input images. The filters/kernels are smaller matrices usually 2×2, 3×3, or 5×5 shape. it slides over the input image data and computes the dot product between kernel weight and the corresponding input image patch. The output of this layer is referred as feature maps. Suppose we use a total of 12 filters for this layer we'll get an output volume of dimension 32 x 32 x 12.

⊙ **Activation Layer:** By adding an activation function to the output of the preceding layer, activation layers add nonlinearity to the network. it will apply an element-wise activation function to the output of the convolution layer. Some common activation functions are RELU: max(0, x), Tanh, Leaky RELU, etc. The volume remains unchanged hence output volume will have dimensions 32 x 32 x 12.

⊙ **Pooling layer:** This layer is periodically inserted in the covnets and its main function is to reduce the size of volume which makes the computation fast reduces memory and also prevents overfitting. Two common types of pooling layers are max pooling and average pooling. If we use a max pool with 2 x 2 filters and stride 2, the resultant volume will be of dimension 16x16x12.

⊙ **Flattening:** The resulting feature maps are flattened into a one-dimensional vector after the convolution and pooling layers so they can be passed into a completely linked layer for categorization or regression.

⊙ **Fully Connected Layers:** It takes the input from the previous layer and computes the final classification or regression task (Fig. 6.10).

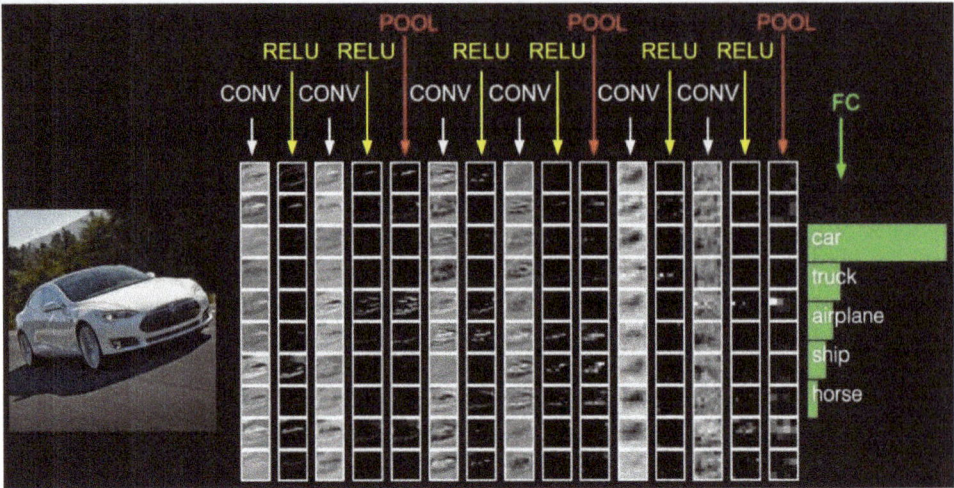

Fig. 6.10 Fully Connected Layers

⊙ **Output Layer:** The output from the fully connected layers is then fed into a logistic function for classification tasks like sigmoid or softmax which converts the output of each class into the probability score of each class.

Example:

Let's consider an image and apply the convolution layer, activation layer, and pooling layer operation to extract the inside feature.

Input image:

Step:

- ⊙ Import the necessary libraries
- ⊙ Set the parameter
- ⊙ Define the kernel
- ⊙ Load the image and plot it.
- ⊙ Reformat the image
- ⊙ Apply convolution layer operation and plot the output image.
- ⊙ Apply activation layer operation and plot the output image.
- ⊙ Apply pooling layer operation and plot the output image.

Advantages of Convolutional Neural Networks (CNNs):

- ⊙ Good at detecting patterns and features in images, videos, and audio signals.
- ⊙ Robust to translation, rotation, and scaling invariance.
- ⊙ End-to-end training, no need for manual feature extraction.
- ⊙ Can handle large amounts of data and achieve high accuracy.

Fig. 6.11 Input image

Disadvantages of Convolutional Neural Networks (CNNs):

- ⊙ Computationally expensive to train and require a lot of memory.

- ⊙ Can be prone to overfitting if not enough data or proper regularization is used.

- ⊙ Requires large amounts of labeled data.

- ⊙ Interpretability is limited, it's hard to understand what the network has learned.

OBJECT DETECTION AND IMAGE RECOGNITION

Object detection is an extension of image classification. It not only tells us if a certain object is present in the picture, but also tells us where.

On the left, we have an example of a classifier. It tells us that there is a cat in the picture.

The object detector, shown on the image to the right, tells us that there's both a cat, a dog, and a duck, and furthermore where they are located.

It starts by analyzing an image and selecting regions in the picture where it "thinks" there is something. It doesn't know what it is but it detects that there is a kind of object, it is not merely background. We call this process region proposal. Let's look at an example.

Object Recognition:

Object recognition is the technique of identifying the object present in images and videos. It is one of the most important applications of machine learning and deep learning. The goal of this field is to teach machines to understand (recognize) the content of an image just like humans do.

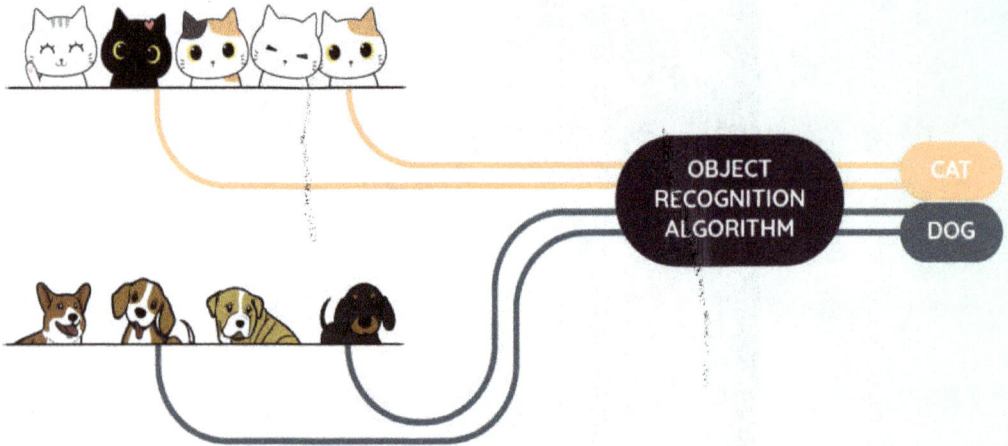

Fig. 6.12 Object Recognition

Object Recognition Using Machine Learning

◉ HOG (Histogram of oriented Gradients) feature Extractor and SVM (Support Vector Machine) model: Before the era of deep learning, it was a state-of-the-art method for object detection. It takes histogram descriptors of both positive (images that contain objects) and negative (images that does not contain objects) samples and trains our SVM model on that.

◉ Bag of features model: Just like bag of words considers document as an orderless collection of words, this approach also represents an image as an orderless collection of image features. Examples of this are SIFT, MSER, etc.

◉ Viola-Jones algorithm: This algorithm is widely used for face detection in the image or real-time. It performs Haar-like feature extraction from the image. This generates a large number of features. These features are then passed into a boosting classifier. This generates a cascade of the boosted classifier to perform image detection. An image needs to pass to each of the classifiers to generate a positive (face found) result. The advantage of Viola-Jones is that it has a detection time of 2 fps which can be used in a real-time face recognition system.

Object Recognition Using Deep Learning

Convolution Neural Network (CNN) is one of the most popular ways of doing object recognition. It is widely used and most state-of-the-art neural networks used this method for various object recognition related tasks such as image classification. This CNN network takes an image as input and outputs the probability of the different classes. If the object present in the image then it's output probability is high else the output probability of the rest of classes is either negligible or low. The advantage of Deep learning is that we don't need to do feature extraction from data as compared to machine learning (Fig. 6.13).

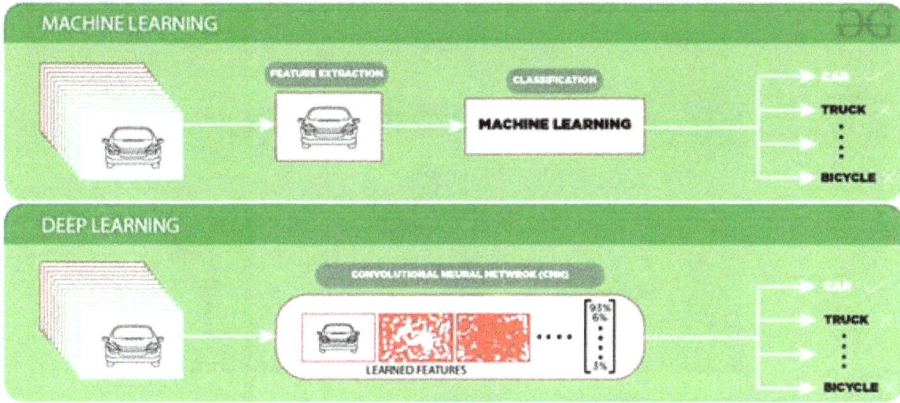

Fig. 6.13 Object Recognition Using Deep Learning

Challenges of Object Recognition:

⊙ Since we take the output generated by last (fully connected) layer of the CNN model is a single class label. So, a simple CNN approach will not work if more than one class labels are present in the image (Fig. 6.14).

⊙ If we want to localize the presence of an object in the bounding box, we need to try a different approach that not only outputs the class label but also outputs the bounding box locations.

Image Classification

In Image classification, it takes an image as an input and outputs the classification label of that image with some metric (probability, loss, accuracy, etc). For Example: An image of a cat can be classified as a class label "cat" or an image of Dog can be classified as a class label "dog" with some probability.

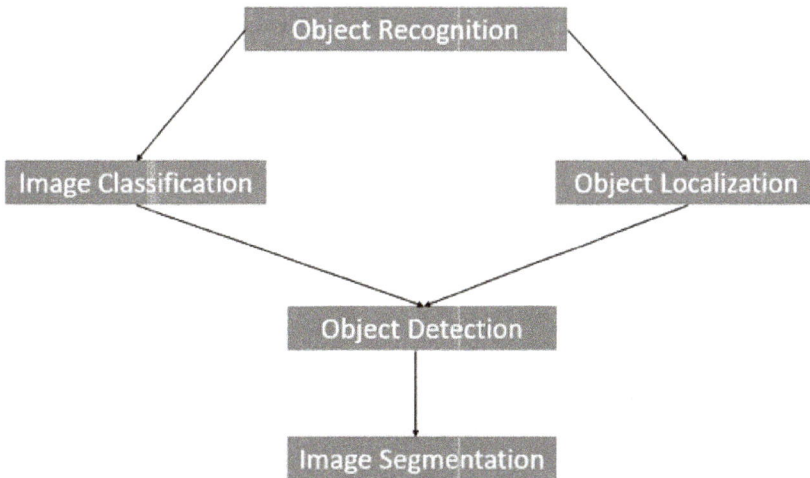

Fig. 6.14 Overview of tasks related to Object Recognition

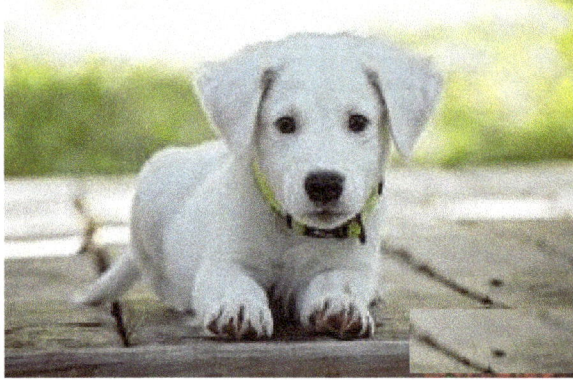

Fig. 6.15 Image Classification

Object Localization: This algorithm locates the presence of an object in the image and represents it with a bounding box. It takes an image as input and outputs the location of the bounding box in the form of (position, height, and width).

Object Detection:

Object Detection algorithms act as a combination of image classification and object localization. It takes an image as input and produces one or more bounding boxes with the class label attached to each bounding box. These algorithms are capable enough to deal with multi-class classification and localization as well as to deal with the objects with multiple occurrences.

Challenges of Object Detection:

- In object detection, the bounding boxes are always rectangular. So, it does not help with determining the shape of objects if the object contains the curvature part.

- Object detection cannot accurately estimate some measurements such as the area of an object, perimeter of an object from image (Fig. 6.16).

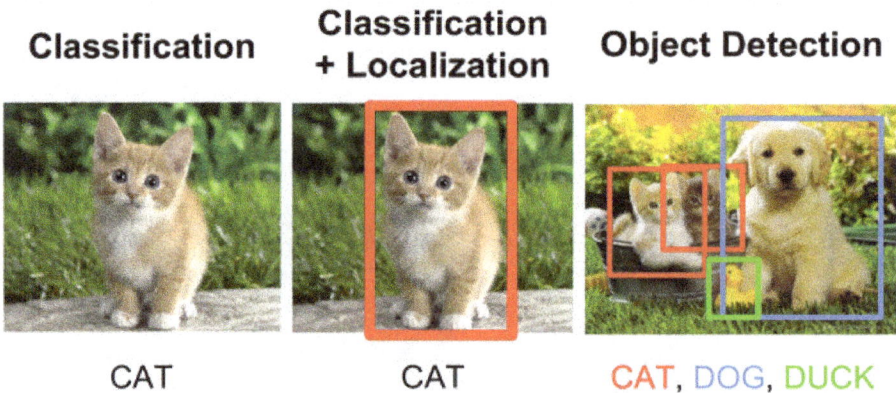

Fig. 6.16 Difference between classification. Localization and Detection

Image Segmentation

Image segmentation is a further extension of object detection in which we mark the presence of an object through pixel-wise masks generated for each object in the image (Fig. 6.17). This technique is more granular than bounding box generation because this can helps us in determining the shape of each object present in the image because instead of drawing bounding boxes, segmentation helps to figure out pixels that are making that object. This granularity helps us in various fields such as medical image processing, satellite imaging, etc. There are many image segmentation approaches proposed recently. One of the most popular is Mask R-CNN proposed by researchers.

There are primarily two types of segmentation:

- Instance Segmentation: Multiple instances of same class are separate segments i.e. objects of same class are treated as different. Therefore, all the objects are coloured with different colour even if they belong to same class.

- Semantic Segmentation: All objects of same class form a single classification, therefore, all objects of same class are coloured by same colour (Fig. 6.18).

Fig. 6.17 Object Detection vs Segmentation

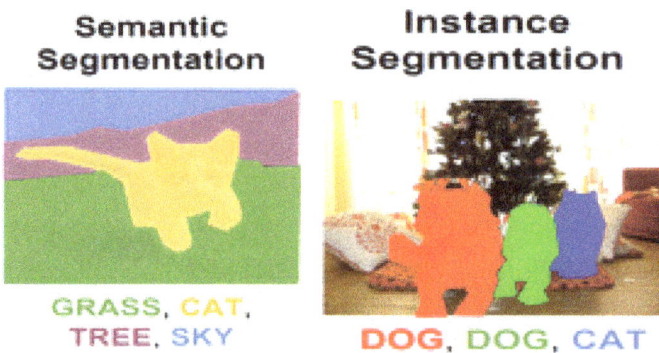

Fig. 6.18 Semantic vs Instance Segmentation

Applications:

The above-discussed object recognition techniques can be utilized in many fields such as:

- ⊙ Driver-less Cars: Object Recognition is used for detecting road signs, other vehicles, etc.

- ⊙ Medical Image Processing: Object Recognition and Image Processing techniques can help detect disease more accurately. Image segmentation helps to detect the shape of the defect present in the body . For Example, Google AI for breast cancer detection detects more accurately than doctors.

- ⊙ Surveillance and Security: such as Face Recognition, Object Tracking, Activity Recognition, etc.

APPLICATIONS OF COMPUTER VISION IN INDUSTRY

Computer vision or machine vision is a field of science that enables computers or devices to recognize different objects just like human beings. the computers need to be trained to detect objects and also some patterns just like you teach a kid to identify the objects but the computers are more efficient as it takes very little time to be trained. Computer vision has applications in all industries and sectors and they are as follows:

- ⊙ **Oil and natural gas:** The oil and natural gas companies produce millions of barrels of oil and billions of cubic feet of gas every day but for this to happen, first, the geologists have to find a feasible location from where oil and gas can be extracted. To find these locations they have to analyze thousands of different locations using images taken on the spot. Suppose if geologists had to analyze each image manually how long will it take to find the best location? Maybe months or even a year but due to the introduction of computer vision the period of analyzing can be brought down to a few days or even a few hours. You just need to feed in the images taken to the pre-trained model and it will get the work done.

- ⊙ **Hiring process:** In the HR world, computer vision is changing how candidates get hired in the interview process. By using computer vision, machine learning, and data science, they're able to quantify soft skills and conduct early candidate assessments to help large companies shortlist the candidates.

- ⊙ **Video surveillance:** The Concept of video tagging is used to tag videos with keywords based on the objects that appear in each scene. Now imagine being that security company who's asking to look for a suspect in a blue van amongst hours and hours of footage. You will just have to feed the video to the algorithm. With computer vision and object recognition, searching through videos has become a thing of the past.

- ◉ **Construction:** Take for example the electric towers or buildings, which require some degree of maintenance to check for degrees of rust and other structural defects. Certainly, manually climbing up the tower to look at every inch and corner would be extremely time-consuming, costly, and dangerous. Flying a drone with wires around the electric tower doesn't sound particularly safe either. So how could you apply computer vision here? Imagine that if a person on the ground took high-resolution images from different angles. Then the computer vision specialist could create a custom classifier and use it to detect the flaws and amount of rust or cracks present.

Healthcare

From the past few years, the healthcare industry has adopted many next-generation technologies that include artificial intelligence and machine learning concept. One of them is computer vision which helps determine or diagnose disease in humans or any living creatures.

X-Ray Analysis

Computer vision can be successfully applied for medical X-ray imaging. Although most doctors still prefer manual analysis of X-ray images to diagnose and treat diseases, with computer vision, X-ray analysis can be automated with enhanced efficiency and accuracy. The state-of-art image recognition algorithm can be used to detect patterns in an X-ray image that are too subtle for the human eyes.

Cancer Detection

Computer vision is being successfully applied for breast and skin cancer detection. With image recognition, doctors can identify anomalies by comparing cancerous and non-cancerous cells in images. With automated cancer detection, doctors can diagnose cancer faster from an MRI scan.

CT Scan and MRI

Computer vision has now been greatly applied in CT scans and MRI analysis. AI with computer vision designs such a system that analyses the radiology images with a high level of accuracy, similar to a human doctor, and also reduces the time for disease detection, enhancing the chances of saving a patient's life. It also includes deep learning algorithms that enhance the resolution of MRI images and hence improve patient outcomes.

Computer Vision in Agriculture

In the agriculture sector, Machine Learning has made a great contribution with its models, including Computer vision. It can be used in areas such as crop monitoring, weather analysis, etc. Below are some popular cases of computer vision applications in Agriculture:

⊙ **Crop Monitoring:** In the agriculture sector, crop and yield monitoring are the most important tasks for better agriculture. Traditionally, it depends on subjective human judgment, but that is not always accurate. With computer vision systems, real-time crop monitoring and identification of any crop variation due to any disease or deficiency of nutrition can be made.

⊙ **Automatic Weeding:** An automatic weeding machine is an intelligent project enabled with AI and computer vision that removes unwanted plants or weeds around the crops. Traditionally weeding methods require human labour, which is costly and inefficient compared to automatic weeding systems. Computer vision enables the intelligent detection and removal of weeds using robots, which reduces costs and ensures higher yields.

⊙ **Plant Disease Detection:** Computer vision is also used in automated plant disease detection, which is important at an early stage of plant development. Various deep-learning-based algorithms use computer vision to identify plant diseases, estimate their severity and predict their impact on yields.

Military

For modern armies, Computer Vision is an important technology that helps them to detect enemy troops and it also enhances the targeting capabilities of guided missile systems. It uses image sensors to deliver battlefield intelligence used for tactical decision-making. One more important Computer Vision application in the areas of autonomous vehicles like UAV's and remote-controlled semi-automatic vehicles, which need to navigate challenging terrain.

Industry

In manufacturing or assembly line, computer vision is being used for automated inspections, identifying defective products on the production line, and for remote inspections of machinery. The technology is also used to increase the efficiency of the production line.

Automotive

This is one of the best examples of computer vision technologies, which is a dream come true for humans. Self-driving AI analyzes data from a camera mounted on the vehicle to automate lane finding, detect obstacles, and recognize traffic signs and signals.

Automated Lip Reading

This is one of the practical implementations of computer vision to help people with disabilities or who cannot speak, it reads the movement of lips and compares it to already known movements that were recorded and used to create the model.

Computer Vision in Transportation

With the enhanced demand for the transportation sector, there has occurred various technological development in this industry, and one of such technologies is Computer vision. Below are some popular applications of computer vision in the transportation industry:

- ◉ **Self-driving cars:** Computer vision is widely used in self-driving cars. It is used to detect and classify objects (e.g., road signs or traffic lights), create 3D maps or motion estimation, and plays a key role in making autonomous vehicles a reality.

- ◉ **Pedestrian detection:** Computer vision has great application and research in Pedestrian detection due to its high impact on the designing of pedestrian systems in various smart cities. With the help of cameras, pedestrian detection automatically identifies and locate the pedestrians in image or video. Moreover, it also considers the variations among pedestrians related to attire, body position, and illuminance in different scenarios. This pedestrian detection is very helpful in different fields such as traffic management, autonomous driving, transit safety, etc.

- ◉ **Road Condition Monitoring & Defect detection:** Computer vision has also been applied for monitoring the road infrastructure condition by accessing the variations in concrete and tar. A computer vision-enabled system automatically senses pavement degradation, which successfully increases road maintenance allocation efficiency and decreases safety risks related to road accidents.

To perform road condition monitoring, CV algorithms collect the image data and then process it to create automatic crack detection and classification system.

Computer Vision in Manufacturing

In the manufacturing industry, the demand for automation is at its peak. Many tasks have already been automated, and other new technology innovations are in trend. For providing these automatic solutions, Computer vision is also widely used. Below are some most popular applications

- ◉ **Defect Detection:** This is perhaps, the most common application of computer vision. Until now, the detection of defects has been carried out by trained people in selected batches, and total production control is usually impossible. With computer vision, we can detect defects such as cracks in metals, paint defects, bad prints, etc., in sizes smaller than 0.05mm.

- ◉ **Analyzing text and barcodes (OCR):** Nowadays, each product contains a barcode on its packaging, which can be analyzed or read with the help of the computer vision technique OCR. Optical character recognition or OCR helps us detect and extract printed or handwritten text from visual data such as images. Further, it enables us to extract text from documents like invoices, bills, articles, etc. and verifies against the databases.

- ⊙ **Fingerprint recognition and Biometrics:** Computer vision technology is used to detect fingerprints and biometrics to validate a user's identity.

- ⊙ Biometrics is the measurement or analysis of physiological characteristics of a person that make a person unique such as Face, Finger Print, iris Patterns, etc. It makes use of computer vision along with knowledge of human physiology and behaviour.

- ⊙ **3D Model building:** 3D model building or 3D modelling is a technique to generate a 3D digital representation of any object or surface using the software. Computer vision plays its role here also in constructing 3D computer models from existing objects. Furthermore, 3D modelling has a variety of applications in various places, such as Robotics, Autonomous driving, 3D tracking, 3D scene reconstruction, and AR/VR.

Computer Vision in Retail

In the retail sector, computer vision system enables retailers to collect a huge volume of visual data and hence design better customer experiences with the help of cameras installed in stores. Some popular applications of computer vision in the retail industry are given below:

- ⊙ **Self-checkout:** Self-checkout enables the customers to complete their transactions from a retailer without the need for human staff, and this becomes possible with computer vision. Self-checkouts are now helping retailers in avoiding long queues and manage customers.

- ⊙ **Automatic replenishment:** Automated stock replenishment is a leading technology innovation in retail sectors. Traditionally, stock replenishment is performed by store staff, who check selves to track the items for inventory management. But now, automatic replenishment with computer vision systems captures the image data and performs a complete inventory scan to track the shelves item at regular intervals.

- ⊙ **People Counting:** Nowadays, various situations occur where we may need the count of people or customers entering and leaving the stores. This foot count or people counting can be done by computer vision systems that analyze the image or video data captured by the in-store cameras. People counting is helpful in managing the people and allowing the limited people for cases such as Covid social distancing.

CHAPTER-7
REINFORCEMENT LEARNING

- Reinforcement Learning is a feedback-based Machine learning technique in which an agent learns to behave in an environment by performing the actions and seeing the results of actions. For each good action, the agent gets positive feedback, and for each bad action, the agent gets negative feedback or penalty.

- In Reinforcement Learning, the agent learns automatically using feedbacks without any labeled data, unlike supervised learning.

- Since there is no labeled data, so the agent is bound to learn by its experience only.

- RL solves a specific type of problem where decision making is sequential, and the goal is long-term, such as game-playing, robotics, etc.

- The agent interacts with the environment and explores it by itself. The primary goal of an agent in reinforcement learning is to improve the performance by getting the maximum positive rewards.

- The agent learns with the process of hit and trial, and based on the experience, it learns to perform the task in a better way. Hence, we can say that "Reinforcement learning is a type of machine learning method where an intelligent agent (computer program) interacts with the environment and learns to act within that." How a Robotic dog learns the movement of his arms is an example of Reinforcement learning.

- It is a core part of Artificial intelligence, and all AI agent works on the concept of reinforcement learning. Here we do not need to pre-program the agent, as it learns from its own experience without any human intervention.

Example: Suppose there is an AI agent present within a maze environment, and his goal is to find the diamond. The agent interacts with the environment by performing some actions, and based on those actions, the state of the agent gets changed, and it also receives a reward or penalty as feedback.

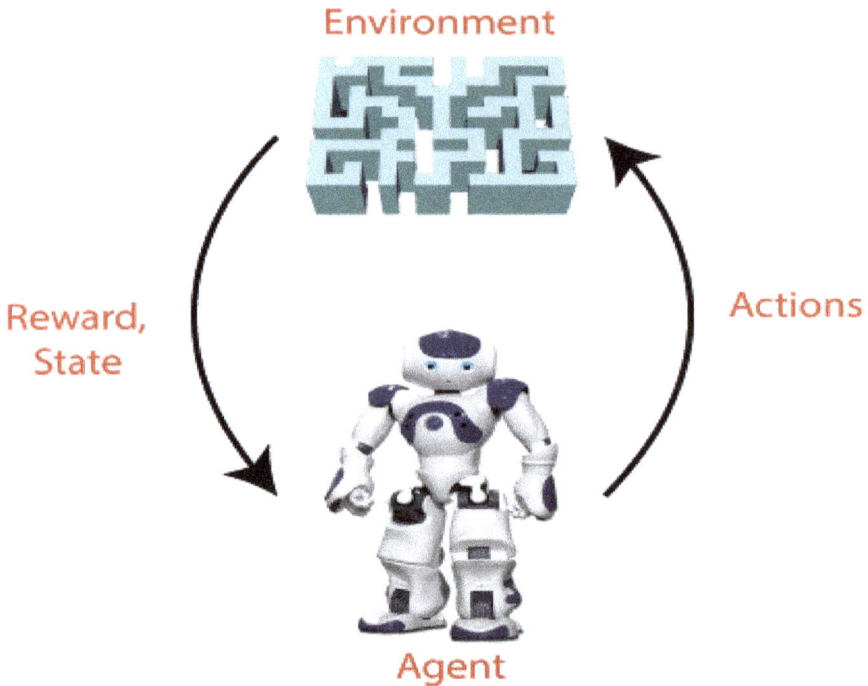

Fig. 7.1

⦿ The agent continues doing these three things (take action, change state/remain in the same state, and get feedback), and by doing these actions, he learns and explores the environment.

⦿ The agent learns that what actions lead to positive feedback or rewards and what actions lead to negative feedback penalty. As a positive reward, the agent gets a positive point, and as a penalty, it gets a negative point.

BASICS OF REINFORCEMENT LEARNING

Basics of reinforcement machine learning include:

⦿ An Input, an initial state, from which the model starts an action

⦿ Outputs – there could be many possible solutions to a given problem, which means there could be many outputs

⦿ The training on deep reinforcement learning is based on the input, and the user can decide to either reward or punish the model depending on the output. The model decides the best solution based on the maximum reward.

⦿ The model considers the rewards and punishments and continues to learn through them.

Reinforcement learning is more general than supervised and unsupervised learning and learn from interaction with the environment to achieve a goal and getting an agent to act in the world so as to maximize its rewards. It allows agents to automatically determine the ideal behaviour within a specific context, in order to maximize its performance. Simple reward feedback is required for the agent to learn its behaviour; this is known as the reinforcement signal.

The motivation behind reinforcement learning is that it allows an agent to learn its behavior based on feedback from the environment. This behavior can be learnt once and for all, or keep on adapting as time goes by. If the problem is modelled with care, some reinforcement learning algorithms can converge to the global optimum; this is the ideal behavior that maximizes the reward.

It is a trial-and-error learning paradigm which learns from rewards and punishments. Reinforcement learning is not just an algorithm but a new paradigm in itself. Its objective is to learn about a system from minimal feedbacklike its behavior, control. It is inspired by behavioral psychology.

As mentioned in Fig. 7.2, the reinforcement learning consists of the agent and the environment. The agent performs the action under the policy being followed and the environment is everything else other than the agent. Reinforcement learning is learning from interaction and it is a goal-oriented learning. It is learning about, from, and while interacting with an external environment. It is a learning which tells you, what to do (what action to take), how to map situations to actions so as to maximize a numerical reward signal.

The general definition of reinforcement learning is as follows "Reinforcement learning is learning what to do - how to map situations to actions - so as to maximize a numerical reward signal. The learner is not told which actions to take, as in most forms of machine learning, but instead must discover which actions yield the most reward by trying them."

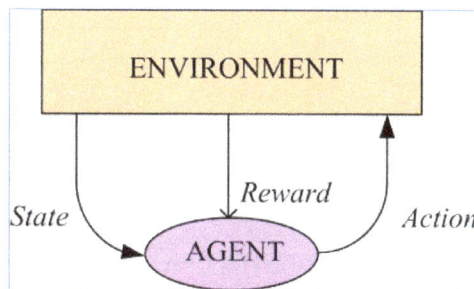

Fig. 7.2 The reinforcement learning consists of the agent and the environment

General Reinforcement Learning Algorithm

The first step is to initialise the learner's internal state. Then the algorithm should repeat forever the following steps

- ◉ Observe current state s

- Choose action a using some evaluation function
- Execute action a
- Let r be immediate reward, s' new state
- Update internal state based on s,a,r,s'.

Here learning is concerned with what to do that is how to map situations to actionsso as to maximize a numerical reward signal. Therefore learning to choose an action based on an evaluation function is the learning part.

Key Features of Reinforcement Learning

The following are the key features of reinforcement learning. The learner is not told which actions to take and in that sense it is a trial-and-error search. It has the possibility of delayed reward (sacrifice short-term gains for greater long -term gains). In reinforcement learning there is a need to explore and exploit. It considers the whole problem of a goal-directed agent interacting with an uncertain environment. The reinforcement model assumes that each percept(e) is enough to determine the State(the state is accessible) and the agent can decompose the Reward component from a percept. Therefore the agent task: to find a optimal policy, mapping states to actions, that maximize long-run measure of the reinforcement.

Agent-Environment Interface

We have the agentenvironment interface as shown in Figure 7.3. Associated with this interface is **st** which is the state at time t, **rt** which is the reward by the environment to the agent at time t and **at** which is the action taken by the agent at time t. After taking the action at time t, the environment goes to the next state **st+1** at time t+1, and gives the reward **rt^{+1}**at time t^{+1}.

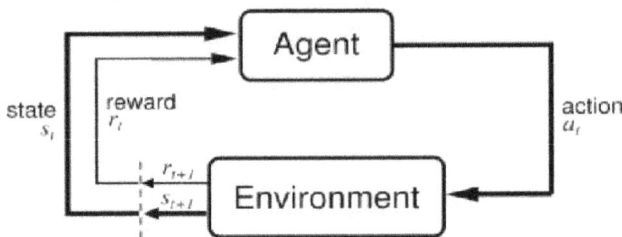

Fig. 7.3 Agent-Environment Interface

The task of reinforcement learning is to learn how to behave successfully so as to achieve a goal while interacting with an external environment and learn through experience from trial and error. Some examples of reinforcement learning are:

- Game playing: The agent knows it has won or lost, but it doesn't know the appropriate action in each state
- Control: a traffic system can measure the delay of cars

A Formal Framework for RL

The agent acts and receives rewards (and new states) from the environment

Problems that are solved via RL tend to be structured in a similar format. Namely, we have an *agent* that is interacting with an *environment*; see above. The agent has a *state* in the environment and produces actions, which can modify the current state, as output. As the agent interacts with the environment, it can receive both positive and negative rewards for its actions. The agent's goal is to maximize the rewards that it receives, but there is not a reward associated with every action taken by the agent! Rather, *rewards may have a long horizon*, meaning that it takes several correct, consecutive actions to generate any positive reward.

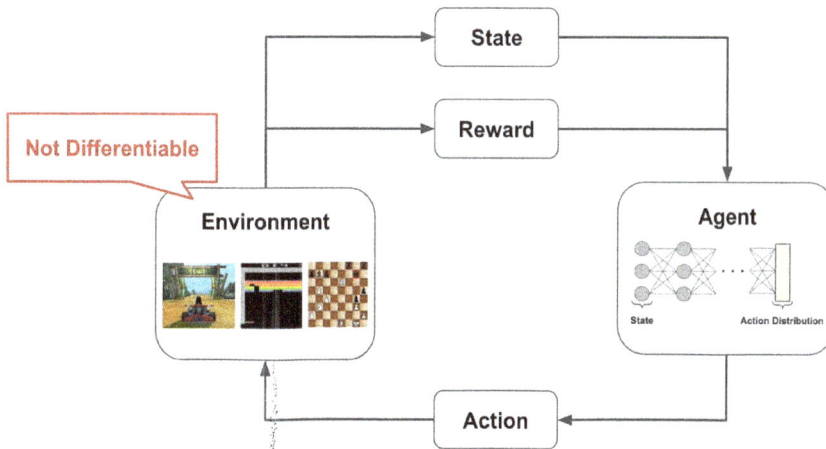

Fig. 7.4 Formal Framework for RL

MARKOV DECISION PROCESS (MDP)

A Markov Decision Process (MDP) model contains:

⊙ A set of possible world states S.

⊙ A set of Models.

⊙ A set of possible actions A.

⊙ A real-valued reward function R(s,a).

⊙ A policy the solution of Markov Decision Process.

What is a State?

A **State** is a set of tokens that represent every state that the agent can be in.

What is a Model?

A Model (sometimes called Transition Model) gives an action's effect in a state. In particular, T(S, a, S') defines a transition T where being in state S and taking an action 'a' takes us to state S' (S and S' may be the same). For stochastic actions (noisy, nondeterministic) we also define a probability P(S'|S,a) which represents the probability of reaching a state S' if action 'a' is taken in state S. Note Markov property states that the effects of an action taken in a state depend only on that state and not on the prior history.

What are Actions?

An **Action** A is a set of all possible actions. A(s) defines the set of actions that can be taken being in state S.

What is a Reward?

A **Reward** is a real-valued reward function. R(s) indicates the reward for simply being in the state S. R(S,a) indicates the reward for being in a state S and taking an action 'a'. R(S,a,S') indicates the reward for being in a state S, taking an action 'a' and ending up in a state S'.

What is a Policy?

A **Policy** is a solution to the Markov Decision Process. A policy is a mapping from S to a. It indicates the action 'a' to be taken while in state S.

Let us take the example of a grid world (Fig. 7.5):

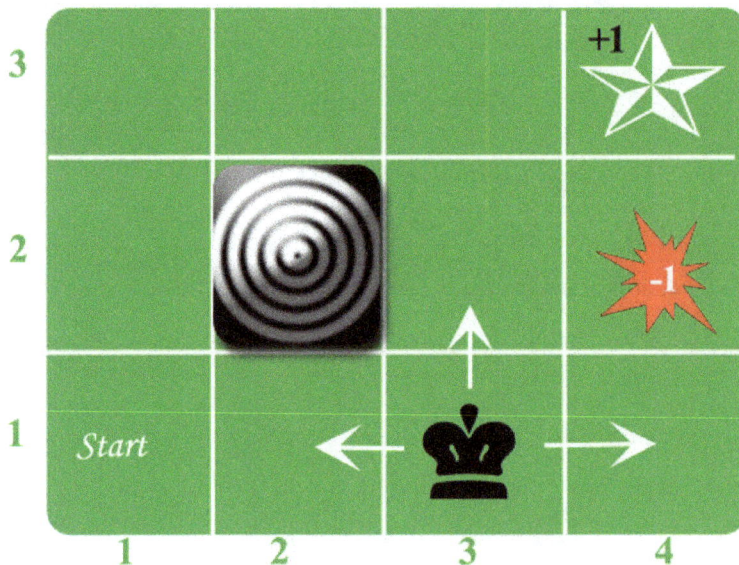

Fig. 7.5 Example of a grid world

An agent lives in the grid. The above example is a 3*4 grid. The grid has a START state(grid no 1,1). The purpose of the agent is to wander around the grid to finally reach the Blue Diamond (grid no 4,3). Under all circumstances, the agent should avoid the Fire grid (orange color, grid no 4,2). Also the grid no 2,2 is a blocked grid, it acts as a wall hence the agent cannot enter it.

The agent can take any one of these actions: **UP, DOWN, LEFT, RIGHT**

Walls block the agent path, i.e., if there is a wall in the direction the agent would have taken, the agent stays in the same place. So for example, if the agent says LEFT in the START grid he would stay put in the START grid.

First Aim: To find the shortest sequence getting from START to the Diamond. Two such sequences can be found:

- ◉ **RIGHT RIGHT UP UPRIGHT**
- ◉ **UP UP RIGHT RIGHT RIGHT**

Let us take the second one (UP UP RIGHT RIGHT RIGHT) for the subsequent discussion.

The move is now noisy. 80% of the time the intended action works correctly. 20% of the time the action agent takes causes it to move at right angles. For example, if the agent says UP the probability of going UP is 0.8 whereas the probability of going LEFT is 0.1, and the probability of going RIGHT is 0.1 (since LEFT and RIGHT are right angles to UP).

The agent receives rewards each time step:-

- ◉ Small reward each step (can be negative when can also be term as punishment, in the above example entering the Fire can have a reward of -1).
- ◉ Big rewards come at the end (good or bad).
- ◉ The goal is to Maximize the sum of rewards.

Q-LEARNING AND DEEP Q NETWORKS (DQNS)

Q-Learning is required as a pre-requisite as it is a process of Q-Learning creates an exact matrix for the working agent which it can "refer to" to maximize its reward in the long run. Although this approach is not wrong in itself, this is only practical for very small environments and quickly loses it's feasibility when the number of states and actions in the environment increases. The solution for the above problem comes from the realization that the values in the matrix only have relative importance ie the values only have importance with respect to the other values. Thus, this thinking leads us to Deep Q-Learning which uses a deep neural network to approximate the values. This approximation of values does not hurt as long as the relative importance is preserved. The basic working step for Deep Q-Learning is that the initial state is fed into the neural network and it returns the Q-value of all possible actions as an output. The difference between Q-Learning and Deep Q-Learning can be illustrated as follows:

Q Matrix

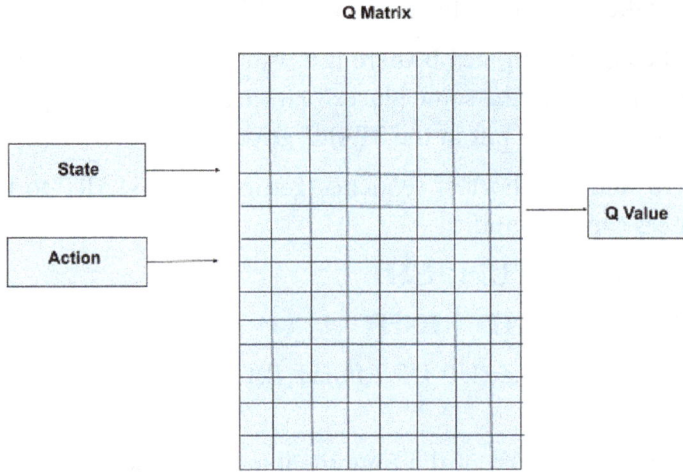

Fig. 7.6 Q-Learning

Deep Neural Network

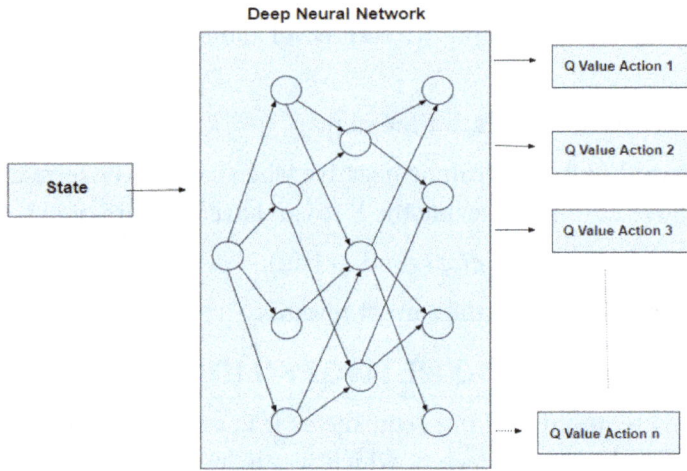

Fig. 7.7 Deep Neural Network

Pseudo Code

Initialize

$Q_0(a, a)$

for all pairs (s,a)s = initial statek = 0while(convergence is not achieved){ simulate action a and reach state s' if(s' is a terminal state) {   target = R(s,a,s') } else {   target = R(s,a,s') +

$gmax_a Q_k(s', a')$

}

$\theta_{k+1} = \theta_k - \alpha \Delta_\theta E_{s'\ P(s'|s,a)}[(Q_\theta (s, a) - target(s'))^2]|_{\theta = \theta k}$

   s = s'}

Observe that in the equation **target = R(s,a,s') +** , the term

$$gmax_{a'}Q_k(s', a')$$

is a variable term. Therefore in this process, the target for the neural network is variable unlike other typical Deep Learning processes where the target is stationary. This problem is overcome by having two neural networks instead of one. One neural network is used to adjust the parameters of the network and the other is used for computing the target and which has the same architecture as the first network but has frozen parameters. After an x number of iterations in the primary network, the parameters are copied to the target network (Fig. 7.8).

Deep Q-Learning is a type of reinforcement learning algorithm that uses a deep neural network to approximate the Q-function, which is used to determine the optimal action to take in a given state. The Q-function represents the expected cumulative reward of taking a certain action in a certain state and following a certain policy. In Q-Learning, the Q-function is updated iteratively as the agent interacts with the environment. Deep Q-Learning is used in various applications such as game playing, robotics and autonomous vehicles.

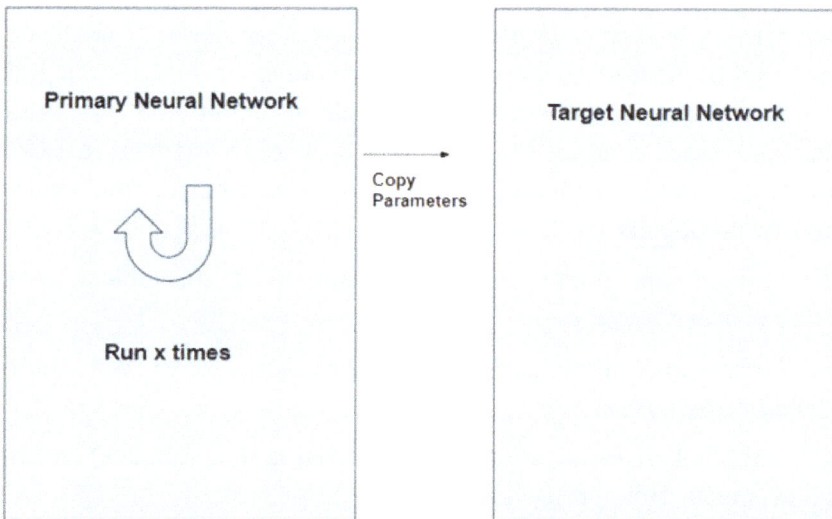

Primary Neural Network

Copy
Parameters

Target Neural Network

Run x times

Fig. 7.8 Copy parameter

Deep Q-Learning is a variant of Q-Learning that uses a deep neural network to represent the Q-function, rather than a simple table of values. This allows the algorithm to handle environments with a large number of states and actions, as well as to learn from high-dimensional inputs such as images or sensor data.

One of the key challenges in implementing Deep Q-Learning is that the Q-function is typically non-linear and can have many local minima. This can make it difficult for the neural network to converge to the correct Q-function. To address this, several techniques have been proposed, such as experience replay and target networks.

Experience replay is a technique where the agent stores a subset of its experiences (state, action, reward, next state) in a memory buffer and samples from this buffer to update the Q-function. This helps to decorrelate the data and make the learning process more stable. Target networks, on the other hand, are used to stabilize the Q-function updates. In this technique, a separate network is used to compute the target Q-values, which are then used to update the Q-function network.

Deep Q-Learning has been applied to a wide range of problems, including game playing, robotics, and autonomous vehicles. For example, it has been used to train agents that can play games such as Atari and Go, and to control robots for tasks such as grasping and navigation.

Don't miss your chance to ride the wave of the data revolution! Every industry is scaling new heights by tapping into the power of data. Sharpen your skills and become a part of the hottest trend in the 21st century.

Deep Q-Learning and Deep Q-Network

One of the main drawbacks of Q-learning is that it becomes infeasible when dealing with large state spaces, as the size of the Q-table grows exponentially with the number of states and actions. In such cases, the algorithm becomes computationally expensive and requires a lot of memory to store the Q-values. Imagine a game with 1000 states and 1000 actions per state. We would need a table of one million cells. And that is a very small state space compared to chess or Go. Also, Q-learning can't be used in unknown states because it can't infer the Q-value of new states from the previous ones. This presents two problems:

First, the amount of memory required to save and update that table would increase as the number of states increases.

Second, the amount of time required to explore each state to create the required Q-table would be unrealistic.

To tackle this challenge, one alternative approach is to combine Q-learning with deep neural networks. This approach is coined as Deep Q-Learning (DQL). The neural networks in DQL act as the Q-value approximator for each (state, action) pair.

The neural network receives the state as an input and outputs the Q-values for all possible actions. The following figure (Fig. 7.9) illustrates the difference between Q-learning and deep Q-learning in evaluating the Q-value.

Essentially, deep Q-Learning replaces the regular Q-table with the neural network. Rather than mapping a (state, action) pair to a Q-value, the neural network maps input states to (action, Q-value) pairs.

In 2013, DeepMind introduced Deep Q-Network (DQN) algorithm. DQN is designed to learn to play Atari games from raw pixels. This was a breakthrough in the field of reinforcement learning and helped pave the way for future developments in the field. **The term Deep Q-network refers to the neural network in their DQL architecture**.

APPLICATIONS IN GAME PLAYING AND ROBOTICS

Game Playing is an important domain of artificial intelligence. Games don't require much knowledge; the only knowledge we need to provide is the rules, legal moves and the conditions of winning or losing the game. Both players try to win the game. So, both of them try to make the best move possible at each turn. Searching techniques like BFS(Breadth First Search) are not accurate for this as the branching factor is very high, so searching will take a lot of time. So, we need another search procedures that improve

- ⊙ **Generate procedure** so that only good moves are generated.
- ⊙ **Test procedure** so that the best move can be explored first.

Game playing is a popular application of artificial intelligence that involves the development of computer programs to play games, such as chess, checkers, or Go. The goal of game playing in artificial intelligence is to develop algorithms that can learn how to play games and make decisions that will lead to winning outcomes.

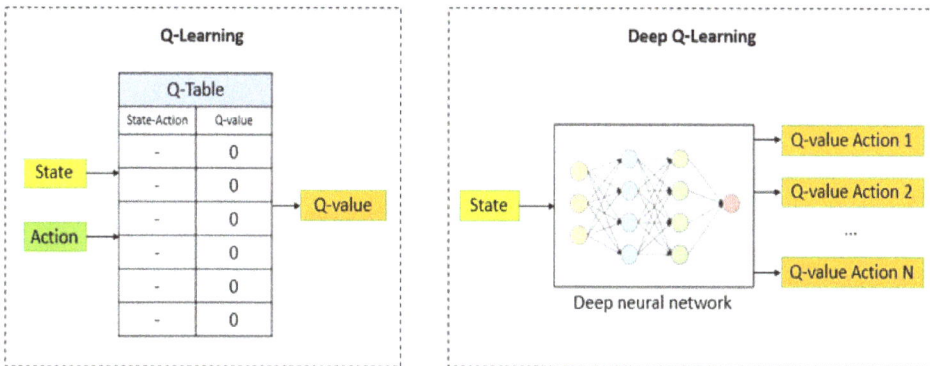

Fig. 7.9 illustrates the difference between Q-learning and deep Q-learning in evaluating the Q-value

One of the earliest examples of successful game playing AI is the chess program Deep Blue, developed by IBM, which defeated the world champion Garry Kasparov in 1997. Since then, AI has been applied to a wide range of games, including two-player games, multiplayer games, and video games.

There are two main approaches to game playing in AI, rule-based systems and machine learning-based systems.

- ⊙ **Rule-based systems** use a set of fixed rules to play the game.
- ⊙ **Machine learning-based systems** use algorithms to learn from experience and make decisions based on that experience.

In recent years, machine learning-based systems have become increasingly popular, as they are able to learn from experience and improve over time, making them well-suited for complex games such as Go. For example, AlphaGo, developed by DeepMind, was the first machine learning-based system to defeat a world champion in the game of Go.

Game playing in AI is an active area of research and has many practical applications, including game development, education, and military training. By simulating game playing scenarios, AI algorithms can be used to develop more effective decision-making systems for real-world applications.

The most common search technique in game playing is Minimax search procedure. It is depth-first depth-limited search procedure. It is used for games like chess and tic-tac-toe.

Minimax algorithm uses two functions:

⊙ **MOVEGEN :** It generates all the possible moves that can be generated from the current position.

⊙ **STATICEVALUATION :** It returns a value depending upon the goodness from the viewpoint of two-player

This algorithm is a two player game, so we call the first player as PLAYER1 and second player as PLAYER2. The value of each node is backed-up from its children. For PLAYER1 the backed-up value is the maximum value of its children and for PLAYER2 the backed-up value is the minimum value of its children. It provides most promising move to PLAYER1, assuming that the PLAYER2 has make the best move. It is a recursive algorithm, as same procedure occurs at each level.

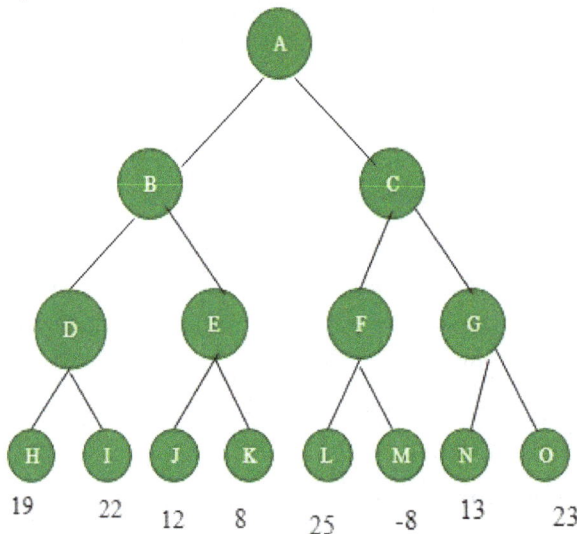

Fig. 7.10: Before backing-up of values

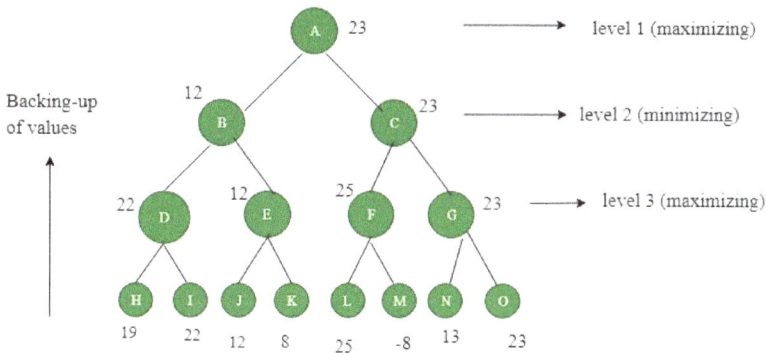

Fig. 7.11: After backing-up of values We assume that PLAYER1 will start the game.

4 levels are generated. The value to nodes H, I, J, K, L, M, N, O is provided by STATICEVALUATION function. Level 3 is maximizing level, so all nodes of level 3 will take maximum values of their children. Level 2 is minimizing level, so all its nodes will take minimum values of their children. This process continues. The value of A is 23. That means A should choose C move to win.

Reference : Artificial Intelligence by Rich and Knight

Advantages of Game Playing in Artificial Intelligence:

◉ **Advancement of AI:** Game playing has been a driving force behind the development of artificial intelligence and has led to the creation of new algorithms and techniques that can be applied to other areas of AI.

◉ **Education and training:** Game playing can be used to teach AI techniques and algorithms to students and professionals, as well as to provide training for military and emergency response personnel.

◉ **Research:** Game playing is an active area of research in AI and provides an opportunity to study and develop new techniques for decision-making and problem-solving.

◉ **Real-world applications:** The techniques and algorithms developed for game playing can be applied to real-world applications, such as robotics, autonomous systems, and decision support systems.

Disadvantages of Game Playing in Artificial Intelligence:

◉ **Limited scope:** The techniques and algorithms developed for game playing may not be well-suited for other types of applications and may need to be adapted or modified for different domains.

◉ **Computational cost:** Game playing can be computationally expensive, especially for complex games such as chess or Go, and may require powerful computers to achieve real-time performance.

CHAPTER-8
ETHICAL CONSIDERATIONS IN AL

Ethics is a set of moral principles which help us discern between right and wrong. AI ethics is a multidisciplinary field that studies how to optimize AI's beneficial impact while reducing risks and adverse outcomes.

BIAS AND FAIRNESS IN MACHINE LEARNING

When machine learning models are being used to make decisions, they cannot be separated from the social and ethical context in which they are applied, and those developing and deploying these models must take care to do so in a manner that accounts for both accuracy and fairness. In this chapter, we will discuss sources of potential bias in the modeling pipeline, as well as some of the ways that bias introduced by a model can be measured, with a particular focus on classification problems. Unfortunately, just as there is no single machine learning algorithm that is best suited to every application, no one fairness metric will fit every situation. However, we hope this chapter will provide you with a grounding in the available ways of measuring algorithmic fairness that will help you navigate the trade-offs involved putting these into practice in your own applications.

Sources of Bias

Bias may be introduced into a machine learning project at any step along the way and it is important to carefully think through each potential source and how it may affect your results. In many cases, some sources may be difficult to measure precisely (or even at all), but this doesn't mean these potential biases can be readily ignored when developing interventions or performing analyses.

Sample Bias

You're likely familiar with sampling issues as a potential source of bias in the contexts of causal inference and external validity in the social science literature. A biased sample can be just as problematic for machine learning as it can be for inference, and predictions made on individuals or groups not represented in the training set are likely to be unreliable. As such, any application of machine learning should start with a careful understanding of data generating process for the training and test sets. What is the relevant population for the project and how might some individuals be incorrectly excluded or included from the data available for modeling or analysis?

If there is a mismatch between the available training data and the population to whom the model will be applied, you may want to consider whether it is possible to collect more representative data. A model to evaluate the risk of health violations at restaurants may be of limited applicability if the only training data available is based on inspections that resulted from reported complaints. In such a case, an initial trial of randomized inspections might provide a more representative dataset. However, this may not always be possible. For instance, in the case of bail determinations, labeled data will only be available for individuals who are released under the existing system.

How does the available training data relate to the population that the model will be applied to? If there is a mismatch here, is it possible to collect more appropriate data? In the example of bail determination, for instance, you only have subsequent outcome data for individuals who were actually released in the past and lack the counterfactual/potential outcomes for those who were detained.

Even if the training data matches the population, are their underlying systemic biases involved in defining that population in general? For instance, over-policing of black neighborhoods might mean the population of incarcerated individuals is unrepresentative of the population of individuals who have committed a given crime and even a representative sample of the jail population might not be the appropriate universe for a given policy or social science question.

For data with a time component or models that will be deployed to aid future decisions, are there relevant policy changes in the past that may make data from certain periods of time less relevant? Pending policy changes going forward that may affect the modeling population?

Measurement here might be difficult, but it is nevertheless helpful to think through each of these questions in detail. Often, other sources of data (even in aggregate form) can provide some insight on how representative your data may be, including census data, surveys, and academic studies in the relevant area.

Label (Outcome) Bias

Regardless of whether your dataset reflects a representative sample of the relevant population for your intervention or analysis, there may also be bias inherent in the labels (that is, the measured outcomes) associated with individuals in that data.

One mechanism by which bias may be introduced is in how the label/outcome itself is defined. For instance, a study of recidivism might use a new arrest as an outcome variable when it really cares about committing a new crime. However, if some groups are policed more heavily than others, using arrests to define the outcome variable may introduce bias into the system's decisions. Similarly, a label that relies on the number of days an individual has been incarcerated would reflect known biases in sentence lengths between black and white defendants.

A related mechanism is measurement error. Even when the outcome of interest is well-defined and can be measured directly, bias may be introduced through differential measurement accuracy across groups. For instance, data collected through survey research might suffer from language barriers or cultural differences in social desirability that introduce measurement errors across groups.

Machine Learning Pipeline Bias

Biases can be introduced by the handling and transformation of data throughout the machine learning pipeline as well, requiring careful consideration as you ingest data, create features, and model outcomes of interest. Below are a few examples at each stage of the process, but these are far from exhaustive and intended only to help motivate thinking about how bias might be introduced in your own projects.

Ingesting Data: The process of loading, cleaning, and reconciling data from a variety of data sources (often referred to as ETL) can introduce a number of errors that might have differential downstream impacts on different populations:

- Are your processes for matching individuals across data sources equally accurate across different populations? For instance, married vs maiden names may bias match rates against women, while inconsistencies in handling of multi-part last names may make matching less reliable for hispanic individuals.

- Nickname dictionaries used in record reconciliation might be derived from different populations than your population of interest.

- A data loading process that drops records with "special characters" might inadvertently exclude names with accents or tildes.

Feature Engineering: Biases are easy to introduce during the process of constructing features, both in the handling of features that relate directly to protected classes as well as information that correlates with these populations (such as geolocation). A few examples include:

- Dictionaries to infer age or gender from name might be derived from a population that is not relevant to your problem.

- Handling of missing values and combining "other" categories can become problematic, especially for multi-racial individuals or people with non-binary gender.

- Thought should be given to how race and ethnicity indicators are collected – are these self-reported, recorded by a third party, or inferred from other data? The data collection process may inform the accuracy of the data and how errors differ across populations.

⊙ Features that rely on geocoding to incorporate information based on distances or geographic aggregates may miss homeless individuals or provide less predictive power for more mobile populations.

Modelling: The model itself may introduce bias into decisions made from its scores by performing worse on some groups relative to others (many examples have been highlighted in popular press recently, such as racial biases in facial recognition algorithms and gender biases in targeting algorithms for job advertisement on social media). Because of the complex correlation structure of the data, it generally isn't sufficient to simply leave out the protected attributes and assume this will result in fair outcomes. Rather model performance across groups needs to be measured directly in order to understand and address any biases. However, there are many (often incompatible) ways to define fairness and Section metrics will take a closer look at these options in much more detail.

Application Bias

A final potential source of bias worth considering is how the model or analysis might be put into use in practice. One way this might happen is through heterogeneity in the effectiveness of an intervention across groups. For instance, imagine a machine learning model to identify individuals most at risk for developing diabetes in the next 3 years for a particular preventive treatment. If the treatment is much more effective for individuals with a certain genetic background relative to others, the overall outcome of the effort might be to exacerbate disparities in diabetes rates even if the model itself is modeling risk in an unbiased way.

Likewise, it is important to be aware of the risk of discriminatory applications of a machine learning model. Perhaps a model developed to screen out unqualified job candidates is only "trusted" by a hiring manager for female candidates but often ignored or overridden for men. In a perverse way, applying an unbiased model in such a context might serve to increase inequities by giving bad actors more information with which to (wrongly) justify their discriminatory practices.

While there may be relatively little you can do to detect or mitigate these types of bias at the modeling stage, performing a trial to compare current practice with a deployed model can be instructive where doing so is feasible.

Keep in mind, of course, that the potential for machine learning systems to be applied in biased ways shouldn't be construed as an argument against developing these systems at all any more than it would be reasonable to suggest that current practices are likely to be free of bias. Rather, it is an argument for thinking carefully about both the status quo and how it may change in the presence of such a system, putting in place legal and technical safeguards to help ensure that these methods are applied in socially responsible ways.

Considering Bias When Deploying Your Model

Ultimately, what we care about is some global idea of how putting a model into practice will affect some overall concept of social welfare and fairness influenced by all of these possible sources of bias. While this is generally impossible to measure in a quantitative way, it can provide a valuable framework for qualitatively evaluating the potential impact of your model.

For most of the remainder of this chapter, we consider a set of more quantitative metrics that can be applied to the predictions of a machine learning pipeline specifically, but it is important to keep in mind that these metrics only apply to the sample and labels you have and ignoring other sources of bias that may be at play in the underlying data generating process could result in unfair outcomes even when applying a model that appears to be "fair" by your chosen metric.

Dealing with Bias

Define Bias

Section bias examples provided some examples for how bias might be introduced in the process of using machine learning to work with a dataset. While far from exhaustive as a source of potential bias in an overall application, these biases can be more readily measured and addressed through choices made during data preparation, modeling, and model selection. This section focuses on detecting and understanding biases introduced at this stage of the process.

One key challenge, however, is that there is no universally-accepted definition of what it means for a model to be fair. Take the example of a model being used to make bail determinations. Different people might consider it "fair" if:

- It makes mistakes about denying bail to an equal number of white and black individuals

- The chances that a given black or white person will be wrongly denied bail is equal, regardless of race

- Among the jailed population, the probability of having been wrongly denied bail is independent of race

- For people who should be released, the chances that a given black or white person will be denied bail is equal

In different contexts, reasonable arguments can be made for each of these potential definitions, but unfortunately, not all of them can hold at the same time. The remainder of this section explores these competing options and how to approach them in more detail.

Definitions

Most of the metrics used to assess model fairness relate either to the types of errors a model might make or how predictive the model is across different groups.

- **True Positives** (TP) are individuals for whom both the model prediction and actual outcome are positive labels.

- **False Positives** (FP) are individuals for whom both the model predicts a positive label, but the actual outcome is a negative label.

- **True Negatives** (TN) are individuals for whom both the model prediction and actual outcome are negative labels.

- **False Negatives** (FN) are individuals for whom both the model predicts a negative label, but the actual outcome is a positive label.

Based on these four categories, we can calculate several ratios that are instructive for thinking about the equity of a model's predictions in different situations (Sections punitive example and assistive example provide some detailed examples here):

- **False Positive Rate** (FPR) is the fraction of individuals with negative actual labels who the model misclassifies with a positive predicted label.

- **False Negative Rate** (FNR) is the fraction of individuals with positive actual labels who the model misclassifies with a negative predicted label.

- **False Discovery Rate** (FDR) is the fraction of individuals who the model predicts to have a positive label but for whom the actual label is negative.

- **False Omission Rate** (FOR) is the fraction of individuals who the model predicts to have a negative label but for whom the actual label is positive.

- **Precision** is the fraction of individuals who the model predicts to have a positive label about whom this prediction is correct.

- **Recall** is the fraction of individuals with positive actual labels who the model has correctly classified as such.

For the first two metrics (FPR and FNR), notice that the denominator is based on actual outcomes (rather than model predictions), while in the next two (FDR and FOR) the denominator is based on model predictions (whether an individual falls above or below the threshold used to turn model scores into 0/1 predicted classes). The final two metrics relate to correct predictions rather than errors, but are directly related to error measurements (that is, recall=1 - FNR and precision=1 - FDR) and may sometimes have better properties for calculating model bias.

Notice that the metrics defined here require the use of a threshold to turn modeled scores into 0/1 predicted classes and are therefore most useful when either a threshold is well-defined for the problem (e.g., when available resources mean a program can only serve a given number of individuals) or where calculating these metrics at different threshold levels might be used (along with model performance metrics) to choose a threshold for application. In some cases, it may also be of interest to think about equity across the full distribution of the modeled score.

Common practices in these situations are to look at how model performance metrics such as the area under the receiver-operator curve (AUC-ROC) or model calibration compared across subgroups (such as by race, gender, age). Or, in cases where the underlying causal relationships are well-known, counterfactual methods may also be used to assess a model's bias (these methods may also be useful when you suspect label bias to be an issue in your data). We don't explore these topics deeply here, but refer you out to the relevant references if you would like to learn more.

Choosing Bias Metrics

Any of the metrics defined above can be used to calculate disparities across groups in your data and (unless you have a perfect model) many of them cannot be balanced across subgroups at the same time. As a result, one of the most important - and frequently most challenging - aspects of measuring bias in your machine learning pipeline is simply understanding how "fairness" should be defined for your particular case.

In general, this requires consideration of the project's goals and a detailed discussion between the data scientists, decision makers, and those who will be affected by the application of the model. Each perspective may have a different concept of fairness and a different understanding of harm involved in making different types of errors, both at individual and societal levels. Importantly, data scientists have an critical role in this conversation, both as the experts in understanding how different concepts of fairness might translate into metrics and measurement and as individuals with experience deploying similar models. While there is no universally correct definition of fairness, nor one that can be learned from the data, this doesn't excuse the data scientists from responsibility for taking part in the conversation around fairness and equity in their models and helping decision makers understand the options and trade-offs involved.

Practically speaking, coming to an agreement on how fairness should be measured in a purely abstract manner is likely to be difficult. Often it can be instructive instead to explore different options and metrics based on preliminary results, providing tangible context for potential trade-offs between overall performance and different definitions of equity and helping guide stakeholders through the process of deciding what to optimize. The remainder of this section looks at some of the metrics that may be of particular interest in different types of applications:

- If your intervention is punitive in nature (e.g., determining whom to deny bail), individuals may be harmed by intervening on them in error so you may care more about metrics that focus on false positives. Section punitive example provides an example to guide you through what some of these metrics mean in this case.

- If your intervention is assistive in nature (e.g., determining who should receive a food subsidy), individuals may be harmed by failing to intervene on them when they have need, so you may care more about metrics that focus on false negatives Section assistive example provides an example to guide you through metrics that may be applicable in this case.

- If your resources are significantly constrained such that you can only intervene on a small fraction of the population at need, some of the metrics described here may be of limited use and Section constrained assistive describes this case in more detail.

Navigating the many options for defining bias in a given context is a difficult and nuanced process, even for those familiar with the underlying statistical concepts. In order to help facilitate these conversations between data scientists and stakeholders. While it certainly can't provide a single "right" answer for a given context, our hope is that the Fairness Tree (Fig. 8.1) can act as a tool to help structure the process of arriving at an appropriate metric (or set of metrics) to focus on.

Punitive Example

When the application of a risk model is punitive in nature, individuals may be harmed by being incorrectly included in the "high risk" population that receives an intervention. In an extreme case, we can think of this as incorrectly detaining an innocent person in jail. Hence, with punitive interventions, we focus on bias and fairness metrics based on false positives.

Count of False Positives

We might naturally think about the number of people wrongly jailed from each group as reasonable place to start for assessing whether our model is biased. Here, we are concerned with statements like "twice as many people from Group A were wrongly convicted as from Group B."

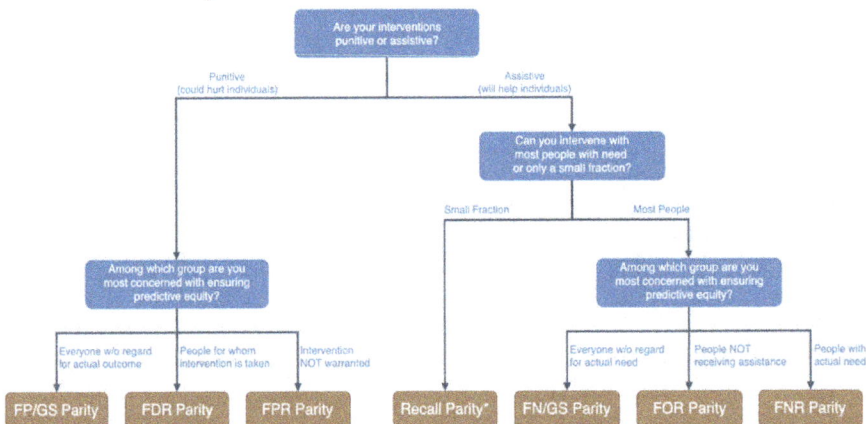

Figure 8.1: Fairness Tree

In probabilistic terms, we could express this as:

P(wrongly jailed, group i)=C $\forall_i$

Where C is a constant value. Or, alternatively,FPi/FPj=1 $\forall_{i,j}$

Where FPi is the number of false positives in group i.

However, it is unclear whether differences in the number of false positives across groups reflect unfairness in the model. For instance, if there are twice as many people in Group A as there are in Group B, some might deem the the situation described above as fair from the standpoint that the composition of the false positives reflects the composition of the groups. This brings us to our second metric:

Group Size-Adjusted False Positives

By accounting for differently sized groups, we ask the question, "just by virtue of the fact that an individual is a member of a given group, what are the chances they'll be wrongly convicted?"

In terms of probability,

P(wrongly jailed| group i)=C $\forall_i$

Where C is a constant value. Or, alternatively,$FP_i/FP_j=n_i/n_j$ $\forall_{i,j}$

Where FPi is the number of false positives and ni the total number of individuals in group i.

While this metric might feel like it meets a reasonable criteria of avoiding treating groups differently in terms of classification errors, there are other sources of disparities we might care about as well. For instance, suppose there are 10,000 individuals in Group A and 30,000 in Group B.

Suppose further that 100 individuals from each group are jail, with 10 Group A people wrongly convicted and 30 Group B people wrongly convicted. We've balanced the number of false positives by group size (0.1% for both groups) so there are no disparities as far as this metric is concerned, but note that 10% of the jailed Group A individuals are innocent compared to 30% of the jailed Group B individuals. The next metric is concerned with unfairness in this way:

False Discovery Rate

The False Discovery Rate (FDR) focuses specifically on the people who are affected by the intervention—in the example above, among the 200 people in jail, what are the group-level disparities in rates of wrong convictions. The jail example is particularly instructive here as we could imagine the social cost of disparities manifesting directly through inmates observing how frequently different groups are wrongly convicted.

False Positive Rate

The False Positive Rate (FPR) focuses on a different subset, specifically, the individuals who should **not** be subject to the intervention. Here, this would ask, "for an *innocent* person, what are the chances they will be wrongly convicted by virtue of the fact that they're a member of a given group?"

The difference between the choosing to focus on the FPR and group size-adjusted false positives is somewhat nuanced and warrants highlighting:

- Having no disparities in group size-adjusted false positives implies that, if I were to choose a random person from a given group (regardless of group-level crime rates or their individual guilt or innocence), I would have the same chance of picking out a wrongly convicted person across groups.

- Having no disparities in FPR implies that, if I were to choose a random *innocent* person from a given group, I would have the same chance of picking out a wrongly convicted person across groups.

Trade-Offs in Metric Choice

By way of example, imagine you have a society with two groups (A and B) and a criminal process with equal FDR and group-size adjusted false positives with:

- Group A has 1000 total individuals, of whom 100 have been jailed with 10 wrongfully convicted. Suppose the other 900 are all guilty.

- Group B has 3000 total individuals, of whom 300 have been jailed with 30 wrongfully convicted. Suppose the other 2700 are all innocent.

That is,

- A randomly chosen individual has the same chance (1.0%) of being wrongly convicted regardless of which group they belong to

- In both groups, a randomly chosen person who is in jail has the same chance (10.0%) of actually being innocent

- HOWEVER, an innocent person in Group A is certain to be wrongly convicted, nearly 100 times the rate of an innocent person in Group B

While this is an exaggerated case for illustrative purposes, there is a more general principle at play here, namely: when prevalences differ across groups, disparities cannot be eliminated from both the FPR and group-size adjusted false positives at the same time (in the absence of perfect prediction).

While there is no universal rule for choosing a bias metric (or set of metrics) to prioritize, it is important to keep in mind that there are both theoretical and practical limits on the degree to which these metrics can be jointly optimized.

Balancing these trade-offs will generally require some degree of subjective judgment on the part of policy makers and should reflect both societal values arrived at with the input of those impacted by model-assisted decisions as well as practical constraints. For instance, if there is uncertainty in the quality of the labels (e.g., how well can we truly measure the size of the innocent population?), it may make more sense in practical terms to focus on the group-size adjusted false positives than FPR.

Assistive Example

By contrast to the punitive case, when the application of a risk model is assistive in nature, individuals may be harmed by being incorrectly excluded from the "high risk" population that receives an intervention. Here, we use identifying families to receive a food assistance benefit as a motivating example. Where the punitive case focused on errors of inclusion through false positives, most of the metrics of interest in the assistive case focus on analogues that measure errors of omission through false negatives.

Count of False Negatives

A natural starting point for understanding whether a program is being applied fairly is to count how many people it is missing from each group, focusing on statements like "twice as many families with need for food assistance from Group A were missed by the benefit as from Group B."

In probabilistic terms, we could express this as:

P(missed by benefit, group i)=C $\forall_i$

Where C is a constant value.

Or, alternatively,

$FN_i/FN_j=1 \ \forall_{i,j} = 1$

Where FN_i is the number of false negatives in group i.

Differences in the number of false negatives by group, however, may be relatively limited in measuring equity when the groups are very different in size. If there are twice as many families in Group A as in Group B in the example above, the larger number of false negatives might not be seen as inequitable, which motivates our next metric:

Group Size-Adjusted False Negatives

To account for differently sized groups, one way of phrasing the question of fairness is to ask, "just by virtue of the fact that an individual is a member of a given group, what are the chances they will be missed by the food subsidy?"

While avoiding disparities on this metric focuses on the reasonable goal of treating different groups similarly in terms of classification errors, we may also want to directly consider two subsets within each group: (1) the set of families not receiving the subsidy, and (2) the set of families who would benefit from receiving the subsidy. We take a closer look at each of these cases below.

False Omission Rate

The False Omission Rate (FOR) focuses specifically on people on whom the program doesn't intervene – in our example, the set of families not receiving the food subsidy. Such families will either be true negatives (that is, those not in need of the assistance) or false negatives (that is, those who did need assistance but were missed by the program), and the FOR asks what fraction of this set fall into the latter category.

In practice, the FOR can be a useful metric in many situations, particularly because need can often be more easily measured among individuals not receiving a benefit than among those who do (for instance, when the benefit affects the outcome on which need is measured). However, when resources are constrained such that a program can only reach a relatively small fraction of the population, its utility is more limited. See constrained assistive for more details on this case.

As with the punitive case, there is some nuance in the difference between choosing to focus on group-size adjusted false negatives and the FNR that are worth pointing out:

- ⊙ Having no disparities in group size-adjusted false negatives implies that, if I were to choose a random family from a given group (regardless of group-level nutritional outcomes or their individual need), I would have the same chance of picking out a family missed by the program person across groups.

- ⊙ Having no disparities in FNR implies that, if I were to choose a random family *with need for assistance* from a given group, I would have the same chance of picking out one missed by the subsidy across groups.

- ⊙ Unfortunately, disparities in both of these metrics cannot be eliminated at the same time, except where the level of need is identical across groups or in the generally unrealist case of perfect prediction.

Machine learning fairness

Machine learning fairness is the process of correcting and eliminating algorithmic bias (of race and ethnicity, gender, sexual orientation, disability, and class) from machine learning models. Machine learning is a branch of artificial intelligence (AI) that stems from the idea that computers can learn from data collected to identify patterns and make decisions that mimic those of humans, with minimal human intervention.

Importances to address fairness in machine learning

Unintentional discrimination in machine learning algorithms is just one of the reasons why it's important to address fairness and AI ethics.

Machine learning is enmeshed in the systems and applications we use to help us buy furniture, find jobs, recruit new hires, apply for universities, listen to music, get loans, find news, search on Google, target ads, and so much more. It enhances our ability to streamline information and provide recommendations, but it can have serious consequences if it is trained on the wrong information and fails to promote fair and equal practices.

To remove these potential biases, data scientists and machine learning experts must look out for them in algorithmic models and correct them. Because machine learning by definition learns by example, it can also "learn" to avoid bias as long as it is given the right data. Used in industries as varied as the criminal justice system to corporate human resources to credit lending, it's important that machine learning adopts fair and ethical processes.

Ways to make machine learning fair and ethical

For those working in data science and artificial intelligence with algorithms, there are a few ways to make sure that machine learning is fair and ethical. You can:

- Examine the algorithms' ability to influence human behavior and decide whether it is biased. Then, create algorithmic methods that avoid predictive bias.

- Identify any vulnerabilities or inconsistencies in public data sets, and assess whether there is a privacy violation.

- Utilize tools that can help prevent and eliminate bias in machine learning.

Tools for machine learning fairness

There are plenty of courses, tools, and processes available to help you integrate machine learning fairness into your organization's workflow and prevent machine learning malpractice. Here are a few you can check out:

- **IBM's AI Fairness 360:** A Python toolkit of technical solutions on fairness metrics and algorithms that helps users and researchers share and evaluate discrimination and bias in machine learning models.

- **Google's What-If Tool:** A visualization tool that explores a model's performance on a data set, assessing against preset definitions of fairness constraints. It supports binary classification, multi-class classification, and regression tasks.

- **Google's Model Cards and Toolkit:** This tool confirms that a given model's intent matches its use case and helps users understand the conditions in which their model is safe and appropriate to move forward with.

- **Microsoft's fairlearn.py:** An open-source Python toolkit that assesses and improves fairness in machine learning. With an interactive visualization dashboard and unfairness mitigation algorithms, this tool helps users analyze the trade-offs between fairness and model performance.

⦿ **Deon:** An ethics checklist that facilitates responsible data science by evaluating and systematically reviewing applications for potential ethical implications, from the early stages of data collection to implementation.

Aequitas - A Toolkit for Auditing Bias and Fairness in Machine Learning Models

To help data scientists and policymakers make informed decisions about bias and fairness in their applications, we developed Aequitas, an open source[97] bias and fairness audit toolkit that was released in May 2018. It is an intuitive and easy to use addition to the machine learning workflow, enabling users to seamlessly audit models for several bias and fairness metrics in relation to multiple population sub-groups. Aequitas can be used directly as a Python library, via command line interface or a web application, making it accessible and friendly to a wide range of users (from data scientists to policymakers).

Because the concept of fairness is highly dependent on the particular context and application, Aequitas provides comprehensive information on how its results should be used in a public policy context, taking the resulting interventions and its implications into consideration. It is intended to be used not just by data scientists but also policymakers, through both seamless integration in the machine learning workflow as well as a web app tailored for non-technical users auditing these models' outputs.

In Aequitas, bias assessments can be made prior to model selection, evaluating the disparities of the various models developed based on whatever training data was used to tune it for its task. The audits can be performed prior to a model being operationalized, based on operational data of how biased the model proved to be in holdout data. Or they can involve a bit of both, auditing bias in an A/B testing environment in which limited trials of revised algorithms are evaluated whatever biases were observed in those same systems in prior production deployments.

Aequitas was designed to be used by two types of users:

⦿ Data Scientists and AI Researchers who are building systems for use in risk assessment tools. They will use Aequitas to compare bias measures and check for disparities in different models they are building during the process of model building and selection.

⦿ Policymakers who, before "accepting" an AI system to use in a policy decision, will run Aequitas to understand what biases exist in the system and what (if anything) they need to do in order to mitigate those biases. This process must be repeated periodically to assess the fairness degradation through time of a model in production.

Aequitas in the larger context of the machine learning pipeline. Audits must be carried out internally by data scientists before evaluation and model selection.

Policymakers (or clients) must audit externally before accepting a model in production as well as perform periodic audits to detect any fairness degradation over time.

Figure 8.2 puts Aequitas in the context of the machine learning workflow and shows which type of user and when the audits must be made. The main goal of Aequitas is to standardize the process of understanding model biases. By providing a toolkit for auditing by both data scientists and decision makers, it makes it possible for these different actors to take bias and fairness into consideration at all stages of decision-making in the modeling process: model selection, whether or not to deploy a model, when to retrain, the need to collect more and better data, and so on.

TRANSPARENCY AND EXPLAINABILITY

Transparency in AI refers to the ability to peer into the workings of an AI model and understand how it reaches its decisions. There are many facets of AI transparency, including the set of tools and practices used to understand the model, the data it is trained on, the process of categorizing the types and frequency of errors and biases, and the ways of communicating these issues to developers and users.

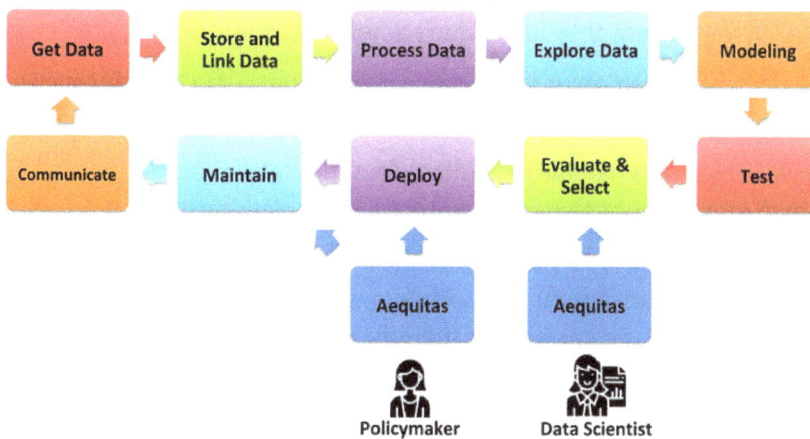

Fig. 8.2: ML pipeline

The multiple facets of AI transparency have come to the forefront as machine learning models have evolved. A big concern is that more powerful or efficient models are harder - if not impossible - to understand since the inner workings are buried in a so-called black box.

Basically, humans find it hard to trust a black box - and understandably so, partner and chief data scientist at business transformation advisory firm Lotis Blue Consulting. "AI has a spotty record on delivering unbiased decisions or outputs."

AI transparency is about clearly explaining the reasoning behind the output, making the decision-making process accessible and comprehensible. At the end of the day, it's about eliminating the black box mystery of AI and providing insight into the how and why of AI decision-making.

Trust, auditability, compliance and understanding potential biases are some of the fundamental reasons why transparency is becoming a requirement in the field of AI. "Without transparency, we risk creating AI systems that could inadvertently perpetuate harmful biases, make inscrutable decisions or even lead to undesirable outcomes in high-risk applications," Masood said.

Working with explainability and interpretability

AI transparency works hand in hand with related concepts like AI explainability and interpretability, but they are not the same.

AI transparency helps ensure that all stakeholders can clearly understand the workings of an AI system, including how it makes decisions and processes data. "Having this clarity is what builds trust in AI, particularly in high-risk applications," Masood said.

By contrast, explainability focuses on providing understandable reasons for the decisions made by an AI system. Interpretability refers to the predictability of a model's outputs based on its inputs. So, while explainability and interpretability are crucial in achieving AI transparency, they alone don't wholly encompass it.

AI transparency also involves being open about data handling, the model's limitations, potential biases and the context of its usage.

Process transparency entails providing documentation and logging of significant decisions made throughout the development and implementation of a system. And it includes the structure of governance and testing practices.

Data and system transparency entails communicating to users or relevant parties that an AI or automated system will use their data. It also alerts users when they directly engage with an AI like a chatbot.

AI explainability and transparency are not easy to achieve, especially for complex and high-dimensional models, such as deep neural networks. Some of the challenges include: the trade-off between accuracy and interpretability, the diversity of stakeholders and their needs, the lack of standards and metrics, the risk of revealing sensitive or proprietary information, and the scalability and usability of explanation methods. Moreover, AI explainability and transparency are not static, but dynamic and contextual, depending on the data, the model, the task, and the situation.

AI explainability and transparency are not only desirable, but also necessary for several reasons. First, they can improve the performance and reliability of AI systems, by enabling developers to debug, optimize, and validate their models. Second, they can enhance the user experience and trust, by allowing users to understand, interact, and control AI outputs. Third, they can foster ethical and responsible AI, by ensuring that AI models comply with legal, social, and moral norms, and that they can be held accountable for their actions.

Explainable artificial intelligence (XAI) refers to a collection of procedures and techniques that enable machine learning algorithms to produce output and results that are understandable and reliable for human users. Explainable AI is a key component of the fairness, accountability, and transparency (FAT) machine learning paradigm and is frequently discussed in connection with deep learning. Organizations looking to establish trust when deploying AI can benefit from XAI. XAI can assist them in comprehending the behavior of an AI model and identifying possible problems like AI (Fig. 8.3).

The need for explainable AI

The need for explainable AI arises from the fact that traditional machine learning models are often difficult to understand and interpret. These models are typically black boxes that make predictions based on input data but do not provide any insight into the reasoning behind their predictions. This lack of transparency and interpretability can be a major limitation of traditional machine learning models and can lead to a range of problems and challenges.

One major challenge of traditional machine learning models is that they can be difficult to trust and verify. Because these models are opaque and inscrutable, it can be difficult for humans to understand how they work and how they make predictions. This lack of trust and understanding can make it difficult for people to use and rely on these models and can limit their adoption and deployment.

Overall, the need for explainable AI arises from the challenges and limitations of traditional machine learning models, and from the need for more transparent and interpretable models that are trustworthy, fair, and accountable. Explainable AI approaches aim to address these challenges and limitations, and to provide more transparent and interpretable machine-learning models that can be understood and trusted by humans.

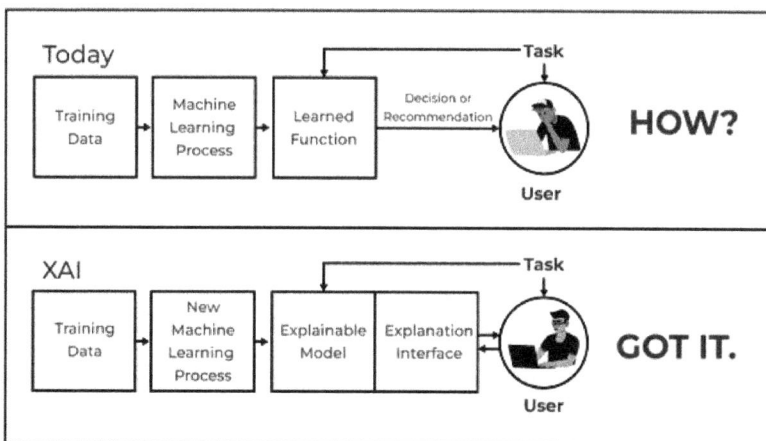

Fig. 8.3 Explainable Artificial Intelligence Concept

Strategies for AI explainability and transparency

When it comes to AI explainability and transparency, there is no one-size-fits-all solution. Rather, there are a variety of approaches and techniques that can be applied depending on the problem and the goal. Designing explainable and transparent models from scratch is one such strategy, which can be achieved by using simpler or more modular architectures, incorporating human knowledge or feedback, or adding explanation layers or modules. Post-hoc explanation methods can also be used to generate visual or textual explanations of model behavior or outcomes.

Additionally, interactive and adaptive explanation systems can be developed by allowing users to query, manipulate, or influence the model, or providing personalized or contextualized explanations based on user preferences or profiles. Finally, it's important to evaluate and improve explanation quality and impact by using quantitative or qualitative methods, such as metrics, surveys, or experiments to measure effectiveness, validity, and satisfaction of explanations, or by using feedback loops or reinforcement learning to update the model or the explanation.

Examples of AI explainability and transparency

AI explainability and transparency are not only theoretical concepts, but also practical applications that can make a difference in various domains and scenarios. For instance, in healthcare, an AI system can explain diagnosis or treatment recommendations to patients or doctors, as well as detect and correct errors or biases in medical image analysis or drug discovery. In finance, an AI system can explain credit score or loan approval to customers or regulators, while also detecting and preventing fraud or money laundering.

Education is another area where AI explainability and transparency can be applied; for example, an AI system can explain learning progress or performance to students or teachers, as well as provide personalized or adaptive feedback or guidance. Lastly, in security, an AI system can explain threat detection or response to operators or authorities while ensuring the privacy and security of the data and the model.

Resources for learning more about AI explainability and transparency

Exploring AI explainability and transparency is an active and evolving research area, with many publications, projects, and tools available for learning more. For instance, there are books such as Interpretable Machine Learning by Christoph Molnar, Explainable AI: Interpreting, Explaining and Visualizing Deep Learning by Wojciech Samek et al., and The Myth of Artificial Intelligence by Erik Larson.

Additionally, journals like the Artificial Intelligence Journal, Machine Learning Journal, and IEEE Transactions on Pattern Analysis and Machine Intelligence are great resources. Conferences like the International Conference on Machine Learning, Neural Information Processing Systems, and ACM Conference on Fairness, Accountability, and Transparency are also helpful. Lastly, websites such as Explainable AI, LIME, and SHAP provide valuable information.

PRIVACY CONCERNS AND DATA SECURITY

Artificial Intelligence (AI) has carved its niche in almost every domain, from entertainment to healthcare. Its transformative capabilities are undeniable. However, with great power comes great responsibility, and the integration of AI brings forth significant challenges, particularly concerning data privacy and security. Have a look at examples explaining the various challenges.

1. Data Breaches due to Weak AI Security Protocols

⊙ *Before AI:* Traditional data breaches typically targeted static databases or systems.

⊙ *The AI Challenge:* AI models, especially those deployed in cloud environments, can become lucrative targets for hackers. A breach in an AI system can compromise vast amounts of sensitive data, impacting both individuals and organizations.

2. Bias in AI Algorithms

⊙ *Before AI:* Human biases in decision-making have always been a concern.

⊙ *The AI Challenge:* AI systems are only as good as the data they're trained on. If this data contains biases, the AI models can perpetuate or even exacerbate these biases, leading to skewed and unjust outcomes.

3. Inadequate Data Anonymization

⊙ *Before AI:* Data anonymity meant removing overt identifiers like names and addresses.

⊙ *The AI Challenge:* Advanced AI algorithms can sometimes de-anonymize data, revealing the identities of individuals from seemingly anonymous datasets. This poses serious privacy concerns.

4. Dependence on Large Data Sets

⊙ *Before AI:* Data collection was often limited to necessary information.

⊙ *The AI Challenge:* The efficacy of many AI models improves with more data, leading companies to hoard vast amounts of user information, sometimes without clear consent, leading to privacy issues.

5. Vulnerability to Adversarial Attacks

⊙ *Before AI:* Traditional systems faced threats from malware or direct hacking attempts.

- ⊙ *The AI Challenge:* AI systems can be compromised through adversarial attacks, where slight, often imperceptible alterations to input data can cause the AI to malfunction or make incorrect predictions.

6. Data Transfer and Storage Concerns

- ⊙ *Before AI:* Data was often stored in local, physical databases.
- ⊙ *The AI Challenge:* AI's integration with cloud platforms means data is regularly transferred and stored online. This raises concerns about data interception during transfer and vulnerabilities in cloud storage.

7. Misuse of Personalized AI

- ⊙ *Before AI:* Personalization was often limited to user settings and preferences.
- ⊙ *The AI Challenge:* AI's ability to curate highly personalized experiences can lead to over-personalization, where users feel their privacy is invaded, or their data is used without explicit consent.

8. AI-Powered Surveillance Overreach

- ⊙ *Before AI:* Surveillance primarily relied on human monitoring, limiting the scope and potential for misuse.
- ⊙ *The AI Challenge:* With the advent of AI-powered surveillance tools, there's an increased risk of unwarranted mass surveillance. These systems can recognize faces, analyze patterns, and track individuals, potentially leading to invasions of privacy and misuse of power, especially without proper regulation.

9. Phishing Attacks with AI-generated Content

- ⊙ *Before AI:* Phishing attacks involved generic deceptive messages crafted by fraudsters.
- ⊙ *The AI Challenge:* Advanced AI tools can craft highly personalized phishing messages that are tailored to specific individuals, making these attacks more convincing and harder to detect. These AI-driven phishing campaigns can dupe users into revealing sensitive information or performing unintended actions.

10. Lack of Transparency in AI Decisions

- ⊙ *Before AI:* Most decision-making systems, though complex, were relatively transparent and could be audited.
- ⊙ *The AI Challenge:* Many AI models, especially deep learning systems, are "black boxes", meaning their decision-making processes aren't easily interpretable. This lack of transparency can lead to trust issues, especially when users aren't sure how their data is being used or processed.

CHAPTER-9

FUTURE TRENDS AND INNOVATIONS

INTRODUCTION

Artificial intelligence is beginning to surpass human-level performance in many situations. To have the option to use these fully leverage in delicate domain completely, the opaqueness of the models needs to be reduced. For example, while using artificial intelligence to help medical experts, language models that interact with medical records to classify sicknesses also need to have the option to output clarifications supporting their cases to be useful. A majority part of respondents shares this opinion in a global CEO study conducted by PwC, where results point to the consensus critical significance of opening up black-box models altogether to involve them in areas, for example, for medical determinations and self-driving vehicles. Using black-box models in high-risk application areas is undesirable, and XAI is broadly viewed as an essential feature.

Explainable artificial intelligence (XAI) is a set of processes and methods that allows human users to comprehend and trust the results and output created by machine learning algorithms.

Explainable AI is used to describe an AI model, its expected impact and potential biases. It helps characterize model accuracy, fairness, transparency and outcomes in AI-powered decision making. Explainable AI is crucial for an organization in building trust and confidence when putting AI models into production. AI explainability also helps an organization adopt a responsible approach to AI development.

As AI becomes more advanced, humans are challenged to comprehend and retrace how the algorithm came to a result. The whole calculation process is turned into what is commonly referred to as a "black box" that is impossible to interpret.

These black box models are created directly from the data. And, not even the engineers or data scientists who create the algorithm can understand or explain what exactly is happening inside them or how the AI algorithm arrived at a specific result.

There are many advantages to understanding how an AI-enabled system has led to a specific output. Explainability can help developers ensure that the system is working as expected, it might be necessary to meet regulatory standards, or it might be important in allowing those affected by a decision to challenge or change that outcome.

EXPLAINABLE AI(XAI)

Explainable AI collectively refers to techniques or methods, which help explain a given AI model's decision-making process. This newly found branch of AI has shown enormous potential, with newer and more sophisticated techniques coming each year. Some of the most famous XAI techniques include SHAP (Shapley Additive exPlanations), DeepSHAP, DeepLIFT, CXplain, and LIME.

Explainability and Interpretability

In a survey by researchers, Explainability and interpretability are portrayed as distinguished concepts. The creators recommend using Explainability while referring to the fulfilment of the result when the model reaction is joined by thinking close about its prediction. In this specific situation, fulfilment alludes to if every one of the applicable pieces of the info is remembered for clarification (note that this is, in some cases, referred to as extensiveness).

Interpretability is recommended when the nature of the clarification depends on how a human interprets it. With this thinking, the creators contend that Explainability can be estimated straightforwardly, contrasting outcomes using a measurement (for example, cross-over-based measurements like IOU, BLEU, or ROUGE). Interpretability - because of its emotional nature - requires a predetermined setting for it to be estimated, for example, the experience of the human specialist.

To incorporate an alternate point of view in their ExNLP review, Luo et al. propose using Explainability and interpretability reciprocally due to how the ideas are accepted and utilized in the field. The definition they give is that it is the ability to make sense of predictions reasonably for people.

Researchers give one more definition, which is intently related, with the distinction that they characterize Explainability as comprising both how people can perceive forecasts and how they can give an understanding of the model. In this work, Explainability will be utilized solely when alluding to the nature of clarifications. As to explainability strategies, there is a qualification to be made whether to think about clarifications of the model's intrinsic prescient interaction or clarifications of detailed forecasts specifically.

Worldwide clarifications allude to the previous, fully intent on uncovering the inward functions of a model, paying little mind to include. In this class, we incorporate models that convey Explainability by plan, which is the situation with, e.g., choice trees and decide-based frameworks that comprise calculations that learn coherent contrasts between information. Examining these consistent standards, a worldwide model clarification can be extricated. Neighborhood clarifications, then again, are characterized as giving thinking to yields given explicit data sources.

This is accomplished by either hard scoring or delicate scoring. The explainability techniques assessed in this venture were both delicate scorings, which implies that they produce loads for input tokens. This is rather than hard scoring techniques, which yield a straightforward determination of tokens or words.

EDGE COMPUTING AND AL AT THE EDGE

Edge Technology aims at making Internet of Things (IOT) with 100 thousand of sensors in next decade, with the increased usage and manipulation of large data it becomes important to get used to this technology which refers to computing on sensor itself. 2019 is predicted as the year of edge technology and will remain so in the coming years. In a variety of situations, edge computing is deployed. One is when IOT devices is centrally connected to cloud due to poor connectivity of devices. By the year 2020, there will be approximately 1.5 GB worth of data is generated per day. With many devices connected to the internet and generating data, its not possible for cloud alone to handle this huge data all by itself.

Edge can relate to the data processing as well as the local processing of real-time data. The various edge components that can be counted upon are Data processing, Rule Engine, Local Database.

Cloud is more concerned with big data processing and data warehousing.

Why Edge Computing?

- ⊙ This technology increases the efficient usage of bandwidth by analyzing the data at the edges itself, unlike the cloud which requires the transfer of data from the IOT requiring large bandwidth, making it useful to be used in remote locations with minimum cost.

- ⊙ It allows smart applications and devices to respond to data almost at the same time which is important in terms of business ad self-driving cars.

- ⊙ It has the ability to process data without even putting it on a public cloud, this ensures full security.

- ⊙ Data might get corrupt while on an extended network thus affecting the data reliability for the industries to use.

- ⊙ Edge computation of data provides a limitation to the use of cloud.

Edge vs Fog Computing: Edge is more specific towards computational processes for edge devices. So, fog includes edge computing, but would also include the network for the processed data to its final destination.

Fig. 9.1 Edge Computing

Real Life Application Of Edge Technology

- **Autonomous Vehicles –** GE Digital partner, Intel, estimates that autonomous cars, with hundreds of on-vehicle sensors, will generate 40 TB of data for every eight hours of driving. Therefore, wheels—edge computing plays a dominant role. Sending all the data to cloud is unsafe and impractical. The car immediately response to the events which has valuable data when coupled into digital twin and performance of other cars of its class.

- **Fleet Management –** Let's example considering a trucking company, the main goal is to combine and send data from multiple operational data points like wheels, brakes, batteries, etc to the cloud. Health key operational components are analysed by the cloud. Thus, essentially a fleet management solution encourages the vehicle to lower the cost.

Key Benefits of Edge Computing

- Faster response time.
- Security and Compliance.
- Cost-effective Solution.
- Reliable Operation With Intermittent Connectivity.
- Reduced latency

Limitation of Edge Computing:

- **Complexity:** Setting up and maintaining edge computing systems can be challenging, especially if there are many devices or a vast geographic region involved.

- **Limited resources:** Edge devices frequently have constrained processing, storage, and bandwidth, which can restrict their capacity to carry out specific activities.

- **Dependence on connectivity:** In order for edge computing to work correctly, connectivity is required. If the connection is lost, the system may not be able to work.

- **Security Concern:** Edge devices may be susceptible to security risks such malware, hacking, and physical interference.

Edge Cloud Computing Services

- IOT (Internet Of Things)
- Gaming
- Health Care
- Smart City
- Intelligent Transportation
- Enterprise Security

Edge Computing Benefits and Challenges

Edge computing helps minimize bandwidth usage and server resources. Bandwidth and cloud resources are limited and expensive. According to Statista, more than 75 billion IoT devices will be installed worldwide by 2025. Supporting all these devices requires moving a lot of computing to the edge.

One of the biggest benefits of moving processes to the edge is low latency. Each time a device needs to communicate with a remote server, there is a delay. By avoiding the need to communicate with that remote server, edge computing achieves much lower latency.

Edge computing can also provide new capabilities not previously available. For example, businesses can use edge computing to process and analyze data at the edge to allow real-time processing.

Downsides of edge computing include new attack vectors. The mix of IoT devices with hardened embedded computers, and the growing variety of smart devices, such as edge servers, create new opportunities for malicious attackers to compromise these devices.

Another disadvantage is that edge computing requires more expensive and complex local hardware. For example, IoT cameras require an onboard computer to send raw video data to a web server, but require a more sophisticated computer with more processing power to run their own motion detection algorithms.

Edge Computing and IoT

The Internet of Things (IoT) refers to the process of connecting physical objects to the Internet. IoT refers to a physical device or hardware system that sends and receives data over a network without human intervention. A typical IoT system works by continuously sending, receiving, and analyzing data in a feedback loop. Analytics can be performed by humans or artificial intelligence and machine learning (AI/ML) algorithms in near real-time, or in batches over an extended period of time.

Edge computing occurs at or near the physical location of users or data sources. By placing computing services closer to these locations, users can enjoy faster, more reliable services and better user experiences, and businesses can better support latency-sensitive applications to identify trends and deliver better products and services.

In the context of IoT, edge computing can place computing power closer to where the physical device or data source actually resides. In order to allow IoT devices to respond more quickly and mitigate issues, analytics should be done at the edge, rather than returning to a central site for analysis.

Edge AI

Edge AI is a combination of edge computing and artificial intelligence (AI). This involves running AI algorithms on local devices with edge computing capabilities. Edge AI does not require connectivity and integration between systems, allowing users to process data in real time on their devices.

Most AI processes today run on cloud-based hubs, because they require significant computing power. The downside is that network issues can cause service downtime or slow down AI services significantly. Edge AI addresses these challenges by making AI processing an integral part of edge computing devices. This saves time, aggregating data and serving users without having to communicate with other physical locations.

Architecture Components of Edge Computing

An edge computing architecture consists of an ecosystem of distributed infrastructure components, spanning an enterprise data center or central server location and multiple edge locations. The ecosystem includes computing and storage equipment, applications, devices, sensors, and network connectivity to a central data center or cloud.

Devices and sensors are where information is collected, processed, or both. Bandwidth, memory, processing power and capabilities, and computing resources are sufficient to collect, process and process data in real time without the help of the rest of the network. Some kind of connection to the network allows communication between the device and the database from a central location.

A scaled-down, on-premises edge server or data center can be easily moved and scaled to a smaller remote location. Flexibility and scalability are critical as your company's needs evolve. Flexible topology options can accommodate smaller footprints or varying environmental requirements, including intermittent network connections.

QUANTUM COMPUTING AND AL

Quantum Computing is the process of using quantum-mechanics for solving complex and massive operations quickly and efficiently. As classical computers are used for performing classical computations, similarly, a Quantum computer is used for performing Quantum computations. Quantum Computations are too complex to solve that it becomes almost impossible to solve them with classical computers. The word 'Quantum' is derived from the concept of Quantum Mechanics in Physics that describes the physical properties of the nature of electrons and photons.

Quantum is the fundamental framework for deeply describing and understanding nature. Thus, it is the reason that quantum calculations deal with complexity. Quantum Computing is a subfield of Quantum Information Science. It describes the best way of dealing with a complicated computation. Quantum-mechanics is based on the phenomena of superposition and entanglement, which are used to perform the quantum computations.

For performing Quantum calculations, a Quantum Computer is used that is dissimilar to a classical computer. Although the concept of quantum computing came earlier, it didn't gain much popularity then.

Superposition and Entanglement

◉ **Superposition:** A Quantum deals with the smallest particles found in nature, i.e., electrons and photons. These three particles are known as Quantum particles. In this, superposition defines the ability of a quantum system to be present in multiple states (one or more) at the same time.

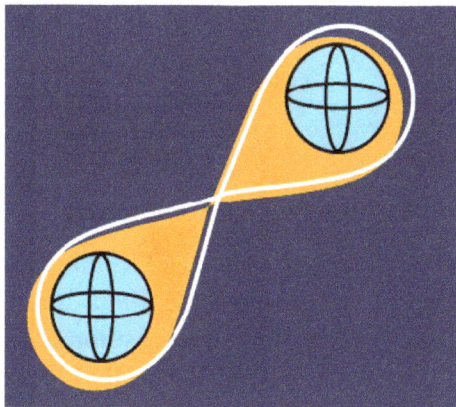

Fig. 9.2 Entanglement

In a quantum Computer, a qubit can exist in a superposition of states. For example, it is able to constitute both 0 and 1 concurrently. This property permits quantum computers to assess a couple of opportunities at the same time. A common analogy is that it's like having a spinning coin. It, without a doubt, is each head and tail till measured.

- ◉ **Entanglement:** Entanglement defines a very strong correlation between the quantum particles. These particles are so strongly linked that even if we place one particle at one end of the universe and one at the other end, both of them dance instantaneously.

Entanglement occurs while qubits become correlated. If you have entangled qubits, measuring one right now determines the country of the opportunity, no matter the space among them. For example, if one qubit is measured as "up," the other is confident to be "down." This belonging is regularly defined as "spooky movement at a distance."

Quantum Computer

A quantum computer is a computer that leverages the principles of quantum mechanics to approach statistics distinctly compared to classical computer structures. Instead of the use of classical bits (0s and 1s), quantum computer structures use quantum bits or qubits, which can exist in superposition and be entangled with exceptional qubits.

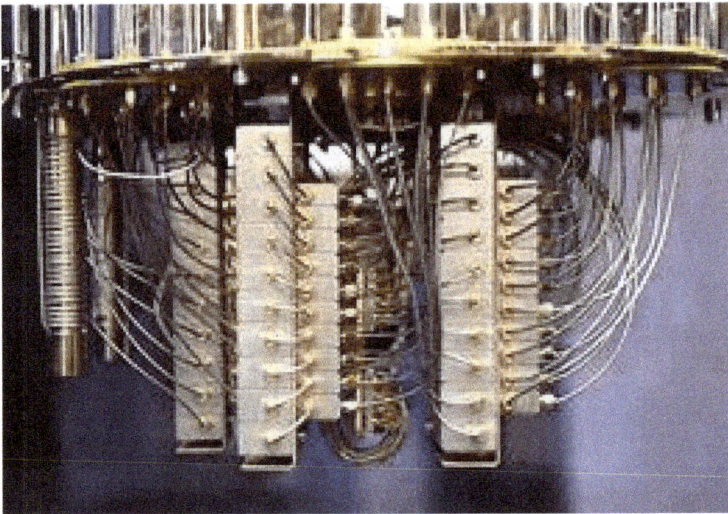

Fig. 9.3 Quantum Computer

Example: Imagine you're fixing a complicated optimization hassle. In classical computing, you would look at one answer at a time. In quantum computing, you could evaluate many answers right now to superposition. Entanglement lets in qubits to artwork collectively in ways that classical bits cannot, potentially locating the fine solution an entire lot faster.

Quantum computers are particularly promising for applications like cryptography, drug discovery, and complex simulations where exploring numerous possibilities simultaneously can lead to significant speed-ups. Currently, researchers are working with Quantum computers in the field of cybersecurity to break codes and encrypt electronic communications to explore better cybersecurity and protected data.

Quantum Bits

Quantum bits, or qubits, are the essential gadgets of statistics in quantum computing. Unlike classical bits that may be either 0 or 1, qubits can exist in a superposition of each zero and 1 concurrently. These specific belongings allow quantum computers to method multiple opportunities in parallel, making them particularly effective for fixing complicated troubles and performing specialized responsibilities in diverse fields. When two qubits of a pair are placed at a far distance, and if the state of one qubit changes, the state of the other will instantaneously change in a predictable manner. A connected group of quantum bits or qubits has much more power than the same binary digit number.

Challenges to overcome in creating a quantum computer

The benefits of quantum computers bring extraordinary advantages, but are equally difficult to maintain. The superposition state produces performance, but it is not stable. To make them stable and manage them, physicists apply many methods - including microwave or laser beams -, need to control the temperature and ensure that there is no interaction of any kind with the working environment.

Fig. 9.4 - Google's Sycamore quantum computer processor was recently at the center of a hotly debate wormhole simulation. Image credits:

With this low resistance to the environment, quantum computers are difficult to maintain. A small difference in one of the elements can jeopardize the entire operation. The process by which dissipation occurs is known as "decoherence".

In short, the more stable the qubits, the more computing power is generated. However, as we increase the number of qubits, the environment becomes more unstable and difficult to control.

At the moment, the most important applications of quantum computing concern the behavior of matter, chemistry and the discovery of materials. But it will take time to understand how we can extend its usefulness. At the current stage of development, our capacity is too limited to imagine the applications in the near future.

Future of Quantum Computing

The future of Quantum Computing seems quite enhanced and productive for world trade. The above-discussed points tell that it is the beginning of the concept and will surely become a part of our life. It is not the mainstream yet. In the future, the quantum systems will enable the industries to tackle those problems, which they always thought impossible to solve. According to reports, the market of quantum computing will grow strongly in the coming decades. Google is showing a great focus and interest in the theory of quantum computing.

Recently, Google has launched a new version of TensorFlow, which is TensorFlow Quantum (TFQ). TFQ is an open-source library. It is used to prototype quantum machine learning models. When it will be developed, it will enable developers to easily create hybrid AI algorithms that will allow the integration of techniques of a quantum computer and a classical computer. The main motive of TFQ is to bring quantum computing and machine learning techniques together to evenly build and control natural as well as artificial quantum computers. Scientists are still facing some new and known challenges with quantum computing, but it will surely lead to software development in the coming years.

INTERDISCIPLINARY APPLICATIONS AND AL ETHICS

Interdisciplinary approach means that people from different scientific fields join forces to address a specific problem. Creative collaboration in exploring and developing artificial intelligence commonly occurs between technical and natural sciences. In biochemistry, AI assists in mapping the 3D structures of human proteins, thereby significantly contributing to disease research and enabling more efficient drug design. In astronomy, AI is used in discovering new objects in the universe. Similarly, in meteorology, AI is harnessed to enhance the precision of weather forecasting.

AI draws on a range of fields, including computer science, mathematics, statistics, psychology, neuroscience, philosophy, and linguistics. To develop AI systems, experts from these fields collaborate to design algorithms, develop models, and train machines to perform specific tasks.

Ethics in AI

Ethics is a philosophical study about moral concepts of good and evil. Ethics in terms of AI is a concept that one need to abide by learning the boundaries of development which includes:

- **Transparency:** The decisions and actions performed by the Artificial Intelligence must be transparent to the humans. Users should be able to understand the internal processions done by AI to get the result. The adaptability of AI is negligible, nevertheless its exceptional knowledge in its trained domain, there is a high possibility of errors that requires transparency to be able to resolve it through human intervention.

- **Security**: AI often deals with sensitive data and performs several operations that relies on the collected data, raising the concerns of data and privacy infringement. Therefore, data security and protection of personal details of a user mustn't be exploited rather preserved throughout the cycle of AI from the collection to the usage.

- **Bias and Fairness:** AI systems can inherit biases from the data they are trained on, leading to unfair or discriminatory outcomes. Such errors must be mitigated by abiding fairness. minimizing bias, stereotypes across demographics, and ensuring equitable treatment for all individuals regardless of their race, gender, ethnicity, age, sexual orientation, or any other characteristic.

- **Responsibility:** AI must ensure accountability for any inherent biases or errors. The developers and deployers must ensure responsibility for its training or design. The users must be responsible for their actions and implementations using AI.

- **Safety:** Since AI is integrated to our lives in every aspect, the development of AI must be carried out by prioritizing safety and evaluation, such that, there is no harm to any factors. The stakeholders and users must be responsible for its safe use.

Ethical challenges of AI

- **Opacity:** Opacity is a key ethical challenge in AI, as AI systems often operate as black boxes, making it difficult for users and stakeholders to understand how decisions are made or why certain outcomes are produced. Lack of transparency usually leads to other challenges such as bias, fairness, etc.

- **Attacks and breaches:** AI is prone to adversarial attacks and since AI solely relies on data, there is a high scope for cyber-attack leads and data breaches. To prevent these, a secure mechanism is cyber-attack *leads* required to safeguard the sensitive data and to promote a secure AI.

- **Algorithmic biases:** Biases present in training data or algorithmic decision-making processes can result in unfair or discriminatory outcomes. Such biased data leads to underrepresentation or overrepresentation which in turn concludes an unethical AI.

- ⊙ **Ethical Accountability:** A minor crept or error in an AI technology can lead to problems such as biases, discrimination, privacy violations, and safety hazards, it is required for a user, stakeholder, deployer or a developer to take the responsibility that involves addressing the ethical dilemmas, concerns, and issues that arise from the development, deployment, and use of AI technologies.

- ⊙ **Risk Management:** Various risks rise during the development, deployment of AI such as system failures, errors, or unintended consequences and addressing these challenges requires careful consideration of safety risks, robust risk management strategies, and the implementation of safety measures to promote the safe use of AI technologies.

The AI Code of Ethics

- ⊙ **Openness and Disclosure:** Transparency in AI refers to a sense of openness of the actions and operations performed by the machine. As per 'Code of Ethics', the provisions of transparency helps the user or developer to understand the actions and decisions taken by the AI internally.

- ⊙ **Data Security Standards:** A secure AI leads to integrity, confidentiality, and availability of AI systems and data. The 'Code of Ethics' provisions include access control and authentication mechanisms to enable security. By prioritizing security in AI, stakeholders can mitigate risks, safeguard user privacy, and ensure the trustworthiness and reliability of AI systems.

- ⊙ **Equity and Unbiased Decision-Making:** Addressing bias and promoting fairness is essential to ensure that AI technologies are developed, deployed, and used in an ethical and responsible manner. The 'Code of Ethics' emphasizes the importance of mitigating biases in AI algorithms and data to prevent unfair or discriminatory outcomes.

- ⊙ **Ethical Responsibilities:** Responsibility refers to the ethical and legal obligations of individuals, organizations, and stakeholders involved in the development, deployment, and use of AI technologies. It refers to the importance of taking accountability for the outcomes and impacts of AI systems.

- ⊙ **Safety and Well-being:** The **'Code of Ethics'** emphasizes the importance of assessing and mitigating potential risks and hazards associated with AI systems, such as system failures, errors, or unintended consequences, to minimize harm and ensure safety of AI technologies.

Implementation of 'Ethics of AI'

While a developer learns the 'Ethics of AI', its crucial for them to address various techniques to mitigate the potential risks and learn how to prevent any unethical errors. The following are the strategies for the management of the 'Ethics of AI':

- ◉ **Strategies to implement Transparency:** The developers can implement transparency in AI by developing tools that helps the AI to explain its decisions and actions. Furthermore , one can develop an AI model that interprets itself, by default. Monitoring and documenting the development process or actions can help us to understand the system's behavior and report if any discrepancies arise.

- ◉ **Strategies to implement Security:** Encrypting any sensitive information is the key to safety that prevents any unauthorized access to the data. Additionally, a developer can apply robust access control mechanisms to handle the permissions and access to specific individuals or they can involve ethical and secure development practices during the training of the model.

- ◉ **Strategies to implement Bias and fairness:** It is required to assess any kind of bias present in the data by proper preprocessing before providing it to the machine. A diverse data sample must be chosen to avoid any kind of underrepresentation. The model must be evaluated to check the fairness and mitigate any risk of potential bias prior to deployment.

- ◉ **Strategies to implement Responsibility:** A set of guidelines must be formed that incorporates principles like privacy, transparency, security, etc., and every developer must adhere to these rules as well as must be educated about risks. A developer must integrate ethical considerations while building an AI model.

- ◉ **Strategies to implement Safety:** The developers need to develop an AI model by following all the ethical guidelines. There must be rigorous validation and testing to mitigate any risk. In case, if there occurs any error, it is suggested to have fall-safe mechanisms to avoid further destruction. After the development, there must be regular monitoring and assessments recordings to evaluate the condition and mitigate any future errors.

Importance of AI Ethics

It is crucial to educate ourselves about every minor detail of any technology, similarly, its essential for us to learn about AI, its working and the impact, this booming technology has on the economy. The following helps us to understand about the importance of AI The well being of the individuals living in the economy is extremely crucial and this must be prioritized while building any technology by educating ourselves about the ethical guidelines and boundaries of development. Any potential harm or risks must be prevented to protect the well-being of the humanity. The ethical guidelines helps the developers to choose the diverse data samples that helps to mitigate any bias or underrepresentation and minimizes negative impacts on the users.

An AI model built on the adherence of all the ethical guidelines is much more trustable among the users. This trust evolves due to transparency, privacy and security concerning the user. Therefore, such technology is promoted by them and AI or any other modern technologies would have sustainable development and world wide adoption for years.

Create and promote more ethical AI

- ◉ It is indeed necessary to create and promote more ethical AI which therefore contributes in further advantages. It is the responsibility of developers and deployers to take up the responsibility of an ethical AI and be accountable of the consequences.

- ◉ **Ethical Guidelines:** Ethical Guidelines refers to a set of regulations that defines the boundaries of development, that deployers and developers need to abide so as to create a more defined form of ethical AI.

- ◉ **Bias Mitigation:** The developer need to acquire a high-quality dataset and check for any bias, underrepresentation or overrepresentation of any and mitigate them. This involves conducting bias assessments, audits and promote fairness.

- ◉ **User Consent and Control:** Since AI relies heavily on data and such sensitive data is obtained from organizations and users, it is required to ask for consent and apply privacy-preserving mechanisms so as to protect their information from any threats or crept.

- ◉ **Ethical Design Principles:** A developer need to create more ethical AI by integrating ethical guidelines, later evaluate to detect any risks and mitigate them beforehand.

- ◉ **Accountability Mechanisms:** Mechanisms that ensure the individuals and organizations are held responsible for the behavior and consequences of AI need to be implemented.

Future of AI ethics

The future of AI ethics is promising to provide ethical guidelines to promote ethical AI. The following contain the key aspects of how future of AI looks:

Advancements in Ethical AI Research: Continued research and development efforts that include developing new algorithms, techniques, and methodologies have the capability of advancing the process of creating ethical AI and ensures responsible development of AI.

Regulatory and Policy Frameworks: Governments, regulatory bodies, and international organizations will play a crucial role in developing and implementing regulatory and policy frameworks to govern the ethical use of AI. This includes promotion of ethical guidelines of responsible and accountable creation of ethical AI.

Ethical Considerations in Emerging AI Applications: As AI technologies are applied in new and emerging domains, there will be a growing need to address ethical considerations for the development of AI applications.

CHAPTER-10

CASE STUDIES AND REAL-WORLD APPLICATIONS

Case studies and real-world applications are useful tools for understanding the effectiveness of theoretical concepts and real-world scenarios. They can help working professionals apply theoretical knowledge to practical situations, enhance critical thinking, and offer experiential learning. Case studies are also useful for students to develop analytical skills and apply their skills to real-world situations. They are especially useful in complex situations where solutions are uncertain.

HEALTHCARE

The integration of AI in healthcare has resulted in expedited diagnosis, personalized care, and predictive analytics. In particular, medical imaging has witnessed a revolutionary shift due to AI capabilities in image recognition and interpretation.

Early Detection of Adolescent Idiopathic Scoliosis

AI and deep learning based on convolutional neural networks (CNN) have been used to help doctors analyze scoliosis patients. The CNN architecture was proposed to detect the location of spinal vertebrae from X-ray images to evaluate the Cobb angle automatically. The proposed method can measure Cobb angles with up to 93.6% accuracy and has excellent reliability compared to manual clinician measurements, making it usable in real-world clinical settings. The method also reduces diagnostic time, leading to faster interventions to treat patients better. Successful integration may encourage other healthcare institutions to explore similar AI-based diagnostic solutions.

Diagnosis of Breast Cancer on Mammograms

Breast cancer is a significant health problem for women globally. Early detection is essential for effective prevention and treatment. A traditional mammogram, an X-ray image of the breast, helps spot the early signs of this cancer. AI can be applied to segmenting areas detected as cancer on mammograms. AI can also help improve image quality and find anomalous patterns. AI is changing the way breast cancer is detected, making the process faster and often more precise. However, AI in medicine can be a tool, not a substitute for human expertise. A doctor and radiologist can do it for further detection and decision-making.

Drug Discovery and Development

Drug discovery and development is a long and expensive process. With AI, this process gets a significant boost. AI algorithms analyze extensive data sets to identify potential drug candidates by predicting how different compounds might interact with biological pathways. So, instead of the traditional trial and error method, researchers can now start by focusing only on the most promising compounds. In addition, AI can help predict potential side effects, making the drug development process safer. AI streamlines and optimizes the journey from the lab to the pharmacy shelf, potentially getting effective drugs to patients faster and more affordably.

Natural Language Processing (NLP) for Medical Records

Medical records often contain large amounts of unstructured text, ranging from doctor's notes to patient histories. NLP, a branch of AI, is designed to understand, interpret, and extract meaningful information from such texts. In the context of medical records, NLP algorithms sift through data, identifying important details such as diagnosis, treatment, and patient outcomes. NLP helps in efficient patient management and research, which provides information for medical studies and strategies. NLP transforms seas of text in medical records into actionable information, improving patient care and healthcare research.

FINAANCE

AI has played a critical role in tackling complex challenges in finance, such as fraud detection and risk assessment. The high volume of financial transactions every day makes manual fraud detection nearly impossible. Financial institutions face a constant battle against ever-evolving fraud techniques. Traditional systems are often reactive, identifying fraud after it has occurred. Financial entities can proactively detect and deter suspicious activity with AI predictive analytics.

Fraud Detection in Real-Time Payment Systems

In a real-time payment system, fraud detection must be instantaneous. Traditional approaches often fail to keep up with this speed and transaction volume. AI methods, such as deep learning, are trained on millions of transactions. These models can detect patterns and anomalies faster than humans.

The AI model can mark high-value transactions from countries where users have never transacted as suspicious. Several financial institutions that integrated AI-based real-time fraud detection observed a reduction in fraudulent transactions of up to 40% while also reducing false positives.

Predicting Credit Card Default Risks

Credit card companies must predict the probability of a default user to decide on credit limits and reduce losses. By training historical data, including past transactions, payment histories, and social factors, AI models can provide more accurate predictions about the likelihood of users defaulting. More advanced models even consider non-traditional data, such as social media activity. Credit card companies using AI-based risk assessment tools can reduce bad loans compared to traditional methods.

Automated Trading and Risk Management

The stock market is notoriously unpredictable. Manual trading strategies cannot always keep up with rapid fluctuations. AI algorithms, trained on large datasets of years of market data, can make real-time trading decisions. By analyzing patterns, AI can predict short-term price changes with greater accuracy. In addition, AI assists portfolio managers in risk assessment by forecasting potential market downturns based on global news and events. Trading companies using AI-based trading strategies consistently outperform traditional methods, some reporting an increase in annual returns of up to 15%.

RETAIL

Physical and digital retailers have turned to AI to enhance the customer shopping experience, offering personalized product recommendations based on individual preferences and browsing history. Modern consumers expect a personalized shopping experience.

Real-Time Personalized Online Shopping Experience

Online shoppers often face many choices, leading to potential shopping cart abandonment. The AI model is trained on users' browsing patterns, purchase history, and click-through rates, dynamically adjusting the online shopping interface. This personalization can range from visual layout adjustments to specific product highlights. E-commerce platforms that have integrated AI personalization tools have reported a 20% increase in conversion rates and a 15% increase in average order value.

In-Store Personalized Recommendations through Augmented Reality (AR)

Brick-and-mortar stores aim to replicate a personalized online experience for in-store customers. Augmented Reality (AR) devices, powered by AI algorithms, analyze a customer's purchase history and store interactions. The AR device then overlays real-time product information and recommendations onto the customer's view. Stores using AR and AI for personalized recommendations have increased in-store sales by 10-15% and increased customer return rates by 20%.

Virtual Try-Ons and Personalized Styling Suggestions

The challenge of choosing the right size and style is familiar to both online and in-store shoppers. With AI and AR, virtual test tools allow customers to wear clothes, accessories, or make-up virtually. AI suggests sizes, colors, and complementary products based on virtual experiences and past purchases. Retailers offering virtual trials and AI-driven style advice saw a 20-40% decrease in product returns and a 3% increase in sales of complementary products.

AGRICULTURE

Modern agriculture seeks to combine traditional wisdom with technological advances. AI has emerged as a vital tool, providing farmers with data-driven insights that were previously inaccessible. Predictive analytics with AI offers solutions to optimize crop yield predictions based on various parameters.

Predicting Yield Based on Weather Patterns

Weather fluctuations have a direct impact on crop yields. Traditional predictive models often lack real-time response to sudden weather changes. Machine learning models, which are trained on historical weather data, crop yields, and satellite imagery, can predict crop yields based on predicted weather patterns. Farms using AI models report yield increases of up to 20% due to timely interventions, optimizing irrigation, and predictive pest control.

Soil Health Analysis and Crop Yield

Soil health, including nutrient content and moisture levels, is a major factor in crop yields. Sophisticated sensors and AI algorithms can analyze soil samples, predicting which plants grow best in certain soil types and conditions. These predictions can also be extended to specific fertilizer or treatment recommendations. By aligning crop planting with soil health recommendations, the farm recorded a 15% increase in crop yields and a 10% reduction in fertilizer and maintenance costs.

Drone-based Crop Surveillance and Yield Prediction

Regular crop monitoring can detect early signs of disease or pest infestation that can affect yields. Drones equipped with AI-based cameras can capture high-resolution images of plants. Then, deep learning models analyze the images to detect abnormalities, predict the potential impact of outcomes, and suggest interventions. Early detection and intervention can reduce crop losses, ensuring more consistent and higher yields.

ENERGY

The energy sector is currently undergoing a transformative AI-driven evolution. As global energy demand increases and the urgent need for sustainable solutions increases, AI delivers innovation, promising efficiency, adaptability, and foresight in diverse energy production, distribution, and consumption fields.

Renewable Energy Forecasting

Renewable energy sources, such as wind and solar, are affected by unpredictable natural factors. AI is used to improve energy production forecasting from these sources. AI models can more accurately predict energy output by analyzing large amounts of data, including weather patterns, historical energy production, and satellite imagery. Thus, the energy network can effectively integrate renewable sources, optimize energy distribution, and reduce dependence on non-renewable reserves. AI-powered forecasting helps maximize the efficiency and reliability of renewable energy, making it a more viable alternative to traditional energy sources.

Energy Efficiency in Buildings

Buildings, such as homes and office spaces, consume much energy. AI plays an essential role in increasing the energy efficiency of these structures. AI algorithms can optimize heating, cooling, and lighting systems in real-time by analyzing data from sensors, past energy usage, weather forecasts and occupancy patterns. AI can ensure that energy is only used when and where needed to prevent wastage. Additionally, AI can predict when a system may need maintenance, avoiding energy inefficiencies due to wear and tear. Therefore, AI is an intelligent manager for building systems, ensuring optimal energy consumption and significantly reducing costs.

Predictive Maintenance in Energy Infrastructure

Energy infrastructure, such as power plants, turbines, and transmission lines, are important assets that require regular maintenance. Traditional maintenance strategies often rely on scheduled inspections or waiting for equipment to fail. The predictive maintenance approach can be applied with AI. AI can analyze data from sensors placed on equipment, identifying patterns and anomalies that hint at potential failure or wear and tear. Foreseeing these problems before they cause damage, operations can continue without interruption, and costly emergency repairs can be avoided. AI ensures energy infrastructure stays in peak condition, reduces downtime, and maximizes efficiency.

AUTOMOTIVE

The automotive field is undergoing a radical metamorphosis powered by AI. As ancient vehicle mechanics are entwined with digital AI prowess, the horizon of automotive possibilities is expanding, ushering in an era of enhanced safety, unprecedented efficiency and reimagined driving experiences.

Autonomous Vehicles

Autonomous vehicles, often referred to as self-driving cars, rely heavily on AI to navigate and make decisions. Using a variety of sensors, cameras and radar, the vehicle is constantly gathering data about its environment. AI processes this data in real-time, helping vehicles recognize obstacles, read traffic signs, and understand road conditions.

Additionally, AI algorithms can predict the actions of pedestrians and other vehicles to make driving decisions, such as when to brake or change lanes. AI, such as deep learning, enables these vehicles to learn from large amounts of driving data and continuously improve their performance. Thus, AI functions as the brain of autonomous vehicles, allowing them to navigate complex urban environments safely and efficiently.

Predictive Maintenance

The automotive industry has applied AI to predict and prevent vehicle breakdowns before they occur. The vehicle continuously delivers performance data by integrating on-board sensors and diagnostics. AI algorithms analyze this data, detecting subtle patterns and irregularities that might indicate potential damage or wear on some parts. Instead of following a fixed service schedule or waiting for a breakdown, car owners are forewarned about which components need attention.

This predictive approach increases vehicle life, ensures safer driving conditions, and can reduce unforeseen repair costs. AI turns vehicles into self-diagnosis systems, offering timely maintenance insights to keep them running optimally.

Intelligent Voice Assistants

Modern vehicles are equipped with AI voice assistants that go beyond basic speech recognition. AI can understand context, preferences and even adapt to individual user voices. Drivers can use voice commands to control navigation, play music, send messages, or get real-time updates on vehicle performance, all without taking their hands off the wheel. AI processes these commands quickly and accurately, ensuring smooth interactions. Over time, these assistants learn from user behavior and can proactively provide suggestions, such as finding a gas station on a long trip or suggesting a faster route. This AI- driven voice assistant enhances the driving experience, making it more intuitive, safe, and enjoyable.

CHAPTER-11

BUILDING A CAREER IN AI AND ML

Here are some educational paths, certifications, industry trends, job roles, professional development, and networking tips to help you build a career in AI and ML:

EDUCATIONAL PATHS

- **Bachelor's degree in computer science, statistics, mathematics, or a related field.:** This will give you a strong foundation in the technical skills you need for a career in AI and ML.

- **Master's degree in AI, ML, or a related field.** This will give you the opportunity to specialize in a particular area of AI and ML and gain the skills you need for more advanced roles.

- **Doctorate degree in AI, ML, or a related field.** This is the highest level of education in AI and ML and is required for some of the most advanced roles in the field.

CERTIFICATIONS

- **Certified Analytics Professional (CAP):** This certification is offered by the Institute for Operations Research and the Management Sciences (INFORMS). It is designed for professionals who want to demonstrate their skills in data analytics and decision-making.

- **Machine Learning Engineer (MLE):** This certification is offered by the Open Group. It is designed for professionals who want to demonstrate their skills in developing and deploying ML models.

- **Data Scientist (DS):** This certification is offered by the Data Science Council of America (DASCA). It is designed for professionals who want to demonstrate their skills in data science and analytics.

INDUSTRY TRENDS

- **The rise of AI and ML in the enterprise.** AI and ML are being used by businesses of all sizes to improve their operations and make better decisions. This is creating a growing demand for AI and ML professionals.

- **The increasing importance of data.** Data are the fuel that powers AI and ML. As businesses collect more data, they will need more professionals who can help them make sense of it.

- **The growing focus on ethics and bias in AI.** As AI and ML become more powerful, it is important to ensure that they are used ethically and responsibly. This is creating a demand for professionals who can help businesses develop and implement ethical AI and ML practices.

JOB ROLES

- **Data scientist**: Data scientists collect, clean, and analyze data to extract insights that can be used to improve business decisions.

- **Machine learning engineer**: Machine learning engineers develop and deploy ML models to solve real-world problems.

- **Research scientist**: Research scientists develop new AI and ML algorithms and techniques.

- **Business intelligence developer**: Business intelligence developers use AI and ML to create dashboards and reports that help businesses track their performance and make better decisions.

- **AI engineer:** AI engineers design, develop, and deploy AI systems.

PROFESSIONAL DEVELOPMENT

- **Stay up-to-date on the latest AI and ML trends**. The field of AI and ML is constantly evolving, so it is important to stay up-to-date on the latest trends and developments. You can do this by reading industry publications, attending conferences, and taking online courses.

- **Network with other AI and ML professionals**. Networking is a great way to learn about new opportunities and get your foot in the door. You can network with other AI and ML professionals by attending industry events, joining online communities, and reaching out to people on LinkedIn.

- **Contribute to open source AI and ML projects**. Contributing to open source projects is a great way to gain experience and build your portfolio. It is also a great way to network with other AI and ML professionals.

NETWORKING

- ⦿ **Attend industry events**. Industry events are a great way to meet other AI and ML professionals and learn about new opportunities.

- ⦿ **Join online communities**. There are many online communities for AI and ML professionals. These communities can be a great way to ask questions, share ideas, and network with other professionals.

- ⦿ **Reach out to people on LinkedIn**. LinkedIn is a great way to connect with other AI and ML professionals. You can reach out to people you know or send connection requests to people you admire.

CHAPTER-12

CONCLUSION: SHAPING THE FUTURE WITH AL AND ML

AI and ML are revolutionizing the way businesses understand their customers. By analyzing vast amounts of data, including purchasing history, online behavior, and demographic information, companies can create highly personalized marketing campaigns.

Artificial Intelligence and Machine Learning represent a paradigm shift in how we leverage data and automation. AI systems, equipped with the ability to learn and adapt, have the potential to augment human capabilities and improve the efficiency and effectiveness of various processes.

Machine Learning, a subset of AI, allows computers to analyze and interpret data, recognize patterns, and make predictions or decisions without explicit programming. This technology has far-reaching applications, from predictive analytics and natural language processing to image and speech recognition.

The future of AI and ML is filled with endless possibilities. These technologies have the potential to drive efficiency, improve decision-making, and unlock new opportunities for businesses across industries.

At Wayvy Labs, we are proud to be at the forefront of this exciting journey, leveraging AI and ML to empower businesses with valuable data insights and informed decision-making capabilities.

KEY CONCEPTS

Artificial Intelligence

Artificial intelligence is any software that mimics our natural intelligence through various methods of AI learning, a prime example from recently being applications of generative AI (like Brancher.ai) or the field of Robotic Process Automation (RPA). For example, a calculator performs a task that we normally do with our intelligence, but it is not mimicking our ability to think. However, when you ask Siri to perform a calculation and she answers your question correctly, that is a very simple form of artificial intelligence.

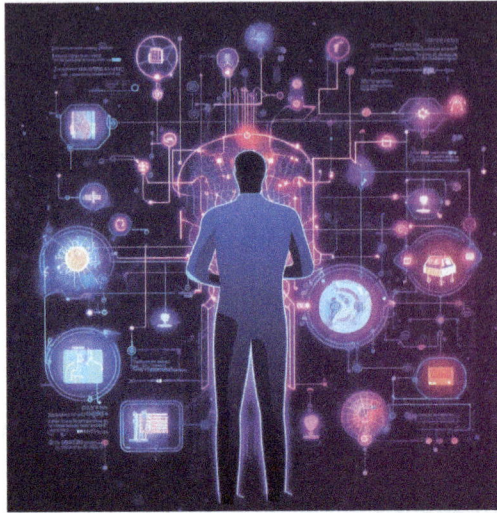

In most forms, AI can observe its environment to some degree (listening to your voice, for example, or in more advanced cases, robots perceiving their environment and navigating challenging environments autonomously) and use the data it gathers to make better decisions. Oftentimes, the interactions AI has with a user are taken as feedback and added to the AI's knowledge base to be used in future decisions, which is a simple type of AI learning.

Machine Learning

Machine Learning (ML) is a subset of AI that focuses on the ability of a program to adapt when given new information. In simpler terms, machine learning often ignores the mimicry typically associated with artificial intelligence and strictly focuses on the learning component. Without any additional coding provided by a programmer, ML software can discover new and better methods to make decisions, which will be essential to the advancement of fields like robotics.

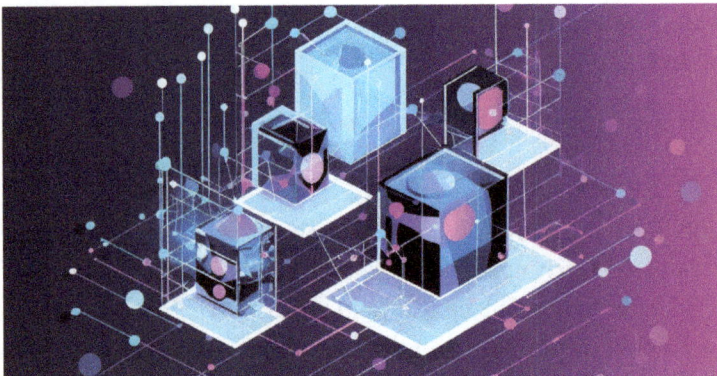

Think of this like the equations you learned in algebra. You start out using equations in specific use cases and eventually realize that they apply more broadly to other areas of math. That realization — the connection between something you've been taught and something you've discovered — is the primary goal of machine learning: to teach software enough that it can begin to teach itself. See our post on MLOps for robots, an example of how to set up systems where machines learn independently when give the right environment.

Neural Network

A neural network is a set of algorithms used in machine learning that model an AI as layers of interconnected nodes. This method of representing a system is loosely based on interconnected neurons in the human brain. In other words, when you hear someone talking about neural networks, just think of it as a really primitive digital brain.

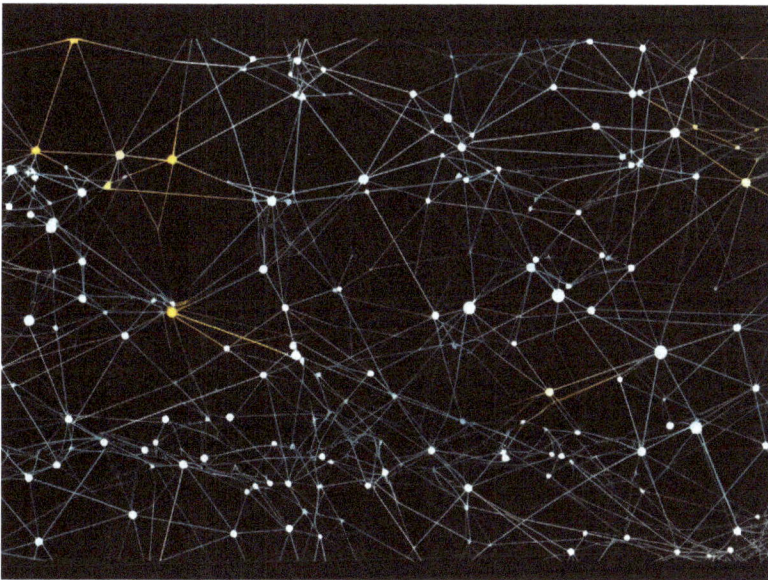

For example, you've likely noticed a feature in your smartphone's photo application that can sort pictures based on the people in each photo. This is accomplished with a neural network built to recognize faces, something that can normally only be done by a human. That "digital brain" can't hold a conversation – it's far too simple. But it can do something that a traditional computer program can't, which is adaptable recognition.

Deep Learning

Deep learning is another subset of machine learning that uses layers of neural networks rather than a single neural network. The word "deep" in deep learning is referring to these layers. You can think of each neural-network-layer as a space where something new is learned from a set of data.

The first one is the input layer — that's where the deep learning software receives data. The second line, layer two, runs the data through an algorithm to learn something about that data. The third layer does the same thing using a different algorithm, which allows the software to learn a second thing about the data. The fourth layer does the same thing, with yet another algorithm, so that the deep learning software now has three things it's learned about the initial input. In the fifth and final layer, the software outputs what it has learned.

The layers in-between the first and last layers are known as "hidden" layers, and most deep learning applications have far more than three hidden layers. But the idea here is that rather than doing one thing with a piece of data, several things are done with it to give the software a deeper understanding of the data.

Supervised and Unsupervised Learning

Supervised learning is a method of teaching artificial intelligence by providing it with labeled training data. For example, you might give an AI a set of images labeled as either "cat" or "dog". Then, by learning from those images, the AI would be able to identify new unlabeled images as "cat" or "dog" on its own. (this type of learning would be especially important in something sophisticated like creating an autonomous fleet of robots)

Unsupervised learning has the same end goal — for the AI to be able to correctly label data — but it's never given the initial training. Let's say you have an AI and you want it to tell the difference between cars and bicycles, but you want it to figure out the difference on its own. So all you do is give it a hundred images of cars and bicycles and say "right" or "wrong" when it labels an image as a car or a bicycle. Eventually, the AI should be able to piece together what makes a "bike" a bike and a "car" a car.

Reinforcement Learning

Reinforcement learning is a type of machine learning that teaches AI through trial and error. Take the lab mouse trying to find the cheese at the end of a maze. On a first attempt, the mouse may struggle to even make it to the end. Each time it is placed in the maze, however, it becomes more and more proficient at the maze, until eventually, it can make consistently perfect runs.

This type of iterative learning is one of the most valuable ways in which humans and other animals learn. We are penalized when we make mistakes and rewarded when we get things right, and eventually learn how to do something (almost) perfectly.

LOOKING AHEAD: OPPORTUNITIES AND CHALLENGES

Looking ahead, the horizon is filled with exciting possibilities for the application of AI and machine learning in the mining sector.

One likely development is the increasing integration of AI throughout all stages of the mining process, creating a more interconnected and automated system. This would involve deeper collaborations between AI systems and human operators, leading to the development of more sophisticated decision support systems. The result could be a significant leap in operational efficiency and a reduction in human error.

Machine learning models are expected to become increasingly accurate as more data becomes available, leading to improved predictions in areas like mineral exploration, ore grade prediction, and safety incident forecasting. We could see the rise of more advanced geostatistical modelling techniques, potentially improving the precision of mineral exploration.

The application of AI in predictive maintenance is also set to grow, with advancements in sensor technology and data processing capabilities allowing for even earlier detection of equipment issues. This could further reduce downtime and extend the life span of expensive machinery.

In terms of safety, we could see the development of AI systems capable of real-time monitoring and alerting, providing instant warnings about potential hazards and allowing quicker responses. These systems could incorporate a range of data, from equipment performance statistics to real-time video feeds.

The use of AI in ESG initiatives is also likely to expand, with AI-powered tools helping to monitor environmental conditions, predict impacts, and guide mitigation efforts. As sustainability continues to be a focal point for the industry, these tools will become increasingly important.

These are just a few of the potential developments we might see in the near future. However, the full potential of AI and machine learning in the mining industry is far from being fully realized, and the journey towards it will not be without challenges.

The Challenges Ahead

While the future of AI and machine learning in mining is promising, it is not without challenges that need to be addressed. One of the primary obstacles is data quality. AI and machine learning models are only as good as the data they are trained on. Mining companies will need to ensure they have robust data collection and management systems in place to facilitate the development of accurate and reliable AI models.

Another significant challenge is the integration of AI systems into existing operations. Mining operations are complex and involve many interconnected processes. Successfully integrating AI systems without disrupting these processes will require careful planning and execution.

Change management is another critical aspect. AI and machine learning will change the way many jobs are done, and this could lead to resistance from employees. It will be important for mining companies to effectively communicate the benefits of these technologies and provide training to help employees adapt to the new ways of working.

Furthermore, ethical considerations are of increasing importance as AI and machine learning models gain more autonomy in decision-making processes. Developing guidelines for AI ethics, ensuring transparency in how models make decisions, and establishing accountability measures for when things go wrong will be crucial.

Lastly, regulations and standards for the use of AI in mining are still evolving. Mining companies must keep abreast of regulatory developments to ensure compliance and avoid potential legal and reputational risks. In some cases, they may also need to work with regulatory bodies to help shape the future rules of AI in mining.

Overcoming these challenges will require a concerted effort from all stakeholders. It's not a journey that can be made alone; collaboration between technology providers, mining companies, employees, regulatory bodies, and other stakeholders will be essential. Despite the challenges, the potential benefits make the journey worthwhile. The future of mining could be more efficient, safer, and more sustainable with the help of AI and machine learning.

Opportunities for AI and Machine Learning

Challenges often serve as catalysts for growth and innovation, and in the case of AI and machine learning in mining, this rings particularly true. These obstacles, while complex, provide an abundance of opportunities for advancements and improvements in the field.

Firstly, the challenge of data quality offers an opportunity to refine data collection and management strategies in mining. This can potentially lead to the development of more robust and precise AI models. Additionally, the push for better data quality can lead to a greater overall understanding of mining operations, as teams must fully comprehend all aspects of the process to gather useful and high-quality data.

Integration issues present an opportunity to develop better and more efficient systems that incorporate AI into mining operations. These could lead to the creation of new jobs, innovative solutions, and more streamlined processes. It also gives the mining industry a chance to rethink and reimagine traditional methodologies.

Resistance to change and the need for change management strategies open avenues for improved communication and training systems within mining companies. Through the right strategies, mining companies can foster a culture of continuous learning and adaptability that extends beyond the implementation of AI.

In terms of ethical considerations, the opportunity lies in leading the discussion and development of ethical guidelines for AI. As pioneers in this field, mining companies and tech providers can help shape a future where AI is used responsibly and ethically in an industrial context. Finally, the evolving nature of regulations and standards presents an opportunity to take part in shaping the future of the mining industry. By actively engaging with regulators and standards bodies, mining companies and technology providers can ensure the creation of a balanced and effective regulatory environment.

The challenges in integrating AI and machine learning in mining are indeed substantial. However, they also present significant opportunities for learning, growth, and innovation, setting the stage for an exciting future.

LOOKING FORWARD: THE ROLE OF AI IN THE FUTURE OF MINING

As we look toward the future, it becomes clear that AI and machine learning will continue to play a pivotal role in the evolution of the mining industry. With potential developments and opportunities abound, these technologies stand to further revolutionize the industry in many ways.

In terms of operational efficiency, we can expect AI to be integrated more fully into various mining processes. From predictive maintenance to extraction sequencing, AI's ability to analyze vast amounts of data and make accurate predictions will continue to streamline operations and reduce costs. With advancements in data collection and integration, these applications of AI will become even more precise and effective.

In the realm of safety and risk management, AI and machine learning will further improve their ability to predict incidents and mitigate risks. Through advanced algorithms and deep learning, these technologies can learn from previous incidents to predict and prevent future ones. As such, mining operations will become increasingly safer, and a proactive approach to safety will become the norm.

As for ESG initiatives, AI's role in environmental management is set to expand. With the ability to predict environmental impacts and aid in remediation efforts, AI will play a critical role in ensuring the mining industry meets its ESG commitments. It will also help mining companies operate more sustainably, reducing their environmental footprint and improving their social impact.

Furthermore, the challenges presented by the integration of AI in mining operations will drive innovation in the sector. As mining companies strive to overcome these obstacles, new solutions and technologies will be developed, pushing the boundaries of what's possible in mining.

Overall, the future of mining, buoyed by the advancements in AI and machine learning, promises to be safer, more efficient, and more sustainable. The integration of these technologies is not a mere trend but an integral part of the mining industry's journey towards a more innovative and responsible future.

THE ROLE OF CONTINUOUS LEARNING IN THE AL LANDSCAPE

In today's fast-paced and ever-changing world, the need for continuous learning has become more important than ever before. Lifelong learning refers to the process of constantly acquiring knowledge and skills throughout one's life, beyond the traditional boundaries of formal education. This blog post explores the immense value of lifelong learning and highlights its impact on personal and professional development, including the positive influence of AI on learning and the transformative changes it brings to businesses.

Adaptability and Improved Problem-Solving Skills

Lifelong learning has always been crucial for adapting to a changing world, but the impact of AI on learning takes it to a new level. Artificial intelligence and machine learning algorithms can analyse vast amounts of data, identify patterns, and generate insights that humans alone may not be able to discover. By leveraging AI-powered tools, lifelong learners can gain deeper insights, enhance problem-solving skills, and make data-driven decisions.

Personal Growth and Development

AI has the potential to enhance personal growth and development by providing personalised learning experiences. Intelligent algorithms can tailor educational content to individual learner preferences, speeds, and needs. This adaptive learning approach ensures that learners receive the most relevant and engaging materials, thereby maximising their learning potential.

Career Advancement and Professional Growth

In the realm of professional growth, AI plays a transformative role. As businesses increasingly adopt AI technologies, lifelong learners who adapt and upskill themselves in AI-related domains gain a competitive advantage. AI-powered automation can handle routine tasks, allowing professionals to focus on high-value activities that require critical thinking, creativity, and problem-solving skills. Lifelong learners who embrace AI can position themselves for new job opportunities and career growth.

Increased Confidence and Resilience

AI's positive impact on learning extends to enhancing learners' confidence and resilience. Intelligent tutoring systems and virtual reality simulations provide interactive and immersive learning experiences, enabling learners to practice and refine their skills in a safe and supportive environment. This builds confidence and resilience by allowing learners to learn from mistakes, experiment with various approaches, and receive personalised feedback that encourages continuous improvement.

Enhanced Social Connections and Networking Opportunities

While AI technologies facilitate online learning, they also create opportunities for social connections and networking. AI-powered platforms can connect learners with similar interests, facilitating group discussions, collaborations, and knowledge sharing. These virtual communities foster a sense of belonging and create networking opportunities, where learners can connect with experts, mentors, and peers from diverse backgrounds and geographical locations.

Conclusion

Lifelong learning in the age of AI brings new dimensions to personal and professional development. AI-powered tools and technologies enhance adaptability, problem-solving skills, and personal growth. They open doors to new career opportunities and empower individuals to embrace change and thrive in the business landscape. Despite advancements in AI, the importance of human engagement and continuous learning remains paramount. By embracing lifelong learning and leveraging the positive impact of AI, we can navigate the evolving landscape with confidence and shape a future that values both human ingenuity and the powerful potential of AI.

GLOSSARY OF TERMS

Adversarial Machine Learning: Adversarial machine learning is a technique employed in the field of machine learning that attempts to make models more robust by exposing them to adversarial (and sometimes malicious) input.

Adaptive Learning: Subject or course material is adjusted based on the performance of the learner. The difficulty of material, the pacing, sequence, type of help given, or other features can be adapted based on the learner's prior responses.

Algorithm: Algorithms are the "brains" of an AI system and what determines decisions in other words, algorithms are the rules for what actions the AI system takes. Machine learning algorithms can discover their own rules (see Machine learning for more) or be rule-based where human programmers give the rules.

Artificial General Intelligence (AGI): Artificial general intelligence has not yet been realized and would be when an AI system can learn, understand, and solve any problem that a human can.

Artificial Intelligence (AI): AI is a branch of computer science. AI systems use hardware, algorithms, and data to create "intelligence" to do things like make decisions, discover patterns, and perform some sort of action. AI is a general term and there are more specific terms used in the field of AI. AI systems can be built in different ways, two of the primary ways are: (1) through the use of rules provided by a human (rule-based systems); or (2) with machine learning algorithms. Many newer AI systems use machine learning (see definition of machine learning below).

Artificial Narrow Intelligence (ANI): AI can solve narrow problems and this is called artificial narrow intelligence. For example, a smartphone can use facial recognition to identify photos of an individual in the Photos app, but that same system cannot identify sounds.

Artificial Neural Network (ANN): Commonly referred to as a neural network, this system consists of a collection of nodes/units that loosely mimics the processing abilities of the human brain.

Black Boxes: We call things we don't understand, "black boxes" because what happens inside the box cannot be seen. Many machine learning algorithms are "black boxes" meaning that we don't have an understanding of how a system is using features of the data when making their decisions (generally, we do know what features are used but not how they are used).

Branch/Sub Tree: A tree formed by splitting the tree.

Chat-based generative pre-trained transformer (ChatGPT) models: A system built with a neural network transformer type of AI model that works well in natural language processing tasks (see definitions for neural networks and Natural Language Processing below). In this case, the model: (1) can generate responses to questions (Generative); (2) was trained in advance on a large amount of the written material available on the web (Pre-trained); (3) and can process sentences differently than other types of models (Transformer).

Computational Linguistics (Text Analytics, Text Mining): Computational linguistics is an interdisciplinary field concerned with the computational modeling of natural language.

Computer Vision: Computer Vision is a set of computational challenges concerned with teaching computers how to understand visual information, including objects, pictures, scenes, and movement (including video). Computer Vision (often thought of as an AI problem) uses techniques like machine learning to achieve this goal.

Convolutional Neural Networks (CNN): A deep learning class of neural networks with one or more layers used for image recognition and processing.

Critical AI: Critical AI is an approach to examining AI from a perspective that focuses on reflective assessment and critique as a way of understanding and challenging existing and historical structures within AI.

Data: Data are units of information about people or objects that can be used by AI technologies.

Data Extraction: Data extraction is the process of collecting or retrieving disparate types of data from a variety of sources, many of which may be poorly organized or completely unstructured.

Deep Learning: Deep learning models are a subset of neural networks. With multiple hidden layers, deep learning algorithms are potentially able to recognize more subtle and complex patterns. Like neural networks, deep learning algorithms involve interconnected nodes where weights are adjusted, but as mentioned earlier there are more layers and more calculations that can make adjustments to the output to determine each decision. The decisions by deep learning models are often very difficult to interpret as there are so many hidden layers doing different calculations that are not easily translatable into English rules (or another human-readable language).

Edge model: A model that includes data typically outside centralized cloud data centers and closer to local devices or individuals — for example, wearables and Internet of Things (IoT) sensors or actuators.

ETL (Entity Recognition, Extraction): Entity extraction is an NLP function that serves to identify relevant entities in a document.

Explainable Machine Learning (XML) or Explainable AI (XAI): Researchers have developed a set of processes and methods that allow humans to better understand the results and outputs of machine learning algorithms. This helps developers of AI-mediated tools understand how the systems they design work and can help them ensure that they work correctly and are meeting requirements and regulatory standards.

Foundation Models: Foundation Models represent a large amount of data that can be used as a foundation for developing other models. For example, generative AI systems use large language foundation models. They can be a way to speed up the development of new systems, but there is controversy about using foundation models since depending on where their data comes from, there are different issues of trustworthiness and bias. Jitendra Malik, Professor of Computer Science at UC Berkeley once said the following about foundation models: "These models are really castles in the air, they have no foundation whatsoever."

Generative AI (GenAI): A type of machine learning that generates content, currently such as text, images, music, videos, and can create 3D models from 2D input. See ChatGPT definition, ChatGPT is a specific example of GenAI.

Hallucinations: An unfortunate but well-known phenomenon in large language models, where the AI system provides a plausible-looking answer that is factually incorrect, inaccurate, or nonsensical because of limitations in its training data and architecture.

Human-centered Perspective: A human-centered perspective sees AI systems working with humans and helping to augment human skills. People should always play a leading role in education, and AI systems should not replace teachers.

Hybrid AI: Hybrid AI is any artificial intelligence technology that combines multiple AI methodologies. In NLP, this often means that a workflow will leverage both symbolic and machine learning techniques.

Intelligence Augmentation (IA): Augmenting means making something greater; in some cases, perhaps it means making it possible to do the same task with less effort. Maybe it means letting a human (perhaps teacher) choose to not do all the redundant tasks in a classroom but automate some of them so they can do more things that only a human can do. It may mean other things. There's a fine line between augmenting and replacing and technologies should be designed so that humans can choose what a system does and when it does it.

Intelligent Tutoring Systems (ITS): A computer system or digital learning environment that gives instant and custom feedback to students. An Intelligent Tutoring System may use rule-based AI (rules provided by a human) or use machine learning under the hood. By under the hood we mean the underlying algorithms and code that an ITS is built with. ITSs can support adaptive learning.

Interpretable Machine Learning (IML): Interpretable machine learning, sometimes also called interpretable AI, describes the creation of models that are inherently interpretable in that they provide their own explanations for their decisions. This approach is preferable to that of explainable machine learning (see definition below) for many reasons including the fact that we should understand what is happening from the beginning in our systems, rather than try to "explain" black boxes after the fact.

LangOps (Language Operations): The workflows and practices that support the training, creation, testing, production deployment and ongoing curation of language models and natural language solutions.

Large language models (LLMs) Large language models (LLMs) Large language models form the foundation for generative AI (GenAI) systems. GenAI systems include some chatbots and tools including OpenAI's GPTs, Meta's LLaMA, xAI's Grok, and Google's PaLM and Gemini. LLMs are artificial neural networks. At a very basic level, the LLM detected statistical relationships between how likely a word is to appear following the previous word in their training. As they answer questions or write text, LLM's use the model of the likelihood of a word occurring to predict the next word to generate. LLMs are a type of foundation model, which are pre-trained with deep learning techniques on massive data sets of text documents. Sometimes, companies include data sets of text without the creator's consent.

Leaf Node: Leaf nodes are the final output node, and the tree cannot be segregated further after getting a leaf node.

Machine Learning (ML): Machine learning is a field of study with a range of approaches to developing algorithms that can be used in AI systems. AI is a more general term. In ML, an algorithm will identify rules and patterns in the data without a human specifying those rules and patterns. These algorithms build a model for decision making as they go through data. (You will sometimes hear the term machine learning model.) Because they discover their own rules in the data they are given, ML systems can perpetuate biases. Algorithms used in machine learning require massive amounts of data to be trained to make decisions.

Natural Language Processing (NLP): Natural Language Processing is a field of Linguistics and Computer Science that also overlaps with AI. NLP uses an understanding of the structure, grammar, and meaning in words to help computers "understand and comprehend" language. NLP requires a large corpus of text (usually half a million words). NLP technologies help in many situations that include: scanning texts to turn them into editable text (optical character recognition), speech to text, voice-based computer help systems, grammatical correction (like auto-correct or grammarly), summarizing texts, and others.

Neural Networks (NN): Neural networks also called artificial neural networks (ANN) and are a subset of ML algorithms. They were inspired by the interconnections of neurons and synapses in a human brain. In a neural network, after data enter in the first layer, the data go through a hidden layer of nodes where calculations that adjust the strength of connections in the nodes are performed, and then go to an output layer.

Parent/Child node: The root node of the tree is called the parent node, and other nodes are called the child nodes.

Pruning: Pruning is the process of removing the unwanted branches from the tree.

Responsible AI: Responsible AI is a broad term that encompasses the business and ethical choices associated with how organizations adopt and deploy AI capabilities. Generally, Responsible AI looks to ensure Transparent (Can you see how an AI model works?); Explainable (Can you explain why a specific decision in an AI model was made?); Fair (Can you ensure that a specific group is not disadvantaged based on an AI model decision?); and Sustainable (Can the development and curation of AI models be done on an environmentally sustainable basis?) use of AI.

Retrieval Augmented Generation (RAG): Retrieval-augmented generation (RAG) is an AI technique for improving the quality of LLM-generated responses by including trusted sources of knowledge, outside of the original training set, to improve the accuracy of the LLM's output. Implementing RAG in an LLM-based question answering system has benefits: 1) assurance that an LLM has access to the most current, reliable facts, 2) reduce hallucinations rates, and 3) provide source attribution to increase user trust in the output.

Robots: Robots are embodied mechanical machines that are capable of doing a physical task for humans. "Bots" are typically software agents that perform tasks in a software application (e.g., in an intelligent tutoring system they may offer help). Bots are sometimes called conversational agents. Both robots and bots can contain AI, including machine learning, but do not have to have it. AI can help robots and bots perform tasks in more adaptive and complex ways.

Root Node: Root node is from where the decision tree starts. It represents the entire dataset, which further gets divided into two or more homogeneous sets.

Self-attention mechanism: These mechanisms, also referred to as attention help systems determine the important aspects of input in different ways. There are several types and were inspired by how humans can direct their attention to important features in the world, understand ambiguity, and encode information.

Splitting: Splitting is the process of dividing the decision node/root node into sub-nodes according to the given conditions.

Training Data: This is the data used to train the algorithm or machine learning model. It has been generated by humans in their work or other contexts in their past. While it sounds simple, training data is so important because the wrong data can perpetuate systemic biases. If you are training a system to help with hiring people, and you use data from existing companies, you will be training that system to hire the kind of people who are already there. Algorithms take on the biases that are already inside the data. People often think that machines are "fair and unbiased" but this can be a dangerous perspective. Machines are only as unbiased as the human who creates them and the data that trains them.

Transformer models: Used in GenAI (the T stands for Transformer), transformer models are a type of language model. They are neural networks and also classified as deep learning models. They give AI systems the ability to determine and focus on important parts of the input and output using something called a self-attention mechanism to help.

User Experience Design/User Interface Design (UX/UI): User-experience/user-interface design refers to the overall experience users have with a product. These approaches are not limited to AI work. Product designers implement UX/UI approaches to design and understand the experiences their users have with their technologies.

BIBLIOGRAPHY

1. Bernatzeder, Petra. "Artificial Intelligence ... »mental intelligence«." *Digitale Welt* 4, no. 1 (December 4, 2019): 15. http://dx.doi.org/10.1007/s42354-019-0224-5.

2. Bostrom, N. (2014). Superintelligence: Paths, dangers, strategies. Oxford, UK: Oxford University Press.

3. Brown, T., Mann, B., et al. (2020) Language Models are Few-Shot Learners. arXiv:2005.14165v4 [cs.CL] 22 Jul 2020. https://arxiv.org/abs/2005.14165

4. Das, Subhashis. "Artificial Intelligence in Diagnosis." *Journal of Clinical and Biomedical Sciences* 13, no. 4 (December 28, 2023): 100–101.

5. Domingos, P. (2012). A few useful things to know about machine learning. Communications of the ACM, 55(10), 78–87.

6. Fernández-Delgado, M., Cernadas, E., Barro, S., and Amorim, D. (2014). Do we need hundreds of classifiers to solve real world classification problems. *Journal of Machine Learning Research*, 15, 3133–3181. h

7. Ferrucci, D., Brown, E., Chu-Carroll, J., Fan, J., Gondek, D., Kalyanpur, A. A., Lally, A., Murdock, J. W., Nyberg, E., Prager, J., Schlaefer, N. & Welty, C. (2010). Building Watson: An Overview of the DeepQA Project. AI Magazine, 31, 59–79.

8. Floridi, Luciano. "Artificial artificial intelligence." *Philosophers' Magazine*, no. 64 (2014): 22–23.

9. Grossman, Maura R., and Gordon V. Cormack. "Technology-assisted review in e-discovery can be more effective and more efficient than exhaustive manual review." Rich. JL & Tech. 17 (2010): 1.

10. Kambur, Emine. "Emotional Intelligence or Artificial Intelligence?: Emotional Artificial Intelligence." *Florya Chronicles of Political Economy* 7, no. 2 (2015): 147–68.

11. Kishorekumar, Mr A., Mr E. Ezhilarasan, and Mr R. Parthiban. "Intelligent Drone based Personal Assistant using Artificial Intelligence AI." *International Journal of Trend in Scientific Research and Development* Volume-2, Issue-3 (April 30, 2018): 1618–21.

12. Markoff, J. (2016). Machines of Loving Grace: The Quest for Common Ground Between Humans and Robots. Ecco; Reprint Edition.

13. McCarthy, J., Minsky, M., Rochester, N., & Shannon, C. E. (1955). A proposal for the Dartmouth Summer Research Project on Artificial Intelligence.

14. Nilsson, Nils J., *The Quest for Artificial Intelligence: A History of Ideas and Achievements* (Cambridge, UK: Cambridge University Press, 2010).

15. Padhy, N. P. *Artificial intelligence and intelligent systems: Artificial intelligence and intelligent system.* Oxford: Oxford University Press, 2005.

16. Rich, Elaine. *Artificial intelligence.* 2nd ed. New York: McGraw-Hill, 1991.

17. Roitblat, H. L. (2020). Algorithms Are Not Enough: Creating General Artificial Intelligence. Cambridge, MA. MIT Press.

18. Roitblat, H. L., Kershaw, A. & Oot, P. (2010). Document Categorization in Legal Electronic Discovery: Computer Classification vs. Manual Review. Journal of the American Society for Information Science and Technology, 61(1):70-80.

19. Rosenblatt, F. (1958). The perceptron: A probabilistic model for information storage and organization in the brain. Psychological Review, 65, 386–408. doi:10.1037/h0042519

20. Russell, S., & Norvig, P. (2020) Artificial Intelligence: A Modern Approach, 4th Edition. Pearson.

21. Samuel, Arthur L. (1959). Some studies in machine learning using the game of checkers. Computation & intelligence: collected readings. American Association for Artificial Intelligence, USA, 391–414.

22. Shafer, G. (1976). A mathematical theory of evidence. Princeton, NJ: Princeton University Press.

23. Singhal, Ankur, and Komal Gupta. "Artificial Intelligence: Transforming Ayurveda." *Indian Journal of Ancient Medicine and Yoga* 15, no. 4 (December 27, 2022): 151–58.

24. Turing, A. M. (1947). Lecture to the London Mathematical Society on 20 February 1947. Reprinted in D. C. Ince (Ed.) (1992), Collected works of A. M. Turing: Mechanical intelligence (pp. 87–105). Amsterdam, the Netherlands: North Holland.

25. Turing, A. M. (1950). Computing machinery and intelligence. Mind, 59, 433–460.

26. Turing, A. M. (1965). On computable numbers with an application to the Entscheidungsproblem. In M. Davis (Ed.), The undecidable (pp. 116–154). New York, NY: Raven Press. (Original work published in Proceedings of the London Mathematical Society, Ser. 2, Vol. 42, 1936-7, pp. 230–265; corrections ibid., Vol. 43, 1937, pp. 544–546).

27. Valor, Josep. "Un-Artificial Intelligence." *IESE Insight*, no. 28 (March 15, 2016): 72.

28. Winston, Patrick Henry. *Artificial intelligence*. 3rd ed. Reading, Mass: Addison-Wesley Pub. Co., 1992.

29. Youm, Jung-seop. "Commercialization of Artificial Intelligence and Artificial Intelligence." *Journal of Korean Association for Buddhist Studies* 85 (March 31, 2018): 65–94.

INDEX